WILD YEARS

THE MUSIC AND MYTH
OF TOM WAITS

WILD YEARS

THE MUSIC AND MYTH
OF TOM WAITS

Jay S. Jacobs

ECW Press

Published by ECW PRESS
2120 Queen Street East, Suite 200, Toronto, Ontario, Canada M4E 1E2

LIBRARY AND ARCHIVES CANADA CATALOGUING IN PUBLICATION

Jacobs, Jay S., 1962-
Wild years: the music and myth of Tom Waits / Jay S. Jacobs – Rev. and updated ed.
Includes bibliographic references, discography and index.
ISBN 1-55022-716-5
1. Waits, Tom, 1949- . 2. Singers – United States – Biography.
3. Actors – United States – Biography. I. Title.
ML420.W145J17 2005   782.42164'092   C2005-907235-0

Front cover photo: Jay Blakesberg
Back cover photo: Ebet Roberts / Redferns
Copy editors: Mary Williams and Crissy Boylan
Cover design: Guylaine Régimbald – SOLO DESIGN
Typesetting: Yolande Martel
Printing: Transcontinental

This book is set in Minion and Univers

DISTRIBUTION

CANADA: Jaguar Book Group, 100 Armstrong Avenue,
Georgetown, Ontario L7G 5S4

UNITED STATES: Independent Publishers Group, 814 North Franklin Street,
Chicago, Illinois 60610

EUROPE: Turnaround Publisher Services, Unit 3, Olympia Trading Estate,
Coburg Road, Wood Green, London N2Z 6T2

AUSTRALIA AND NEW ZEALAND: Wakefield Press, 1 The Parade West
(Box 2266), Kent Town, South Australia 5071

PRINTED AND BOUND IN CANADA

ECW PRESS
ecwpress.com

CONTENTS

ACKNOWLEDGMENTS

I would like to thank all those people who played either small or large parts in the creation of this book. It would have been impossible without them.

To Leslie Diamond and Debbie Jacobs, thanks for always being there with advice, help, and the occasional kick in the backside when I needed it.

To Robert Lecker, Holly Potter, Emma McKay, Mary Williams, and the people of ECW Press, thank you for this wonderful opportunity and for having so much faith in me.

To Gary Tausch, thank you so much for your tireless assistance with my research, for sharing your encyclopedic knowledge with me, and for giving me access to your vast library. You were truly indispensable.

To Craig Morrison, I am very grateful for all of your editorial advice and suggestions. You have played a vital role in making this book what it is.

To Bones Howe, Jerry Yester, David Geffen, Mike Melvoin, Francis Ford Coppola, and everyone else who so generously shared their feelings about, and memories of, Tom Waits (both on and off the record), thank you. Also, to Barney Hoskyns, David Zimmer, Mark Rowland, and the good people at *Rolling Stone* and KCRW radio, thank you for allowing me to draw on your work.

To Lou Hirshorn, Mark and Marie Healy, Bob, Roni, and Colleen McGowan, Drew Bergman, Sam Bergman, John Ruback, Damian Childress, Phil Green, Ron Sklar, Mary Aloe, George Wagner, Ken and Terry Sharp, Lucille Falk, Frances Zucker, Wayne Diamond, Alan and Sandra Feroe, Dave Feroe, Kathy Feroe, Christina Feroe, Sheila Graham, Ron Merx, and so many others, thank you for taking me away from the computer for the occasional stiff drink (or whatever) and listening to me bitch on and on about things without telling me to shut up. It's appreciated more than you know.

Lastly — and most importantly — to Tom Waits, thank you for being such an inspiration, both as an artist and a man, for so many years. I know that your next fifty years will be as fascinating as your last fifty have been.

PERMISSIONS

INTRODUCTION
Little Trip to Heaven

A seedy skid-row bar. A defective neon beer sign sputters and a television drones on, unwatched. A tired bartender with a hard face mops the bar top with a towel. A cocktail waitress, aged before her time, sits alone, occasionally casting glances at the joint's only patron. He motions once in a while for a refill and continues to gaze at the battered, varnished wood of the bar and the little bubbles in his glass.

Such scenarios come to most people's minds when they think of Tom Waits. A 2:00 A.M. world where the disenfranchised struggle to forget life's little indignities. Here, love is a fleeting ideal. Dreams never come true, but they are relentlessly manufactured, a comfort, a way to get through the night.

Tom Waits is the poet laureate of homesick sailors, down-on-their-luck traveling salesmen, dance-hall girls — anyone seeking refuge from life's disappointments at the bottom of a glass. Waits's vision is an American Gothic of three-time losers, lost souls, and carnival folk. Driving this vision is the artist's understanding of such people. He refuses to look down on them. Some of his critics have said that he has sentimentalized them, but this is rarely true. Waits habitually respects his subjects because of — not despite — their faults and weaknesses. To him there has always been a shabby nobility about surviving in a hard, cold world. And sometimes the bravest thing a person can do is stay the course and hold on to his dreams and ideals.

In 1976, Waits told *Newsweek*, "There's a common loneliness that just sprawls from coast to coast. It's like a common disjointed identity crisis. It's the dark, warm, narcotic American night."[1] This, more than anything else, is what intoxicates Tom Waits. Not alcohol, not drugs, not fame, not fortune . . . but maybe love. He's inspired and challenged by the endless

15

possibilities, the desperation, the hurried compromises made in order to survive and maybe even grab a little happiness.

The irony of Tom Waits's career is that *after* he found happiness, love, and sobriety, his music became more and more experimental. Starting with *Swordfishtrombones* in 1983, his work became increasingly primitive and sensual. The melodic conventions and piano-based instrumentation of his earlier albums gave way to a much more radical sound.

Then, in 1999, the album *Mule Variations* brought Waits's project full circle. The two extremes of his music — the jazzy saloon ballads and the weird Harry Partch–meets–Bertolt Brecht dance-hall music from hell — came together in a unified, breathtaking whole. Critical acclaim for his work intensified. In the meantime, Waits had abandoned his low-life urban hipster persona and been reborn as a nice, contented, slightly eccentric gentleman farmer, husband, and dad.

Still, as his music and his persona underwent these transformations, Waits's focus on the common man never wavered. And the consistency of his themes signaled to some members of the record-buying public that little had changed. "I seem to have a wide reputation," Waits admitted to writer Mark Rowland in 1993, "but my records don't sell a lot. A lot of people seem to have bought one record or heard one record a long time ago and got me down, so they don't have to check in anymore: 'Oh, that guy. The one with the deep voice without a shave? Know him. Sings about eggs and sausages? Yeah, got it.'"[2]

Even Waits himself acknowledges that he has created such an overpowering legend for himself that it's sometimes difficult to distinguish fact from fiction — real-life events from the elements of what he thought would make, at one time or another, a cool story. Waits is a very funny man and an entertainer at heart. When he does interviews, imparting the truth is not nearly as important as spinning a yarn. He'll gladly tell an obvious fib if it makes the tale more interesting or sets up a joke. Sometimes he seems motivated by the desire to relieve the monotony of answering the same questions over and over again. Waits once told Gavin Martin of *New Musical Express*, "Music paper interviews, I hate to tell you but two days after they're printed they're lining the trash can. They're not binding. They're not locked away in a vault somewhere tying you to your word."[3]

Of course Waits doesn't simply tell stories to amuse himself and his audience; he also tells them to shield himself because, although he is a very forthright character, he is also an intensely private man. He has allowed few hard facts about his personal life to escape into the arena of public knowledge; those details of his past that he does — only occasionally — make mention of he downplays, tosses off. Minor bits of information, such as his mother's first name (which is Alma) or where he went to school (Hilltop Junior and Senior High Schools in Chula Vista, California), have been unearthed — with difficulty, and despite Waits's efforts to conceal them — but they provide little real insight. The stories that Waits has built up around himself as a protective device have done their job. And if you want to piss Tom Waits off, pry a little.

Then there is the rear guard: Waits's friends are fiercely protective of him. Not one of them will utter a negative word about the man. Which doesn't necessarily mean that they're all covering something up. Many will tell you that Waits is just a good man at heart and bears few people any ill will. Perhaps he's just what he seems to be — a genial guy and a loyal friend. As Bones Howe, who produced seven albums with Waits, from *The Heart of Saturday Night* (1974) to the soundtrack to the film *One from the Heart* (1982), put it, "He's the only artist I've worked with throughout this forty-three-year career that I miss being around and hanging out with. He's my favorite."

Waits does deserve a private life. So in this biography I have tried to respect the boundaries he has struggled to establish and to delve, instead, into his music and the dynamic legend that he has created for himself. I haven't dragged any skeletons out of his closet or speculated about his sex life. This book is a celebration of a brilliant storyteller — a man who happily reinvented himself as a beatnik purveyor of squalid urban hip. And the process of reinvention continues. I have to acknowledge right off the bat that many of the things described in the coming chapters quite possibly never happened — except in the mind of a compelling self-mythologizer. But it's important to realize that they are still vital pieces of the puzzle that is Tom Waits.

"I've got a personality that an audience likes," Waits said in 1976. "I'm like the guy they knew — someone raggedy and irresponsible, who never really amounted to much but was always good for a few laughs. A victim, just a victim. But I don't mind the image."[4] Because of all this, Waits has taken on a larger-than-life quality. Legend has it that Tom Waits has lived life to its fullest, stared down his demons, and awoken countless times not knowing where he was. Often, tales of his exploits have a strong basis in truth. And even when they don't, they really should . . .

1

OLD SHOES AND
PICTURE POSTCARDS

There are certain people in this world who are difficult to imagine as children. Tom Waits is certainly one of them. In fact, in the 1973 press-kit bio for his first album, *Closing Time*, Waits claimed that he was born in a taxicab with three day's growth of beard. As soon as he popped out, he told the driver to head for Times Square on the double. In other interviews, he maintained that the driver wouldn't let him out of the cab until he had come up with the fare — which was pretty tough since he didn't have pockets.

This tall tale evolved into stage patter. At a show Waits gave in Princeton, New Jersey, on April 16, 1976, he treated the audience to the following version: "I was born at a very young age in the backseat of a yellow cab in the Murphy Hospital parking lot in Whittier, California. It's not easy for a young boy growing up in Whittier. I had to make decisions very early. First thing I did was pay, like, a buck eighty-five on the meter. As soon as I got out of the cab I went out looking for a job. The only job I could land was as labor organizer at a maternity ward for a while. I got laid off, got a little disenchanted with labor."[1]

Since then, the story that Tom Waits was born in a taxi outside a hospital has become official — the Gospel According to Saint Tom. Is it true? Quite possibly not, but the people who would know aren't talking (even the County of Los Angeles seems to be in on the conspiracy, accepting payment for a copy of Waits's birth certificate but failing to deliver it).

The taxi story didn't make it into the brief birth announcement that appeared on the society page of the *Pomona Progress-Bulletin* on December 9, 1949: "WAITS — To Mr. and Mrs. Jesse F. Waits, 318 N. Pickering Street, Whittier, a son, Thomas Alan, 7 pounds, 10 ounces, born December 7 at Park Avenue Hospital." But how else could that announcement read? "Born in a Tijuana taxi double-parked in a loading zone?" Not likely. In the end, it doesn't really matter. The fact is that even if Tom Waits wasn't born in a taxi, the notion feels right. It's the way it should have been.

So what do we know? He was born Thomas Alan Waits on December 7, 1949 at a hospital in the sleepy Los Angeles suburb of Pomona, not far from Whittier. Waits has often said in interviews — he did at the Princeton show — that he was born at the Murphy Hospital, and there is little reason to doubt it, despite the published birth announcement, which indicates he was born at the Park Avenue Hospital. The hospital-name discrepancy may be explained as a typo, a trick of memory, an institutional name change — it's not that important.

Waits's parents, Frank (after whom Tom named one of his most enduring musical characters) and Alma, were schoolteachers. They both taught for years, although in at least one television interview Waits claimed that his father was a bail bondsman and his mother was a fan dancer — his, he insisted, was a typical show-biz clan.[2] Alma's family was Norwegian; Frank was of Scottish and Irish descent. Frank was actually named Jesse, after his own father, Jesse Waits, but he always went by Frank, his middle name. Tom has said that the name Jesse Frank was a tribute to Old West outlaws Frank and Jesse James — the James Brothers; but as a young man Jesse Junior started using his middle name because he liked the cachet of having the same handle as the Chairman of the Board, Frank Sinatra. The bobby-soxers just wouldn't fall so easily for a Jesse.

In concert, Tom Waits has claimed that he was "conceived one night in April 1949 at the Crossroads Motel in La Verne, California [northwest of Pomona], amidst the broken bottles of Four Roses, the smoldering Lucky Strike, half a tuna-salad sandwich, and the Old Spice."[3] Where could a couple of young parents go from there? As it turns out, the Waits family lived for most of Tom's first ten years in Whittier, a town that is probably best known as the home of Richard Milhous Nixon.

Tom had two sisters, and the childhood they passed together was fairly unremarkable. Frank was a frustrated guitarist, and he instilled in young Tom an appreciation of music. Despite his Anglo origins, Frank was fascinated by all things Mexican. By day he taught Spanish at a local school, and by night he played guitar in a mariachi band. Waits's earliest musical memories are of the mariachi, romantica, and ranchera music Frank would play on the car radio. Alma was also of a musical bent, singing whenever she had a chance. Tom, however, never really felt that he came from a musical family. When Mark Rowland asked him about it for a

Musician magazine interview, Waits cracked, "Not like Liza Minelli, all right? Contrary to popular belief, we don't have the same mother. I took her out a couple of times, nothing ever happened."[4]

The same Princeton audience that heard Waits relate the myth of his birth was also told a touching story of how Alma Waits nurtured her son's musical curiosity. She got him his first musical instrument. "I remember it was Christmastime . . . As the snow fell down all over Whittier, I was coming home from work in the factory. I was right by Palace Pawnshop. There was a piano in the window. It was right next to an old bent-up saxophone, old Toro mowers, some dentures and shit. I knew I had to get my hands on that sucker. And it being Christmastime, I ran all the way home, pulled on my mother's coat . . . [and] I said, 'I just got to get my hands on that piano so I can get double-parked on Easy Street.' Well, Mother, bless her soul, ran all the way down to Palace Pawnshop. The moon was high — she stood out in front of the pawnshop and goddamn if she didn't throw a brick through the window and get it for me. What can I say? The rest is history."

Tom had a gang of neighborhood buddies. They engaged in standard kid stuff — "hanging around in the Sav-On parking lots and buying baseball cards," was how Waits described it to Rich Wiseman of *Rolling Stone*.[5] Waits learned to play the piano at a neighbor's house, and he tells the story of how he learned to play the guitar in a minor key from a childhood friend named Billy Swed. Billy also provided his pal with a verbal demonstration of the hard-luck lifestyle that has continued to enthrall Waits over the years. A twelve-year-old dropout who already drank and smoked, Billy lived with his overweight mother in a trailer on a polluted lake over by the local hobo jungle. Tom idolized Billy; he was convinced that the writing on Billy's blue jeans was some secret musical code that he was incapable of cracking. One day, Tom went down to the lake to see his friend, but Billy and his mother had vanished. Tom insisted that he learned more from Billy than he ever did in school.[6]

He also received some life instruction from a young friend named Kipper. Kipper was handicapped — confined to a wheelchair. When they were both about ten, Tom and Kipper would hang out together, often racing each other to the school bus. Years later, Tom memorialized Kipper, and his neighborhood in general, in the song "Kentucky Avenue," named for a Whittier thoroughfare.

Waits introduced that song during a 1981 concert with this childhood reminiscence: "I grew up on a street called Kentucky Avenue in Whittier,

California. My dad was teaching night school at Montebello. I had a little tree fort and everything. I had my first cigarette when I was about seven years old. It was such a thrill. I used to pick 'em up right out of the gutter after it was raining. My dad smoked Kents. Now, I never liked Kents — I tried to get him to change brands. I used to repair everybody's bicycles in the neighborhood. I was the little neighborhood mechanic. There was a guy called Joey Navinski who played the trombone, and a guy called Dickie Faulkner whose nose was always running. And there was a woman called Mrs. Storm. She lived with her sister. She used to sit in her kitchen with her window open and a twelve-gauge shotgun [sticking] out of it . . . so we took the long way around."[7]

Waits has said that the musical persona he adopted was a slightly idealized version of his own father, and he's also maintained that his musical tastes were influenced by two of his uncles, Vernon and Robert. Through the decades, the exploits of this pair of uncles have recurred regularly in Waits's tales, and they have gradually reached Bunyanesque dimensions. Uncle Vernon had a hard, raspy voice. Young Tom wished he could sound just like him; and the adult Waits insists that he came up with his trademark vocals by imitating Vernon. His uncle's voice was affected by throat surgery he underwent as a child. Family lore has it that the doctors left gauze and a small pair of scissors inside him when they closed him up. Tom says that years later, during Christmas dinner, these surgical relics again saw the light of day — Uncle Vernon, choking on his food, coughed them up.[8]

Uncle Robert was a botanist who also played the pipe organ for the local church, and Tom was intrigued by what he could do with the instrument. When Robert played the organ, the building would actually vibrate from the sheer force of it. The problem was, Uncle Robert's music kept getting louder and more experimental, prompting members of the congregation to complain. Old favorites became swirling masses of sound. Cherished hymns ended up resembling "Lady of Spain." The organ's vibrations were stripping the paint off the walls. Finally, Uncle Robert was fired, but he never stopped playing. The church was eventually torn down, and Uncle Robert had the pipe organ delivered to his house, where the pipes extended right through the ceiling. Uncle Robert also had a piano that had — somehow — been left out in the rain. Most of the keys no longer worked, so Tom learned to play it using only the black keys.

Waits has described how taken he was with Uncle Robert's house, which was in an orange grove. The place was a disaster area, clothes and trash strewn everywhere, but this was romantic clutter to Tom, a squalor born of long nights, hard work, and not enough money. The image of a downtrodden man in a downtrodden environment appealed to Tom so much that at one point he asked his mother why he couldn't let his room get as messy as Uncle Robert's. His mother pointed out that Uncle Robert was blind.[9]

One of Waits's most famous remarks is that he slept through the sixties. In the early seventies most music-world denizens were still either on a post-Beatles psychedelic high or in a Southern California Jackson Browne folk-rock navel-gazing mode. Tom Waits seemed like such an anachronism — a grizzled, drunken hipster cat in roach-killers and a filthy beret who looked and acted like he'd just driven across town from skid row — that one could almost believe in that marathon sleep. But Tom's sixties experience was actually much more unsettling than his glib comment suggests.

The sixties began with upheaval for Tom. In 1959, when he was ten, his parents were divorced. Frank soon became involved with another woman; Alma remained single for years, and then she married a private investigator. After the breakup, Alma and the three children moved to Chula Vista, California, where Tom quickly became fascinated with nearby National City, a grimy suburb of San Diego near the Mexican border. "It was a tiny community," he told a concert audience. "The main drag was a transvestite and the average age was deceased."[10] There, Waits became indoctrinated into a whole new world. He started hanging out with adults: pool hustlers, vinyl-booted go-go dancers, traveling salesmen, and assorted gangsters. As he tells it, National City was a sailor town, and the kids he knew had dads who spent more time at sea than they did at home. This made it a bit easier for him to deal with the absence of his own father — absent fathers were the norm.

"I guess most entertainers are, on a certain level, part of the freak show," Waits told Barney Hoskyns of *Mojo* in 1999. "Most of them have some kind of wounding early on, either a death in the family or a break-up of the family unit, and it sends them off on some journey where they find themselves kneeling by a jukebox, praying to Ray Charles. Or you're out looking for your dad, who left the family when you were nine. And you know he drives a station wagon and that's all you've got to go on, and in some way you're gonna become a big sensation and be on the cover of *Life* magazine and it'll somehow be this cathartic vindication or restitution." After the divorce, Frank Waits continued to teach Spanish, and he still took his son on excursions south of the border. In Mexico, Tom would get a haircut, experience the culture, and learn a little of the language. "That's when I started to develop this opinion that there was something Christlike about beggars," he explained. "See a guy with no legs on a skateboard, mud streets, church bells going . . . these experiences are still with me at some level."[11]

Alma took the boy to church, but Tom just never warmed to the undertaking. For a while he went along to keep his mother happy, but that didn't last very long. Which is not to say that Waits never pondered the existence of a higher power or a deeper meaning to life. He just sensed that what he was looking for could not be found in organized religion, and he refused to credit the notion of heaven and hell.

"I don't know what's out there or up there," he told Chris Douridas of KCRW-FM's *Morning Becomes Eclectic.* "Maybe a little office. Like when your car gets towed in New York . . . You have to go down to Pier 74, and it's four in the morning, and there's a Plexiglas shield. It's three inches thick with bullet holes in it and an old woman with bifocals, sitting there at a typewriter. You can see it, chain-ganged to hundreds of other cars over there. Your car looks ashamed and embarrassed. And you realize she's got your destiny in her hands. [Religion's] probably something like that. I mean, after you die . . . people think it's gonna be simple, but, please . . . It's gonna be an organizational nightmare . . ."[12]

A neighbor gave Tom an old piano, and they installed it in the Waits garage. Soon Tom had memorized all kinds of songs. He had an ear for music: he could play any tune he heard, despite the fact that he hadn't yet learned to read music. Somehow feeling that he should have mastered this skill, he faked it, and no one was the wiser. He'd just commit a song to memory and pretend that he was reading the notes as he played along.

A favorite haunt of Tom's at about this time was a local movie theater, the Globe. Seeking escape and inspiration, he'd sometimes spend the whole day there, catching ten films, hopping from screening room to screening room, subjecting himself to the manager's weird programming choices, soaking it all in. Waits recalls seeing a Globe double feature of Disney's *101 Dalmatians* and a gritty urban drama called *The Pawnbroker*, starring Rod Steiger. Cruella DeVil of *Dalmatians* has frightened countless young children, but Steiger's Holocaust survivor who sets up shop in Harlem is in a whole other league. Waits later remarked that whoever was in charge of programming at the Globe either had an extremely offbeat perspective on life or was completely deranged.[13] Still, such experiences were shaping Tom. He was catching some tantalizing glimpses of life's broad spectrum and starting to sense rich possibilities for art and entertainment.

Early in his career, Waits said that he first acquired appreciation for the blues while attending an all-black junior high school. He'd sneak out at night, head over to Balboa Stadium, and see shows by the likes of James Brown and the Famous Flames. Young Tom also became a huge fan of Ray Charles. Once, years later, while in the bathroom of a club in East St. Louis called the Dark Side of the Moon, he spotted some graffiti that read, "Love is blind. God is Love. Ray Charles is blind. Therefore Ray Charles must be God."[14] Tom Waits was already a believer.

Tom was an industrious boy. "I had a lot of different jobs when I was a kid," he told the crowd at a 1990 concert. "I used to deliver papers. I had two routes because the first route was such a washout. It . . . didn't make me feel like a paperboy. It made me feel like a guy who just throws papers away. It started to get to me so I got another route — it was called the *Independent*. When I used to have to go collect for the *Independent* it was always so sad. A nice woman would come to the door and she'd say, 'Wait a minute.' She'd say, 'Bob, they're collecting for the *Independent*,' and off in another room I'd hear, 'Fuck him!' It did nothing for my self-image."[15]

By the time he was fourteen Tom was working on the graveyard shift at Napoleone's Pizza Parlor, an establishment he would later immortalize in the song "The Ghosts of Saturday Night." Back in 1965, you got to Napoleone's by following National Avenue, past the infamous Mile of Cars, up to the north end of the strip. On the Mile Tom bought a 1955 Buick Roadmaster for $150, and it turned out to be such a lemon that he'd put another $3,500 into it by the time a dealer gave him $12 for the parts. National Avenue was also home to the Golden Barrel, Wong's Chinese Restaurant, and Escalante's Liquor Store. Napoleone's could be found between the Burge Roberts Mortuary and a Triumph motorcycle dealership.

The pizza parlor had been operating for twenty-five years before Tom Waits showed up, and few significant changes had been implemented during that time. Nor has Napoleone's changed all that much in the decades since. Of course the jukebox now plays CDs instead of 45s — for some reason the featured Tom Waits CD is not *The Heart of Saturday Night*, which contains Waits's tribute to the place — but Napoleone's has retained a strangely comforting forties feel. Maybe this in some way explains why the teenaged Waits regularly made the five-mile trek to Napoleone's instead of seeking employment closer to home.

Joe Sardo and Sal Crivello, the man who still runs the place, gave Tom the job. Waits says that he was hired because the guy who washed dishes at Napoleone's was so large that only a skinny little runt could squeeze into the kitchen with him. Tom fit the bill,[16] and his long nights of flipping dough, waiting tables, and swabbing the bathrooms began. His shift didn't end until 4:00 A.M. He had lots of time to think, lots of time to read, lots of time to study people. In 1999 he told Hoskyns that he'd gotten his first two tattoos while working at Napoleone's. "I got a map of Easter Island on my back. And I have the full menu of Napoleone's Pizza House on my stomach. After a while, they dispensed with the menus. They'd send me out, and I'd take off my shirt and stand by the tables."[17]

On several occasions Waits has asserted that he never had any desire to escape that life — in fact, he harbored dreams of eventually owning his own restaurant. "In my formative years," he told David McGee of *Rolling Stone* in 1977, "my ambitions didn't go much beyond just working in a restaurant, maybe buying into a place. Music was just such a vicarious thing. I was a patron. No more, no less."[18]

More than twenty years later he told Hoskyns, "I'm still not convinced I made the right decision. I go back and forth. I'm doing this children's work. 'What do you do?' 'I make up songs.' 'Uh, okay, we could use one of those, but right now what we actually need is a surgeon.' In terms of the larger view, there's no question that entertainment is important. But there are other things I wish I knew how to do that I don't." Waits began writing while he was working at Napoleone's, but looking back, he's not convinced that those early works could really be described as songs. "Mostly they parodied existing songs with obscene lyrics."[19]

Sal Crivello remembers it a little differently. He allows that Tom was a hard worker, but it was apparent even at that stage what his young employee truly wanted from life. Crivello insists that Tom was determined to become a musician. "He was fifteen years old. He was doing songwriting. He was playing several clubs then . . . coffeehouses and things like that. We'd always talk about it while we were working. I saw him going in that direction. I knew he was talented, but I just never thought he'd be that big."

During his Napoleone's years, Waits never saw Sal out of uniform: an old apron splattered with marinara sauce, a paper chef's hat, and black rubber-soled shoes. Then one night — he thinks it may have been Christmas Eve — he was shocked to see his boss in an entirely different getup. Sal had arranged to go bowling with a girl he knew, so when his shift was done he disappeared into the back of the restaurant, changed his clothes, and reemerged. Waits says it was like witnessing Superman exiting a phone booth. Somewhere in the back of his mind, Waits had always pictured Sal going everywhere in that stained apron, and he was captivated by the unexpected revelation. Surfaces, he could now see, were likely to be deceptive.[20]

Across the street from Napoleone's was Wong's Chinese Restaurant. When the Napoleone's staff got tired of eating pizza they'd set up a little trade with Wong's. Waits told David Fricke of *Rolling Stone* that he'd shuttle a pizza across the street and "they'd give me Chinese food to take back. Sometimes Wong would tell me to sit in the kitchen, where he's making all this food up. It was the strangest galley; the sounds, the steam, he's screaming at his coworkers. I felt like I'd been shanghaied. I used to love going there."[21]

Throughout this period Waits was still attending school, but he admits that he was just going through the motions. "I really started to shine after school," he says, but while school was in session he drifted along, earning mediocre grades and getting into the occasional conflict with his teachers.[22] Frank and Alma Waits, schoolteachers themselves, had little sympathy for him and refused to chalk it up to normal youthful rebellion. Despite their displeasure, Tom was unwilling to play the game any longer. Only music had the power to fire his imagination, and so he dropped out of school, took on more hours at Napoleone's, and began writing songs in earnest. "I thought high school was a joke," he told Wiseman. "I went to school at Napoleone's."[23]

Later, Waits cut his way through a series of dead-end jobs — janitor, cook, dishwasher, cabdriver, fireman, delivery guy, gas-station attendant — he even sold night crawlers to fishermen. He toiled at all kinds of jobs that involved wearing a hair net and rubber gloves. Waits later described himself during this era as being "a jack-off-of-all-trades."[24] But all these jobs were just a means to an end. The money he made permitted him to explore San Diego's nighttime netherworlds in his free time, and to him it was a good way of life.

When he finally landed a doorman job at the Heritage, a small club and coffeehouse in the Mission Beach area of San Diego, he found himself in a prime position to experience a wealth of musical styles. Budding rockers played the Heritage, as did folk singers, bluesmen, jazz musicians, and country singers. Anything that a given act might want to do was okay.

Officially, Waits was supposed to be the Heritage's ticket taker, but he quickly realized that he was also expected to serve as the bouncer. He was issued a chair leg to defend himself with and instructed to get rid of the undesirables — obnoxious conventioneers and caffeine-buzzed punks.

Music was everywhere, on the job and off. Waits's friends were into whatever was in heavy rotation on AM radio, generally content to catch a wave with The Beach Boys or zone out with the incense and peppermints of The Strawberry Alarm Clock. Waits hung back. Love-ins and peace signs didn't do it for him; he failed to idolize Jimi Hendrix; his bedroom remained unadorned with psychedelic posters. His decor choice was actually quirkier than that. Obsessed with lyrics, he pinned the words to Bob Dylan songs all over his walls. He also started listening to some of his parents' old 78-RPM records and was blown away by the Tin Pan Alley tunes of Cole Porter and George Gershwin. "I wasn't thrilled by Blue Cheer, so I found an alternative, even if it was Bing Crosby," he told David McGee. Waits also came to love jazz, discovering Mose Allison and Dizzy Gillespie.[25]

While his buddies were lining up for tickets to see big acts like The Beatles, The Who, and The Kinks, Waits was off indulging his less mainstream tastes. Over time, however, he has developed an appreciation for some of the music of the sixties. As he puts it, "The thing about a record is that it's a record: if you don't want to listen to it right now, don't listen. Listen in thirty years . . . In a sense, you put a record on and there it is. There's that moment they captured . . . I just heard 'Kicks' by Paul Revere and the Raiders on my way here, and that's a cool song! 'Wild Thing.' 'Louie Louie.' I heard 'Son of a Preacher Man' the other day, and it just killed me. There's a point in the song where [Dusty Springfield] just kind of whispers 'The only one who could ever love me' really smoky and low. That's a sexy song! Hey, it's all out there."[26]

The teenaged Tom Waits was deeply interested in story songs. It consistently amazed him to hear a whole, complicated yarn condensed into a set of lyrics. Country artist Bobby Gentry's 1967 pop crossover classic "Ode to Billie Joe," a tale of passion, deceit, and suicide in the American heartland, was a prime example. It had more layers than an onion, and Waits was intrigued. Like Gentry, he wanted to tell stories that would draw people in and entertain them.[27]

Some nights at the Heritage, Waits was asked onstage to supplement the scheduled entertainment — usually bluegrass, country, folk, or traditional blues players. He'd either bring a guitar along or sit at the club's piano and perform covers of Mississippi John Hurt and Reverend Gary Davis tunes. Since the Heritage was a local joint employing mainly local acts, very few of which had any original material, Tom didn't do much of his own music.

When the annual San Diego Folk Festival was on Waits could also be found there, checking out the local talent and the national acts that passed through. Blending with the crowd, digging the sounds, Waits couldn't have known that in a few short years he'd be playing that very gig himself.

All of this exposure to live musical performance was fueling Waits's desire to command the spotlight in his own right. He formed a band; an R&B cover outfit called The Systems. Speaking to Hoskyns, he reminisced, "I did an all-Schoenberg program for the first year . . . no, I played 'Hit the Road, Jack,' 'Are You Lonesome Tonight?' It was pretty lame, really . . ."[28] Another highlight of The Systems' lineup was James Brown's "Papa's Got a Brand New Bag," which years later Waits would sometimes treat his concert audiences to.

Frank and Alma were somewhat bemused by their son's career choice. "I think when children choose something other than a life of crime, most parents are encouraging," Waits told Mark Rowland of *Musician* magazine in 1987. "Music was always around when I was a kid, but there wasn't a lot of 'encouragement' — which allowed me to carve my own niche." Waits went on to describe how, as a fledgling performer, he had a sense of the inherent dangers of his mission but very little ability to focus, or to determine where the boundaries were. "When you're young, you're also very insecure. You don't know if you can lean on that window, if it'll break . . . I didn't really know what I was doing when I started. I have a better idea now. In a way, I'd like to start now. A lot of great guys, only one-third of them is visible, the rest is beneath the ground. Took them ten years just to break the surface." The fear — engendered in Waits at this early stage — of the risks involved in standing up to perform has persisted through the decades. "I still have nightmares about the stage where everything goes wrong. The piano catches fire. The lighting comes crashing to the stage. The curtain tears. The audience throws tomatoes and overripe fruit. They make their way to the front of the stage, and my shoes can't move. And I always play that in my head when planning a tour. The nightmare that you will come completely unraveled."[29]

The time came when San Diego started feeling kind of small to Waits. He later remarked, obliquely, that "At a certain age, you realized the cool thing about San Diego was that there were a lot of tattoo parlors, and when you were ready, you knew exactly where you were going." By way of explanation, Waits then related a conversation he'd had with Paul Reubens (the comedian, formerly known as Pee Wee Herman, and one of Tom's costars in the movie *Mystery Men*). "He said that he grew up in Sarasota, Florida, and hated it. But then he went one night to a diner, and the whole place was populated by circus people. He went, oh, what a cool place to live. So, there's a certain place where you make that identification with your community. And then, the next thing it's like, jeez, I gotta get the hell out of here!"[30]

In order to "get the hell out of" San Diego, Waits began making his way up the coast to Los Angeles on a regular basis. It was the late sixties. The city's nightlife was rocking full tilt, and its effects were notoriously harsh. Waits threw himself into it. He'd work till three in the morning, party till dawn, sleep till noon. Speaking to Dave Zimmer of *Bam*, he admitted that he'd settled on singing and songwriting as a profession, "because I was basically lazy, irresponsible, impatient, unorganized, a terrible planner, and liked to sleep late."[31]

The burgeoning L.A. narcotics scene did not attract him, however: alcohol had become his drug of choice, and it eased his entry into the urban night of seductive women, shabby taprooms, and untold possibilities. He hit the club circuit and was up to speed in no time, spending night after night in a range of seedy joints, getting hammered, watching a succession of bands struggle to capture the attention of their audiences. It occurred to Waits that this was something he could do. This epiphany, he told *Buzz* magazine, was actually triggered by an encounter with, of all people, Sir Monti Rock III, an openly gay Puerto Rican singer and celebrity hairdresser who went on to front the seventies drag-queen group Disco Tex and The Sex-O-Lettes. Rock also played the part of the DJ at the 2001 Odyssey disco — where John Travolta's character Tony Manero dazzled them on the dance floor — in the movie *Saturday Night Fever*. (It was Rock who uttered the classic line, "Look at that chick! She be dancin', man. She groovin'!")

Waits caught Rock's show in a disreputable little Sunset Strip establishment called Filthy McNasty's. The place was nearly empty — Rock and his band, decked out in shocking-pink jumpers, were playing to the bar staff, Waits, and a handful of wayward businessmen. As Waits describes it, Rock was in the middle of a "bitter and distracted" version of "The Tennessee Waltz" when he suddenly stopped singing. Then he grabbed his drink, hurled it against the wall, and started screaming at the suits, calling them "a bunch of damned bloodsuckers." Sweat pouring from his brow,

Rock launched into a long, rambling, brilliant, but "purely psychotic confession" that was like a "cross between an execution and a striptease."

Waits, of course, was enthralled. Here was Sir Monti Rock III, testifying like a preacher and sweet-talking like a pimp, spinning stories for that uncomprehending crowd about his experiences in Puerto Rico, about being a hairdresser, about his dreams of Hollywood stardom. Lighting up a cigarette, Rock then performed an a capella version of Ben E. King's R&B lament "I (Who Have Nothing)." The suits didn't get it at all, but Tom Waits did. He knew just where Rock was coming from. And it dawned on him right then and there that it was time to stop spinning his wheels. He had to get into show business as fast as he could.[32]

At about this time Waits also discovered the writings of Jack Kerouac, Gregory Corso, Charles Bukowski, Allen Ginsberg, William Burroughs, and the other Beat Generation writers. It was an enormous revelation. Waits had found an entire set of kindred spirits and he wanted to share their energy and richness with the world. He explained to Barney Hoskyns that "It's like when you buy a record, and you hold it under your arm and make sure everyone can see the title of it . . . I felt I'd discovered something that was so rich, and I would have worn it on the top of my head if I could have . . . I incorporated it into what I was."[33]

Waits devoured the unofficial Beat bible, Kerouac's *On the Road*, and he was hooked. He tracked down as many of Kerouac's writings as he could, in the process flipping through some rather esoteric publications — the kind whose readers tend to insist that they really do subscribe for the articles. Kerouac had no interest in filling the pages of such highbrow journals as *Gentleman's Quarterly* and the *New Yorker*, so he became a contributor to the type of publication favored by the common man — fifties stroke magazines with names like *Cad* and *Rogue*. Kerouac was real. He was human. He bled, he sweated, he fucked, he drank too much, and he wrote about it. Waits was right there with him.

Kerouac had coined the term "Beat" in 1948, but it achieved buzzword status in 1952, when Kerouac's friend and fellow writer John Clellon Holmes published a story in the *New York Times Magazine* called "This is the Beat Generation." And it was then that this small, tightly knit group of writers began to work its way into the American literary canon.

The Beat movement had two centers: New York City and San Francisco. Ginsberg (the poet who went on to become a sixties cultural guru), Burroughs (who penned the classic surreal novel of drug addiction called *Naked Lunch*), and Kerouac had studied together at New York's Columbia

University in the forties, and this triumvirate presided over the flourishing East Village Beat Scene. In San Francisco, Beat blossomed at the City Lights Bookstore in North Beach under the nurturing hand of poet, publisher, and store owner Lawrence Ferlinghetti. (City Lights is still one of the world's most respected purveyors of alternative literature.)

Entrenched on both coasts, the Beat writers set about mixing two distinct artistic viewpoints. They immersed themselves in the unique structures of American poetry and fell under the powerful influence of Walt Whitman, particularly revering Whitman's lyric-epic poem *Leaves of Grass* (first published in 1855). With Whitman's breadth of vision, his notions of meter and verse, the Beats blended ideas of rhythmic improvisation and syncopation gleaned from the jazz musicians they worshipped, including such legends as Charlie Parker, Miles Davis, and Thelonious Monk. But the Beats represented something more than a literary style. They created a distinct lifestyle, one that was drastically out of step with its context — the button-down Eisenhower years. The Beats adamantly rejected middle-class values, materialism, nonpacifist approaches, and sped off in search of the artistic, sexual, and spiritual self. Along the way they ingested plenty of drugs, engaged in casual sex, explored jazz and Zen Buddhism.

The first true Beat novel was published in 1952 — *Go*, by John Clellon Holmes. Then, in 1956, Ginsberg's *Howl* became the poetic manifesto of the Beat movement; in 1957, the government tried — and failed — to censor it through the courts. The vibrant, three-part, stream-of-consciousness epic drew on a range of older influences — Whitman, the scriptures — to create something unlike anything anyone had seen before. It revolutionized contemporary poetry. Kerouac's *On the Road* came out the next year, and Beat culture entered its heyday.

In the sixties the works of the Beat authors were embraced by the hippies, whose radical new set of counterculture values dovetailed with those the Beats had promoted in the previous decade. Beat influence was reflected in the work of many sixties cultural icons like Ken Kesey, Hunter S. Thompson, Tom Wolfe, and The Grateful Dead. And Tom Waits recast his life in order to live the Beat lifestyle and philosophy.

With a buddy named Sam Jones, Waits packed a car with the necessary gear and went on the road, Kerouac-style. They would see the country, get drunk, get laid, live high, have some great adventures. But the call of the music was too strong — Jones and Waits soon made their way back to California.

His energies renewed, Waits applied himself to his project of musical self-expression. He wrote, drawing on such diverse influences as Irving Berlin, Johnny Mercer, and Stephen Foster[34]; contributing to this nourishing mix were Mose Allison, Nat "King" Cole, Cab Calloway, Frank Sinatra, Ray Charles, and Randy Newman, not to mention George Gershwin and Jerome Kern. All helped to shape the distinctive Waits persona. Perhaps not surprisingly — considering his penchant for clever stage patter — Waits has also, over the years, cited comedians Rodney Dangerfield, Wally Cox, Harry the Hipster, Redd Foxx, Lord Buckley, and Lenny Bruce as early career influences.

Still, Waits had to develop the lyrical content of his songs. To that end, he became adept at eavesdropping. While working at the Heritage, he'd move around listening to patrons' conversations, taking notes. "When I put them together," he later explained, "I found some music hiding in there."[35]

At this point, Waits has said, he labored over his original material, constantly tweaking his songs, willing them to be better. Gradually, he pulled together a repertoire. He had an act. It was time to pound the pavement and scare up a few gigs. Waits played some very seedy joints and was usually paid about enough to get drunk after the show. Every Monday night he'd drive north to L.A., hoping to take part in Hoot Night, an amateur event at the popular Troubadour Club, but he never managed to get onstage. Most of his gigs were in San Diego, including the occasional showcase at the Heritage.

The songs Waits was performing had more of a folk vibe than the jazzy numbers that would become his specialty a few years down the road, and his voice was just kind of gruff; it hadn't yet been ravaged by alcohol and cigarettes to achieve that signature world-weary quality. His voice was, however, decidedly different. Speaking to Mark Rowland of *Musician* in 1987, Waits said that he'd never troubled himself with questions like, "'Are you gonna fit in? Are you gonna be the only guy at the party with your shirt on inside out?' I was never embarrassed, but I'm liking [my voice] more now. Learning how to make it do different things."[36]

After over a year of playing the local dive circuit, Waits was getting nowhere fast. The gigs were getting fewer and further between. Money was scarce, and most of it went toward funding his nights on the town and picking up a little extra hair of the dog to keep the world at bay. By now Waits was living in his car — an old fifties boat that was probably as spacious as many L.A. apartments. Frustration, and then desperation, set in.

It was at this low ebb that Waits finally got himself onto the Troubadour stage. After months of standing on the sidewalk outside the club with a mob of other Hoot Night hopefuls, he was allowed to come inside and try to prove that he had what it took to entertain the audience. "It was frightening to hoot, to be rushed through like cattle," he told Rich Wiseman. "And at the Troubadour, it's like the last resort. You see old vaudeville cats, bands that have hocked everything to come out here from the East Coast just to play the Troub one night. You also meet a lot of carnival barkers, smoking Roi-Tans and giving you some long Texas routine. They say, 'Hello, sucker.' And I was a sucker. But, you're desperate, you're broke."[37]

That night another classic rock-and-roll success story was written according to the usual formula. It so happened that a rock manager was in the club, and he caught Waits's set. Herb Cohen handled Frank Zappa and The Mothers of Invention, Tim Buckley, Fred Neil, Captain Beefheart, as well as an up-and-coming songstress named Linda Ronstadt. Listening to Waits, he became convinced that he'd found a diamond in the rough, a singer who was talented and eclectic enough to make an impact. The next day Waits had a songwriting contract and three hundred dollars in his pocket.

"You bust your chops to get hold of something," Waits told David McGee. "Get chumped again and again to where you become bitter and cold-blooded and suddenly someone's saying, 'Okay, here.' You can't offer any kind of rebuttal. You just have to take it, along with the responsibility. That was frightening."[38] Frightening but exhilarating. Waits was finally able to move to Los Angeles. There, Cohen supported him for a few years, shepherding his talent, giving him a chance to write.

Slowly, Waits's reputation started to build. His songs began to make inroads. The quality of his music and lyrics was apparent to those in the business, and some of Tom's musician friends appropriated a few of his tunes for their own sets. This was how Jerry Yester first heard a Tom Waits song. Yester — who was later handpicked by Herb Cohen to produce Tom's debut album, *Closing Time* — was doing production work for Tim Buckley, The Turtles, and The Association, the pop outfit responsible for such smash sixties singles as "Along Comes Mary," "Windy," and "Cherish." Prior to that, Yester had been a member of, and producer for, the pop-folk group The Lovin' Spoonful. Joe Butler, a founding member of the Spoonful, performed a Waits number for him.

"I heard 'Grapefruit Moon' quite a while before I met Tom," Yester recalls. "So it rang a big bell when I heard it by Tom the first time in my living room. Joe Butler had met Tom somewhere along the line. Butler was in town and he did some recording out at the Association Clubhouse.

That's where I was, weaseling my way into the place so that I could use it while they were on the road . . . which they let me do. They asked me to help some friends out, and Joe was one of them . . . He played that song . . . I remember thinking, 'Yeah, I like that song.' Then when I heard Tom do it, it was like the Technicolor version. I could see into the song about a mile deeper."

Waits recorded at least twenty-four tracks for Cohen and Zappa's Bizarre/Straight label. Against Tom's wishes, Cohen released these tracks as the two-volume set *The Early Years* in 1991 and 1992, but they weren't originally intended for release. They were essentially two-track demos through which Tom could work out his various kinks and learned about the recording process; Cohen used them to shop Waits's material around to the record labels and to other artists. Several of the songs that would appear on Waits's first two albums came from these sessions, including "Ol' 55," "I Hope That I Don't Fall in Love with You," "Ice Cream Man," and "Shiver Me Timbers." In their crude, original form, these songs are undoubtedly interesting to listen to, but their later, more refined incarnations are better examples of Waits's art.

A number of those first recordings were never officially released. "Mockin' Bird" is a stunning synthesis of Waits's Tin Pan Alley jones and the popular folk rock of the time. "Looks Like I'm Up Shit Creek Again," despite its unfortunate title (which seems to bear the Zappa influence), is actually quite a beautiful and moving Hank Williams–esque country weeper. "I'm Your Late Night Evening Prostitute" is a beautiful preview of Waits's future forays into folk and jazz. Some of the songs probably deserved to fade into obscurity though: "Had Me a Girl," for example, is one of the few songs Waits ever wrote with painfully awkward lyrics — "Had me a girl in L.A. / I knew she could not stay"; "Had me a girl in Tallahassee / Boy she was a foxy lassie"; "Had me a girl from Mississippi / She sure was kippy." But even this song is almost redeemed by its bluesy chorus —"Doctor says it's gonna be all right / But I'm feelin' blue."

The Bizarre/Straight recordings served their purpose well in the end. Making them was excellent training for Waits — training he'd soon be drawing on. Big things were in store for Tom Waits. In 1972 he was signed to Asylum Records.

2

ASYLUM YEARS

Tom had become a Troubadour regular by 1972. He often made his
way onto the club's tiny stage, wearing ratty black jeans, a crumpled jacket,
and shoes with holes in them. He'd flick the ashes of his Viceroy onto the
floor as he regaled the assembled L.A. nightlifers with his tales of triumph
and woe. Waits fit right in — his image meshed with that of the venue.
Despite — or maybe because of — its run-down aspects, the Troubadour
had a certain disheveled trendiness, and being invited to play there was
quite a break for an unsigned artist.

Waits says, "They'd put a big picture of you in the window. In those
days, if you sold out the Troubadour, that was it. People weren't playing in
sports facilities. They announced your name and picked you up with a
spotlight at the cigarette machine and they'd walk you to the stage with
the light. It was the coolest thing . . . like Ed Sullivan, without Ed. Anyone
could get up. It got very thrilling, because you would find people who'd
hitchhiked to this spot for their twenty minutes."[1]

One night, while Tom was participating in a Troubadour hootenanny,
David Geffen happened by. The boy-wonder music exec had discovered
Laura Nyro, The Eagles, and Joni Mitchell (who was so fond of her mentor that she immortalized him in her song "Free Man in Paris"). Geffen
began his career as an agent for William Morris, and his nose for talent
had propelled him to the top of the heap. From there he ventured off on
his own, establishing an artist-management company with partner Elliott
Roberts. The two were a powerful combination — they constituted a yin-
yang of rock-and-roll promotion. Roberts was the slightly scruffy former
hippie who felt most comfortable when he was among musicians, drinking,
hanging out, and staging impromptu gigs. Geffen was the savvy business-
man with a remarkable ability to sell his well-chosen stable of artists to

the masses. Geffen was also more attracted to deal making than engaging in the day-in, day-out business of recording.

Eventually Geffen and Roberts were recruited to run Asylum Records. Asylum and its sister label, Elektra, had a reputation for discovering and nurturing esoteric talent. The acts that had sprouted up under the Elektra/ Asylum banner reflected a range of musical styles — from The Doors to The Eagles to Iggy Pop and The Stooges to Joni Mitchell. Geffen would go on to form his own prestigious label, Geffen Records, for which he'd sign up such acts as Guns N' Roses and Beck. In the late nineties, Geffen made yet another major career move, joining forces with movie moguls Steven Spielberg and Jeffrey Katzenberg to form the superstudio Dreamworks SKG.

Geffen wasn't planning on staying long when he dropped by the Troubadour that night in 1972, but he quickly changed his mind. Commanding the stage was a guy who looked more like a vagabond than a rock musician. But Geffen had barely taken his seat before Waits's seductive aura had encompassed him. "He was singing a song called 'Grapefruit Moon' when I heard him," Geffen recalled recently. "I thought it was a terrific song, so I listened to the set." He watched, he listened, and the wheels started turning. Here was an artist who could make some intriguing records. "After [the show], I said that I was interested in him. He said, 'Well, I'll have my manager, Herb Cohen, call you.'"

Geffen left the Troubadour thinking that since Cohen had his own record company, this would be "the end of it." But, to his surprise, Cohen did finally call: "He was interested in making a deal with me for Tom . . . Herb had said that he didn't really think that it was right for him to make the record. My making the record would help him with the publishing. So I made a deal for [Tom]. And he made a great first record."

Geffen got Elliot Roberts involved in signing Waits to Asylum. Roberts, who is now Neil Young's manager, was happy to facilitate the process. "Waits was different than any act out there," he told Hoskyns — "he'd reinvented himself as a beatnik."[2]

Once Tom had been signed to Elektra/Asylum, Herb Cohen contacted Jerry Yester. Cohen had been impressed with Yester's production work, and he felt that Yester could bring out the best in his young protégé. Not knowing what to expect, Yester agreed to meet with Tom and asked Cohen to send the young musician to his home.

Yester still remembers the occasion clearly. "He came over and I said, 'Let's hear your songs.' He started playing. Marlene [Yester's wife] was in the bathroom, washing the tub or something. She heard this guy playing and just threw the sponge down, astonished. It was amazing. The songs were just undeniable, just absolutely wonderful. So I knew it was going to be a terrific project." Waits himself mentioned the same meeting to Barney Hoskyns, concluding, "Jerry Yester was a great producer. The first guy whose house I ever went to and found a pump organ."[3]

Yester maintains that he was unfazed by Tom's beatnik-jazzbo-hipster-bohemian image. "Nothing surprised me in '72 because it was in the new decade. We'd gone through the sixties and got through so much weird shit that nothing really surprised me. [Waits] just looked like a nice young fellow, which he was. During the album, he started going to the skid-row image. And he cultivated that for an album or two . . . until it started to catch hold. [Then] he just looked at it and snapped right out of it. He recognized that it was destructive. It was amazing to see. He just said, 'Okay, that's enough of that.' And on he went to something else. Because it definitely was a character, it wasn't him. But his characters are so good and he draws on them with such faith."

Closing Time, which was released the year after Waits signed his recording contract, included many standards from his live sets. The album is probably his most accessible, and some hardened Waits fans find it too slick, but *Closing Time* is, in fact, a uniformly strong collection of songs and a very impressive recording debut. The voice hasn't yet reached the degree of gruffness it will later achieve, but the songwriting chops are there in abundance. "I was just blown away by the material," says Yester.

In fact, the entire *Closing Time* project seemed blessed from the outset. Strong material was the starting point; then, as the recording sessions got under way, it became clear that the chemistry was right, too. "Tom's real easy to work with," Yester remarks. "We had a real good relationship. I really wasn't interested in telling him what to do. I just wanted to get the music out of him. That was the important thing. So, we talked about how he wanted to do it and I would make suggestions. There was a very good relationship between all of the band members. That album was absolutely the easiest one I've ever done in my life. It was done in, like, a week and a half . . . in the studio at Sunset Sound. One reason it was good, I think, was we couldn't get the nighttime hours that I was looking for. We had to come in from ten to five every day. It took two days to get used to it, but once we did it was great. We were even awake when we got there, and it was like a job. Everybody was real alert and into it. We took our lunch breaks, came back and worked again. And we had the evening to do something with. It was like being human, you know?"

The *Closing Time* cut that seemed to attract the most attention was "Ol' 55," a subtle ode to that most American of infatuations, the car, and to the freedom it represents. On a *VH1 Storytellers* segment taped in 1999, Waits shed some light on what had inspired him to write "Ol' 55." He got the idea from a buddy of his named Larry Beezer. The two had hooked up at the Tropicana Motel, where Waits had lived for several years. Beezer knocked on Waits's door in the middle of the night. He was on a date with a very young girl, he had to get her home to her parents, and he was out of gas. Beezer wanted Waits to lend him some gas money. In exchange, he promised, he'd supply Waits with some jokes for his act. Waits, of course, agreed. Beezer's car, Waits then explained, was a '55 Caddy, and it could only go in reverse. So Beezer drove his seventeen-year-old date home backwards along the Pasadena freeway.[4]

Waits's passion for cars was enormous. By the early seventies, many Americans had become much more conservative in their gasoline consumption, and suddenly little foreign cars were everywhere. But Waits's taste in automobiles remained stubbornly traditional. He was always in the market for an American classic, a big old boat that got two miles per gallon and could house a small family. Or, as he himself put it during a 1976 concert at Boston Music Hall, "Climb aboard that Oldsmobile and let it take you for a ride. No, thank you, on the economy car. I don't like to ride around in the fetal position all night. I like the large one that's about a half a block long."[5] The kind of car that Frank Waits would have dreamed of owning when it was the latest thing to hit the showroom floor. Now it was just a few blocks ahead of the tow truck. Bald tires, broken turn signals, several shades of primer — these Tom regarded as assets. Somehow it all made sense, given his worldview. He was attracted to cars — and to people — that had once been beautiful and full of promise but had fallen on hard times.

In a 1975 radio interview, Waits outlined his approach to car ownership. For one thing, the idea of forking over more than $150 or $200 for a car violated his principles. He'd rather pick up a twenty-five-dollar special and drive the thing until it cried uncle.[6] Jerry Yester went with Waits on one of his car-hunting expeditions. "I helped him buy his '52 Cadillac," he laughs. "It was like a work of art and he trashed it on purpose. There were newspapers in it and old paper plates and plastic forks. Beer cans. It was a mess. Kind of an Andy Warhol thing."

The most Tom ever spent for a car was $150. That bought him a 1955 Buick Roadmaster on National City's Mile of Cars. He claimed that he "got snookered" on the purchase price, but he was in love with that Roadmaster and he had to have it. He kept it for three years, traveling a few miles here and there between breakdowns. During that time he poured $3,500 into repairs. One day, when the Roadmaster was parked in front of the local dry cleaner's, its brakes finished, a stack of unpaid parking tickets jammed into its glove box, Waits knew that he'd had enough. He sold the thing to Ace Wrecking for twelve bucks.[7]

Despite Tom's *VH1 Storytellers* yarn about Beezer, many people have insisted that the Roadmaster was the real inspiration behind "Ol' 55." Yester says, "I just love that song." Recalling the *Closing Time* sessions, he explains, "we could sink our teeth into 'Ol' 55' and get our pop rocks off. We were sitting around listening to the first take of it and Johnny [Seiter, who also drummed on the track] started singing harmonies to it. To hear Johnny's voice singing with it, it was like, 'Oh, jeez, get out there in front of a mike.' Tom loved it and they sounded so great together."

Waits has referred to his songs as short stories, and *Closing Time* is rife with tales of lost love and dashed dreams. "I Hope That I Don't Fall in Love with You" is an evocation of pure loneliness. A barfly contemplates a woman sitting by herself farther down the bar. He begins to imagine the possibilities. Could she be interested in him? How should he approach her? Could they become lovers? Would he break her heart? Would she break his? He hunches over his glass of stout, failing to make his move. Finally the woman goes off alone into the night. "That's one of those great story songs," comments Yester. "I loved the way [Tom] played the guitar, because it was so unusual . . . It was always a surprise, even though I knew he was going to do it."

Another one of *Closing Time's* musical short stories was more of an imaginative stretch for Waits. "Martha" is about an elderly man who looks up his first sweetheart fifty years after their breakup. The narrative has an undeniable nostalgic charm, and Waits — despite his age — is convincing in his portrayal of a man who surveys his life and comes to a sad realization. Although he's had a good ride, something has eluded him. Waits also wears his heart on his sleeve in the gorgeous "Grapefruit Moon." It's a simple tale of a man trying desperately to forget the woman he has lost; every time he comes close to succeeding, however, he hears their favorite song and he is wrecked anew. But love doesn't always evade Waits's dreamers: "Little Trip to Heaven (On the Wings of Your Love)" is a serene hymn of love and devotion. Then Waits gets frisky and playful, dishing up some funky blues laced with sexual innuendo in "Ice Cream Man."

Closing Time fades out on the title track, a delicate instrumental suite that came dangerously close to not being recorded. Waits and Yester were working on a tune that just wasn't coming together. Says Yester, "Then we said, 'Well, what about "Closing Time?"' I just started making phone calls. It was a Sunday evening or a late afternoon and [the problem] was just finding who was available. I found Jesse Ehrlich to play cello, and Jesse said, 'Well, I got a young guy [Arni Egilsson] plays bass. He's just wonderful. Here's his number.' I called him and he was in the middle of an afternoon barbecue and he'd had a few beers. He was feeling — he wasn't drunk, but he was just really laid back. He came down, and Tony Terran was on trumpet."

Yester describes what transpired as "one of those magical sessions that happens once in a great while where no one wants to leave once it's over. Because it was so good and it happened so quickly. There wasn't any pain, any strain at all. It just flowed out of everybody." Yester continues: "Richie Moore recorded it live to track. We listened . . . and it was great. We just kept listening to it. I think we stayed for like three hours after we recorded the song."

The songs that make up *Closing Time* are, in Yester's estimation, still revolutionary. And he has never been able to pick a favorite. "Truthfully, all of them," he smiles. He points out that "in early '72, no one was doing stuff like that. 'Virginia Avenue,' give me a break. And 'Ice Cream Man,' and great stuff like that. And 'Martha' — who the hell was doing songs like that, except maybe Dave Van Ronk? Nobody was writing them. Tom was. His writing gift was huge. Obviously huge. And the way he played the piano, it was like Hoagy Carmichael, for Christ's sake . . ."

One night while Waits was in Denver, Colorado, playing a little blues club called Ebbett's Field, he had a brief conversation with a member of the house band. Guitarist Chuck E. Weiss had been hanging out at the club since he was a teenager, and he'd been lucky enough to play with veteran bluesman Lightnin' Hopkins. Hopkins became Weiss's mentor, and he took the skinny young guitarist with him on tour. Soon Weiss was playing with blues royalty — Muddy Waters, Howlin' Wolf, Dr. John — not to mention established rockers like Spencer Davis. In a 1999 interview broadcast on Colorado's KBCO Radio, Waits recalled that Weiss had initially caught his eye because he was dressed in a chinchilla coat and towering platform shoes. They were outside the club, it was icy, and the shoes were like skates. Weiss was scrambling to stay on his feet.[8] Intrigued, Waits struck up a conversation with Weiss, and he was impressed when he learned of the Hopkins connection. At sixteen, Waits had seen the blues legend perform live. Waits and Weiss met up with one another again soon afterward, when Weiss moved to Hollywood, and the two became fast friends.

During the interval between signing with Elektra/Asylum and releasing *Closing Time*, Waits's involvement in the nightlife intensified. He wanted to live the marginal Charles Bukowski barfly lifestyle to its fullest. He wanted to frequent tough, smoky joints, shoot pool, mourn lost loves and opportunities. He wanted to search out beauty in squalor. On many nights, he could be found in some one-horse taproom where Budweiser was a sissy drink and if a woman wasn't mistreating you, it just meant you couldn't find one. Only in these havens for hard drinkers could he mix with the kind of people he felt compelled to write about. He was feeding his understanding of them.

"We used to go play pool a lot. We used to go drinking a lot — when drinking was fun instead of suicidal," Yester laughs. "There was a place in Burbank that was fifty cents an hour for a nine-foot table covered with cigarette burns. And cheap beer, cheap Coors. Tom really loved those kinds of places. It had that kind of funkin' atmosphere."

When Waits looks back on this era, he does so with amusement and a tinge of regret. In 1982 he told Dave Zimmer of *Bam*, "During that period, it was like going to a costume party and coming home without changing. I really became a character in my own story. I'd go out at night, get drunk, fall asleep underneath a car. Come home with leaves in my hair, grease on the side of my face, stumble into the kitchen, bang my head on the piano and somehow chronicle my own demise and the parade of horribles that lived next door."[9]

Even though Waits was committed to witnessing and engaging in as many different experiences as he could, he wasn't endlessly resilient, and he did suffer the occasional jolt. Yester says that one of his favorite memories of Tom came out of an incident that occurred early on while they were working on *Closing Time*. Yester was mixing the album at Wally Heider Recording, which was located right in the middle of one of Hollywood's shabbier districts, a neighborhood that Waits had yet to explore. "We'd start working on the tunes and he didn't like to hang around," says Yester. "He didn't want to hear it that many times. He was out just soaking up the atmosphere of Coyne and the Boulevard, which was hookers and all the strange population down in Hollywood at that time — God, it's a hundred times weirder now! It was very colorful." One day, Yester explains, "Tom was gone for an hour, and he came back in and he was like . . . white. And just shaking a little. I said, 'Jesus, Tom, what's the matter?' And he's, like, 'I just came on to a guy.'" Laughs Yester, "He's like, 'This guy was one of the most beautiful women I ever saw in my life! We were going to go up to her place, and right before she said, "You know I'm a man?"' That really shook [Tom's] foundation."

Waits took his show on the road, but when he wasn't touring he was in Los Angeles working on *Closing Time*. He had a little one-bedroom house in the Silver Lake district of L.A., and he described his setup to Rich Wiseman of *Rolling Stone* like this: "I live in a predominately Mexican-American neighborhood and I get along fine there. My friends won't come over. It's a hovel. My landlord is about ninety. He's always coming over and asking if I live here. And my neighbor up front is a throwback to the fifties, an old harlot. She wears these pedal pushers and gold-flecked spiked heels and has a big bouffant hairdo. She has one of the worst mouths I've ever heard. I wake up to that. I need a place that is cluttered so I can see the chaos. It's like a visual thesaurus."[10]

Chuck E. Weiss was also living in Silver Lake then, but he eventually moved into the Tropicana Motel, a funky little fleabag on Santa Monica Boulevard in West Hollywood. The Tropicana was a rock-and-roll landmark. There, music-world banditos rubbed shoulders with groupies, rock-star wannabes, hard-luck cases, and drunken traveling salesmen. Record labels put up touring bands at the Tropicana. Andy Warhol filmed his cult movie *Heat* at this atmospheric locale, and Jim Morrison lived there for years during the glory days of The Doors — he was a Tropicana resident most of the time between 1966 and 1969, at which point he moved to the slightly more upscale Alta Cienega Motel on La Cienega Boulevard. Van Morrison wrote "T.B. Sheets" and several other songs while staying at the Tropicana. Fred Neil was registered there when he recorded "Everybody's Talkin'." Big Brother and the Holding Company, Rhinoceros, Bob Marley and the Wailers, and Alice Cooper all made the Tropicana their Hollywood base of operations at one time or another.

Rumors circulated that all sorts of crimes and misdemeanors — ranging from rampant drug use to deviant sex — were being committed at the Tropicana, but as long as you didn't kill anyone and you paid the rent on time, the management couldn't care less. Even the Hollywood cops didn't want to know about it unless the mayhem started spilling out into the streets.

Music and film producer Mary Aloe lived at the Tropicana when she first moved to Los Angeles. "There was this divey hole called the Tropicana," she recalls, "but it was in the heart of West Hollywood and I wanted to be in the heart of West Hollywood . . . It was like a Motel 6 with shag carpeting. Barely a good, working T.V. . . . old cigarette-butt holes burned in different things. There was a gold bedspread. Who knows if it had ever been washed? Met a lot of characters, mostly in the music business. Of course, I was some little debutante girl coming in with money. They tried to get me to invest in their projects." Aloe says that some rooms had several people living in them; others were rented by those who needed some place "for a quickie — they'd picked up some trick in Hollywood." At the Tropicana, she continues, you could mingle with "the famous and the infamous. Then you'd get your people who would stumble in there along the way and had no idea, like me."

In October of 1970 Janis Joplin was found dead in a "suite" of a seedy Hollywood motel. Rumors spread quickly that it was the Tropicana, although some other stories have suggested that it might have been Landmark Motor Hotel in L.A. or the more upscale Chateau Marmont in Beverly Hills (where just over a decade later, comedian John Belushi would also die from an overdose). Tainted by the word of its part in the tragedy, the Tropicana fell on hard times for a while. It became a curiosity, a stop on the tour itinerary of morbid fans eager for a glimpse of the place where Janis supposedly drew her last breath. Actress Sylvia Miles, while starring in Warhol's *Heat*, stayed in the room where the death was believed to have taken place, and she claimed that she was often awakened in the wee hours by thrill-seekers in pursuit of the ghost of Janis.[11]

But Chuck E. Weiss did not choose to become a Tropicana resident because of the motel's storied past. The deciding factor for him was the little greasy spoon next door — Duke's. Weiss fell in love with both the menu and the atmosphere. Duke's became his favorite hangout. "I was driving from Silver Lake to there every day to eat," explains Weiss, "and I thought, 'I'll just move in there.' About seven, eight months later Tom moved in. There were a lot of different people there. Sam Shepard, the playwright, was living there. The Dead Boys were there. Levi and the Rockats were living there. Pretty soon, Blondie would stay there. I'm sure this was because of Tom. As soon as he moved in the place started to get an international reputation."[12]

Waits further boosted the motel's "international reputation" by mentioning the fact that he lived at the Tropicana in the liner notes of his 1976 album *Small Change*. This triggered one of the most persistent of all the Waits myths. Nearly every Waits fan has heard a variation of it: late one night, a friend of a friend of a friend, feeling drunk and melancholy, dials the number. A barely awake Waits answers, and the fan gushes on for a minute or two about the brilliance of Waits's work and how Waits is the only one who truly understands the caller. Waits finally replies, irritably, "Yeah, well, that's great, but I'm trying to sleep here," and hangs up.

While this did, in fact, occur from time to time, if it happened as often as the mythmakers claimed, Waits wouldn't have had a good night's sleep through the late seventies. In a 1980 interview included in the press kit for his album *Heartattack and Vine*, Waits conceded that it had been a dumb idea to advertise his location. He added that lots of people with "clinical problems" had phoned, and he had no idea what he was supposed to have said to them.[13]

Tom's rent at the Tropicana was nine dollars a night. He has said that in the nine years he lived there he was never provided with clean sheets or towels, but he never complained because he didn't want to make waves.[14] He brought in a piano, stuck it in the back room, and the Tropicana became a funky little homestead for him. That homestead soon became as spectacularly cluttered as the one at Silver Lake had been. Sheet music and beer cans and empty food containers and clothes and nudie mags and wine bottles and cigarette packages and records were all drawn into the vortex.

Acquiring a new cachet as the living quarters of Tom Waits, the Tropicana filled up with struggling musicians. A pre–Fleetwood Mac Stevie Nicks and Lindsey Buckingham holed up at the Tropicana when they came to Hollywood and got their first recording contract; their debut album, *Buckingham-Nicks*, was released in 1973. Punk and New Wave acts like The Dickies, The Dead Boys, The Ramones, and Blondie all stayed at the Tropicana when they were in town. Tom Petty's Heartbreakers lived there, too, though Petty himself chose a little dive in East Hollywood called the Hollywood Premiere — which he describes as even less "luxurious" than the Tropicana.[15] Somehow, the Tropicana had become the preferred address of the rock scene, and Tom Waits was the establishment's unshaven figurehead.

By the time Waits's debut album was delivered to Asylum, Geffen knew that he had something special on his hands. "I always thought that [Tom] would become an important artist," says Geffen, "because his songs were so great — although his records tended to become slightly more esoteric, one after the other. There was never, I think, an album with quite the collection of commercial songs that were on his first album."

Closing Time quickly started generating a buzz within the recording industry. Part of that buzz involved a linking of Waits with another singer/songwriter whose debut album had also just come out. The two new artists found themselves being heralded as nothing less than the future of rock and roll. In retrospect, it's hard to imagine how such profoundly different musicians could have been lumped together in such a way: Tom Waits and Bruce Springsteen? *Closing Time* and *Greetings from Asbury Park NJ*? Then everyone started trying to figure out which of the two would be the next rock superstar. Waits dismisses the whole thing. "They always try to create scenes — just making connections so that they can create a circuitry. It all has to do with demographics and who likes what. If you like that, you'll like this. If you like hair dryers, you'll like water heaters. Then you try to distinguish yourself in some way, which is essential — you find your little niche. When you make your first record, you think that's all I'm gonna do is make a record. Then you make a record and you realize now I'm one of a hundred thousand people who have records out. Okay, now what? Maybe I oughta shave my head."[16]

Closing Time's producer didn't buy into the hype, either. Yester was convinced that they'd created a great album — "I knew that for an absolute fact" — and that's all that mattered. He didn't have to be told by the cultural pundits that Tom Waits was here to stay: "I knew it the first time that I met him and he was in my living room, playing the stuff. You'd have to be a dummy to miss it. All I had to do was keep out of the way. That was the whole point of the thing. That's what I try and do with an artist. With Tom and Tim Buckley — it was the same kind of case. The talent is so big that it's really easy to keep out of the way. I just feel very fortunate that I was there. I [only] feel that way about a couple of albums. [*Closing Time* is] definitely one, and *Goodbye & Hello* by Tim Buckley."

Neither *Closing Time* nor *Greetings from Asbury Park* enjoyed immediate commercial success, but both turned out to be sleepers, selling steadily for years. Springsteen, of course, did evolve into the icon the media had predicted he would become, in the process filling stadiums worldwide, selling millions of albums, and spawning countless imitations. Waits has always been quite comfortable with the way things worked out: "I saw Bruce in Philadelphia when I was about twenty-five, and he killed me — just killed me. I don't know, no one sits down to write a hit record. I got to a point where I became more eccentric — my songs and my worldview . . . Everybody's on their own road, and I don't know where it's going."[17]

It's evident, however, that commercial success is no barometer of influence. The list of artists who cite Waits as an inspiration is long and impressive. To name a few, there are grunge leader Eddie Vedder of Pearl Jam, hip-hop folkie Beck, Les Claypool and the alternative pop-rock funk-metal band Primus, Paul Westerberg of the pioneering Minneapolis band The Replacements, and punk-Irish traditionalists Shane McGowan and The Pogues. Also identifying Waits as one of the best singer/songwriters around are rock experimentalists Sparklehorse, country singer/songwriter and producer Rodney Crowell, alternative chanteuse P. J. Harvey, rapper Everlast of House of Pain, and even actor/singer Mandy Patinkin.

Multiplatinum Canadian singer/songwriter Sarah McLachlan, founder of the all-woman Lilith Fair tour, says that *Closing Time* touched her deeply when she was growing up, and it still has a hold on her imagination. "I don't get an opportunity to listen to music too much," she admits, "so when I feel the need to listen to music, I put on my old faithful [albums] that I know are going to work for me. I have ten CDs I've had for years and years . . . like Tom Waits's *Closing Time*. I'll never, ever tire of that record. It's timeless." McLachlan covered "Ol' 55" on her EP *The Freedom Sessions*.

David Geffen envisioned building Waits's reputation by offering his songs to other artists. Creating exposure for a fledgling artist by inviting more established acts to record his or her material was a strategy that Geffen had implemented for years, dating back to the days when he managed Laura Nyro. Pop songstress Nyro had, like Waits, been adored by the critics from the outset of her career, but she'd had trouble accessing a broad audience, so Geffen went to work convincing some big-name acts to record her songs. As a result, Laura Nyro songs became hits for such luminaries as The Fifth Dimension ("Blowin' Away," "Wedding Bell Blues," and "Stoned Soul Picnic"), Three Dog Night ("Eli's Comin'"), Blood, Sweat and Tears ("And When I Die"), and Barbra Streisand ("Stoney End").

Now it was Tom Waits's turn, and Geffen flexed his networking muscles. "I turned Bette Midler on to his music. And a lot of other people. I put The Eagles together with his music. I tried to get Rod Stewart to record one of his songs." Geffen suggested to The Eagles that they record "Ol' 55." In a Hollywood bar one night, Tom ran into an Eagle who told him that the band had heard the song and was thinking of recording it. Waits was flattered. Shortly afterward, he hit the road for about three months. He didn't hear another thing about it until "Ol' 55" showed up on The Eagles' 1974 album *On the Border*. The band also released "Ol' 55" as a single (the flip side was a tribute to actor James Dean).

The Eagles' version of "Ol' 55" was solid, well recorded, but it was characterized by the band's Southern California country-rock vibe, and it didn't approach the depths of Waits's own recording. For The Eagles, "Ol' 55" was just a car, but for Waits it was a lifeline. An unimpressed Waits called the *On the Border* version of his ode to the automobile "antiseptic" and then remarked that the only good thing he could think of to say about your average Eagles album was that it kept the dust off the turntable. Soon afterward, Fairport Convention and Matthews Southern Comfort alumnus Ian Matthews gave "Ol' 55" a shot, as did folk singer Eric Andersen. Tom finally concluded that he much preferred his own version.[18]

In the meantime, Herb Cohen had employed the Geffen strategy and talked Tim Buckley into trying his hand at recording a Tom Waits song. Buckley was himself a respected songwriter with several acclaimed albums under his belt — *Happy Sad* (1969), *Starsailor* (1970) — and a cult following to boot, so some industry insiders were surprised at his decision to include a version of Waits's "Martha" on his 1974 album *Sefronia*. But the decision turned out to be a wise one. Buckley added his own twist to this gentle, wistful tune without sabotaging Waits's intentions.

As his old songs, for better or for worse, took on new life, Waits was moving ahead. He'd taken his act on the road, winning new fans by delivering the goods in person. He'd been writing some new songs. *Closing Time* was launched, and now it was time to record a new album.

3

LOOKING FOR THE HEART OF SATURDAY NIGHT

In the summer of 1974, Waits hunkered down to work on his follow-up album. It's conventional wisdom in the music industry that if an artist's first album is a hit then the second will disappoint; after all, he's had years to work on the first album but the countdown's on for the second (in publishing, it's called the second-novel syndrome). Waits was well aware of this, and he resolved not to fall victim to the sophomore jinx.

David Geffen wanted to hook Waits up with a new producer and immediately thought of Dayton Burr "Bones" Howe, who had engineered or produced a string of acts, ranging from Elvis Presley to The Association. The tall, gangly Bones — who'd been given his nickname as a school-boy — was probably best known for shaping the pop-soul sound of The Fifth Dimension. Geffen and Howe had worked together for years, ever since Geffen, highly impressed with The Association's sound, had offered to manage that band for free. Geffen felt that Howe and Waits would be a good match, "because Bones had a background in jazz. I thought that he was a perfect mix of jazz and pop for Tom."

Howe recalls Geffen's approach: "He said, 'I want you to produce an artist that's just strictly an album artist. The guy's never going to have a hit single, so you just concentrate on making great albums with him.'" Waits was in the studio at the time working on demos for his new album, so Geffen urged Howe to listen to a few of them and see what he thought. If Howe liked what he heard, Geffen would set up a meeting with Tom.

"He sent me the demo tape, and I listened," says Howe. "I heard all this Jack Kerouac in there. This is something I really know about. In my engineering days, when I was engineering mostly jazz records, sitting in a motel room in Miami, just going on into the tape recorder, I had put together an album of about four hours of Kerouac. I had gone through all that material and put an album together for him. It was called *The Beat Generation* . . . I was really familiar with Kerouac's work, so David set up the meeting with Tom."

Geffen had also filled Waits in on Howe, describing his larger projects — the work he'd done with The Association, The Turtles, and The Fifth Dimension — but Waits wasn't very excited by Howe's credentials. They sounded a lot like Jerry Yester's, and the plan had been to attempt something new in the recording process. Still, Tom did agree to meet with Bones. "I started talking to him about Jack Kerouac," Howe reminisces. "Then I told him I'd engineered all these jazz records. I guess David had told him the other things I'd done. But that was really the cement. The glue with Tom and me was jazz and Kerouac. He said, 'Do you know that Kerouac once made a record with Steve Allen?' I didn't. And he said, 'Well, I have a tape of it somewhere and I'll get it.'"

That particular album — which was called *Kerouac/Allen* — was one of Waits's favorites. He'd slip it onto the turntable and hear Kerouac intoning tales of hard times and life on the road while the original *Tonight Show* host and piano player wove in a little unobtrusive jazz. Waits loved the way Kerouac's stories were transformed by the music. As he spoke over the melody, Kerouac's poetry and prose metamorphosed into song. Waits had started exploring this dynamic in his own work. He gave Bones a copy of *Kerouac/Allen* and was happy to see that the album had a similar effect on him. "It was one of those things," remembers Howe. "We were trading tapes and talking about music. Do you know this saxophone player? It was just that kind of natural thing. We decided to do *The Heart of Saturday Night* together."

Interviewed by Barney Hoskyns of *Mojo* in 1999, Waits remarked that "In those days, nobody would even think of sending you into the studio without a producer. In their minds, they give you thirty grand, you might disappear to the Philippines and they never see you again. They're not giving you thirty grand, they're giving [it to] this guy who plays tennis and wears sweaters and lives in a big house. They're giving him the money and he's paying for everything. Just show up on time and stay out of jail."[1] So the guy who wore sweaters and the guy who was managing to stay out of jail got down to it. Waits and Howe held late-night meetings at Duke's Coffee Shop, where they would throw ideas onto the table and discuss the songs that Tom was writing. Then they would head over to Wally Heider Recording. Recalls Howe, "The funny thing was that at one point David

[Geffen] said to me, 'Don't make a jazz record with it.' And of course that's what I made."

One of the first agreements that Tom and Bones struck was that this album was going to be a lo-fi product — a gritty assortment of expressions bearing no trace of studio polish. Even the artwork for *The Heart of Saturday Night* would have that low-life after-hours feel — a drawing of a tired and slightly dazed-looking Waits being sized up by a blonde hooker as he steps out of a neon-lit cocktail lounge at closing time.

Howe needed an arranger for Tom's new compositions, someone who could instinctively relate to what he and Waits were trying to achieve. He approached Michael Melvoin, legendary studio musician whose job list reads like a who's who of twentieth-century popular music (Frank Sinatra, John Lennon, Barbra Streisand, Peggy Lee, The Beach Boys, Michael Jackson, Harry Nilsson, The Partridge Family, Bing Crosby, Quincy Jones, John Williams, Burt Bacharach, Dean Martin, Herb Alpert, Bette Midler, Cher — and there are many more).[2] Melvoin was so widely respected in the music business that he was voted president of the National Academy of Recording Arts and Sciences, the organization that presents the Grammy Awards, and he was the first practising musician to land this position. (Melvoin's children have made their own mark on the industry: Wendy was a member of Prince's band, The Revolution, and then formed her own group, Wendy and Lisa, with fellow revolutionary Lisa Coleman; Jonathan was a member of Smashing Pumpkins in 1998 when he died, tragically, of an overdose.)

Howe and Melvoin had worked together before — with The Fifth Dimension and several other acts — and despite the fact that Melvoin hadn't yet heard of Tom Waits, Howe felt that he had the sensitivity and the expertise to help them shape *The Heart of Saturday Night*. When Howe gave him a preliminary taste of Waits's material, Melvoin says, "I knew that I was dealing with an extraordinary, different kind of talent. There were a couple of things about it. First of all, the lyrics . . . I would describe them as top-rank American poetry. I thought then, and I still believe, that I was dealing with a world-class poet. My degree from school was in English literature, so I felt that I was in the presence of one of the great Beat poets." As a student Melvoin had played jazz behind Beat poet and essayist Kenneth Rexroth. Tom's work was "a counterpoint to that experience. I was amazed by the richness of it. The musical settings that he was using reminded me of certain roots jazz experiences that I thought were very, very appropriate for that."

Melvoin never had a moment's hesitation about taking on the *Heart of Saturday Night* project. "It seemed like a very good fit for my background. It amazed me how well [Tom and I] got on, immediately. I thought I understood what he was doing right away, and I felt great affection for him personally and professionally. My enthusiasm was full-blown right away."

The Heart of Saturday Night signals its difference in its opening notes. Waits plays a bawdy barrelhouse New Orleans piano intro to "New Coat of Paint" that would do Dr. John, his future friend and legendary Big Easy ivory-tickler, proud. Over a strutting, preening peacock of a tune floats Waits's voice (by now even raspier). The singer is planning a memorable night of drunken carousing with his sweetheart because their relationship is turning stale. Maybe a little wine, dancing, romancing somewhere in this sleepy old town can save them. This initiates the album's unofficial theme. The songs of *The Heart of Saturday Night* form a loose chronology of a descent into loneliness: the singer and his lover set out together on an evening ripe with promise; they slide deeper and deeper into the night world; they wind up drunk, forlorn, alone together in an all-night restaurant.

The next cut, "San Diego Serenade," is a love song to Waits's hometown, and it wouldn't have been out of place on *Closing Time*. "Depot, Depot" evokes late nights at the Greyhound Bus Terminal in downtown Los Angeles, an ideal spot, so Waits has claimed, to take your date — but be sure to bring along a bunch of quarters to insert into the T.V. chairs.[3] "Shiver Me Timbers" is a sincere tribute to sailors. "Diamonds on My Windshield" was scribbled on the back of a tour itinerary in a single spontaneous burst, and it recalls Tom's days of shuffling between San Diego and Los Angeles, stopping regularly for a cup of coffee, a bathroom break, or a car repair. Pulling out this scrap of paper in the studio, Tom began to wrestle with his jotted lyrics, but "Diamonds" just wouldn't click. Finally, the session musicians caught a vibe that Tom liked. The bassist, Jim Hughart, hit on a cool bass line, and the drummer, who that day was Jim Gordon, pulled out the brushes and delivered a hot shuffle beat. Gordon, a brilliant studio musician, was once a member of Eric Clapton's supergroup, Derek and the Dominoes; he cowrote the rock anthem "Layla" with Clapton. Years later, in a fit of dementia, he killed his mother, and he was forced to spend his later years in a mental hospital. But that day at Wally Heider Recording the atmosphere was unclouded by specters of tragedy. Waits, Hughart, and Gordon nailed "Diamonds on My Windshield" on the first take.

The album's title track is yet another celebration of the freedom to drive, to step into your car with a six-pack and a dream and go see what the sprawling Los Angeles night can offer. The cut's opening car-horn effects were created by setting up a tape recorder during rush hour on Hollywood's Cahuenga Boulevard. From twenty minutes of tape the best traffic sounds were extracted. It may not have been the most sophisticated recording technique, but, in its inspired simplicity, it worked. The edited street noises import an immediacy to the track, an authenticity, as Waits's lyrics communicate doubt and desperation and chronicle the attempt to turn it all around by combing your hair and washing your face and becoming a better person.

The album winds down as the sun comes up. Waits's disheartened revelers face a new day. "The Ghosts of Saturday Night (After Hours at Napoleone's Pizza House)" is a clear-eyed and moving look at the deflated patrons of Waits's former workplace couched in lyrics reminiscent of Charles Bukowski's poetry — an American Gothic of tormented but unbowed contenders. Sal Crivello recognized the song for what it was: Waits's tribute to Napoleone's and those who pass through it. "I enjoyed it and I thanked him for it."

All told, *The Heart of Saturday Night* was an enormous step forward in artistic terms. *Closing Time* had been an impressive debut, but this was an album for the ages. Shortly after *The Heart of Saturday Night* had been recorded, Waits said that he expected the album to be a smash.[4] He was proud of what he and his team had accomplished, and this made him confident. Experience would eventually make him more wary, less prone to making such glowing predictions.

In a just world, *The Heart of Saturday Night* would have been a smash. The fact that it wasn't could indicate that it was too far ahead of its time. Or too far behind. In hindsight it seems unrealistic to have expected such a creation to take flight in an era when middle-of-the-road pop stars like Helen Reddy, Neil Sedaka, and Bo Donaldson and the Heywoods dominated the charts. "I'm on the wrong end of the wheelbarrow every time," Waits wryly remarked to David Fricke of *Rolling Stone*.[5]

Time, however, has a way of making up for slights like these. Over the years, *The Heart of Saturday Night* has gained in stature. Many now consider it a masterpiece. It is still selling, but Reddy, Sedaka, and Donaldson have long since faded into relative obscurity. Mike Melvoin sensed that *The Heart of Saturday Night* had staying power. "I knew I was working with a genius. I knew that this was of serious, real value. It wasn't of ephemeral value." Admittedly, Melvoin has worked with artists he considered "wonderful talents" who generated some interest but ultimately failed to take off. There's no calling it. Still, Melvoin insists, "Tom's work is intrinsically timeless."

While *The Heart of Saturday Night* demonstrated how much Waits had grown as a musician in the studio setting, his live act needed an overhaul. The problem was that despite his growing reputation, few people in the music business knew which niche he belonged in. Was he rock? Was he jazz? As a result Waits was booked into a series of tours as the opening act for artists he couldn't possibly mesh with. Live performance became an ordeal for him — he was booed off the stage by fans of acts he had no business sharing a bill with. In the early seventies he toured with a diverse assortment of entertainers, including comedians Redd Foxx, Martin Mull, and Richard Pryor; Bette Midler in her "Boogie Woogie Bugle Boy" phase; country-rock outfit Poco; and fifties guitarist Link Wray.

Waits also opened for the likes of country-and-blues singer Charlie "The Silver Fox" Rich (whom Tom acknowledged was one damn good singer), former Byrds leader Roger McGuinn, and the doo-wop funk collective The Persuasions. Then there was adult-contemporary singer/songwriter Melissa Manchester, funk pianist (and one of several unofficial Beatles) Billy Preston, and blues belter Big Mama Thornton.

"It was the old case of the one-size-fits-all industry push on a new songwriter," Waits complained to David McGee of *Rolling Stone*. "Throw you out there and see what you can do. I didn't know what the hell I was doing."[6] One of the few pairings that actually made some sense was Tom Waits and Bonnie Raitt. Waits had sung backing vocals for the song "Sweet and Shiny Eyes" on Raitt's *Home Plate* album, along with a collection of other still-unproven Elektra/Asylum artists — including Jackson Browne — and he and the young singer/blues guitarist shared a certain affinity. Touring with Tom, Raitt told *Newsweek*, was an enriching experience: he kept her band in touch with life on the street; he was like a portal to a world they didn't usually get to visit.[7]

Waits often complains to interviewers that he was even obliged to be the warm-up act for fifties' T.V.-puppet-show maestro "Buffalo" Bob Smith and his wooden better half, Howdy Doody. Chances are that this is just part of the comic hard-knocks mythology that Waits enjoys building for himself — there is no real evidence that Tom Waits ever did meet Howdy Doody. But Waits continues to spin it out, maintaining that he still breaks into a cold sweat when he remembers plying his trade at 10:00 A.M.

for a studio full of polyester-clad suburban hausfraus and their bored Brady Bunch kids. "I wanted to kill my agent. And no jury would have convicted me. Bob and I didn't get along. He called me Tommy. And I distinctly remember candy coming out of my piano as I played."[8]

But all of this was just fun and games. Waits's real trial by fire came when he was recruited to open for the stars of Herb Cohen's stable — brilliant, anarchistic joke-rocker Frank Zappa and his cohorts, The Mothers of Invention. Waits's Tin Pan Alley piano ballads about whiskey, love, and loss didn't do it, to put it mildly, for audiences all pumped up to hear "Broken Hearts Are for Assholes," "Weasels Ripped My Flesh," and "Don't Eat the Yellow Snow." Zappa heads lit into the young Waits with wolflike ferocity. "Zappa — that was my first experience of rodeos and hockey arenas," Waits told David Fricke. "The constant foot stomping and hand clapping: 'We! Want! Frank!' It was like *Frankenstein*, with the torches, the whole thing."[9]

Many years later the memory still preyed on Waits. In 1999 he said to Barney Hoskyns, "I was always rather intimidated by Frank. There was so much mythology around him, and he had such confidence . . . When I toured with him, it was not well thought out. It was like your dad saying, 'Why don't you go to the shooting range with your brother Earl?' I was like, I don't really want to. I might get hurt. And I did get hurt. I went out and subjected myself to all this really intimidating criticism from an audience that was not my own. Frank was funny. He'd just say: 'How were they out there?' He was using me to take the temperature, sticking me up the butt of the cow and pulling me out. Kind of funny in retrospect. I fit in, in the sense that I was eccentric. Went out every night, got my forty minutes. I still have nightmares about it. Frank shows up in my dreams, asking me how the crowd was. I have dreams where the piano is catching fire and the audience is coming at me with torches and dragging me away and beating me with sticks . . . so I think it was a good experience."[10]

Bones Howe thinks that dealing with Zappa actually did help Waits as a touring artist. "I saw him open for The Mothers a few times, and he would get heckled. I know it was uncomfortable for him, but it was a good baptism. He learned to banter with the audience. There were always a few people in the audience that he would hook . . . and he'd end up talking with them. He would develop a rapport with the people in his audience who really liked him. Little by little, he built his following that way. But he was always much better at a small venue."

One person Tom had impressed in the small-venue setting would eventually play a key role in exposing him to a national audience. Don Roy King caught Waits's show in 1973 at a Manhattan club called Reno McSweeney's. King was there to see the headliner — "a lovely, thin-voiced flight attendant turned cabaret singer" whose name King has long since forgotten. Waits, King thought, had "a great hook . . . He started his set in character, sort of a half-buzzed derelict with the voice of a bulldozer, slurring his way through a metaphor-rich stream of semiconsciousness. I couldn't wait for him to drop the act, to see what he was really like, to hear how he really sounded. Well, song after song went by. Each one rich and gutsy. Each with its own syncopated stutter-step of urban images and dark-side tales. Some were brash. Some were tender. All were captivating. The moods swung and flipped and flayed. But Tom never changed. He played the role straight through. He never looked at us. Never smoothed out the gravel. Never put out his cigarette. He did balance it on his stool once when he sat down to play the piano. The whole set was that derelict. A gutsy, shrewd act."[11]

A few years later, when he was directing *The Mike Douglas Show*, King would give Tom his first shot on the daytime talk-show circuit, but in 1973 Waits was at a low point. He was impressing the likes of King with his "gutsy, shrewd act," opening minds to a new style of performance, but it was costing him. "I was sick through that whole period," he said to David McGee. "I'd get onstage at Reno's and be thrown off by the fancy surroundings. It was starting to wear on me, all the touring. I'd been traveling quite a bit, living in hotels, eating bad food, drinking a lot. Too much. There's a lifestyle that's there before you arrive and you're introduced to it. It's unavoidable."[12]

So, if you can't avoid it, meet it head on. If his record company booked him a room at the Holiday Inn or the Ramada, Waits would cancel the reservation and seek out more comfortably sordid accommodations. In a hotel room where the window shades were torn, where cigarette burns dotted the carpet, where the mattress was hard and lumpy, where maid service was a low priority, and where the stench of stale beer and urine permeated the air, Waits could begin to relax. In short, as long as the place had an hourly rate it was okay by him.

In a 1988 issue of *Playboy*, Waits listed some of his favorite flophouses.

PLAYBOY: While L.A. may be your stomping grounds, your other great love is the wee-hours world of America's big cities. From all your travels, what have been your favorite dives?

WAITS: The Sterling Hotel, in Cleveland. Great lobby. Good place to sit with the old men and watch Rock Hudson movies. Then there's the Wilmont Hotel, in Chicago. The woman behind the desk, her son's the Marlboro man. There's the Alamo Hotel, in Austin, Texas, where I rode in an elevator one night with Sam Houston Johnson. He spit tobacco juice into a cup while we talked. Let's see: The Swiss American Hotel is San Francisco's insane asylum. The Paradise Motel, right here on Sunset in L.A. It's nice in the summer when there's a carnival across the street. And, oh, the Taft. I think they're a chain. You can probably get off a train in just about any town, get into a taxi and say, "Take me to the Taft Hotel," and wind up somewhere unsavory.[13]

Early on, Waits checked into hotels under his own name, but after learning firsthand — while fielding those late-night phone calls at the Tropicana — the joys of anonymity, he altered his approach. He adopted the dramatic road alias of Montclaire de Havelin, thereby ensuring that people he didn't know and didn't want to know couldn't find him.[14]

Waits also hit on a virtually foolproof means of locating the most atmospheric hostelries in the country. At random, he'd choose an American president and then ask a cabbie to take him to the hotel bearing the man's name. He'd ask to go to the Eisenhower or the Cleveland, and it always worked. "Invariably, there would be a Cleveland," he told David Fricke. "I would wind up in these very strange places — these rooms with stains on the wallpaper, foggy voices down the hall, sharing a bathroom with a guy with a hernia. I'd watch T.V. with old men in the lobby. I knew there was music in those places — and stories. That's what I was looking for."[15]

Like Neal Cassady and Jack Kerouac, or even Hunter S. Thompson, Waits soaked up the country. He explored America from the inside, shunning the tourist traps and seeking out the places where, he was convinced, real life was unfolding — a taproom in the Bowery or a Mexican restaurant in South Central. He thrived on urban action. He wanted to immerse himself in life and walk close to death. He loved the fact that if he really needed a Johnny Walker Red at 4:00 in the morning he could always find a place to buy one.

But because the world Waits was perpetually searching for was, very consciously, the substance of his art, a certain amount of idealization was unavoidable. The film-noir existence that he created for himself could never be as squalid as the real thing. Despite his best intentions, Waits was a tourist in that late-night world of vagabonds and cheap diners and flop sweat. The fact that he had never been imprisoned by poverty and failure and mental instability made all the difference. Anytime he wanted to he could hop back into his Ol' 55 and drive himself out of there. His music was primarily inspired by a fifties black-and-white dream of skid row, a social underbelly that reflected Raymond Chandler's sensibility more accurately than his own experience.

The inhabitants of Waits's romanticized underclass tended to be white and to wear retro gear like fishnet stockings and battered Stetson hats. The trappings of urban poverty and crime circa 1974 — the food stamps, the drug paraphernalia — were foreign to them. But Waits was able to bring these existences into stark, often brilliant focus. Through them he could present a poetic truth, not necessarily a slice of life.

When it came right down to it, though, as long as that night world Waits was roaming around in — however idealized, anachronistic, limited — served as a conduit for poetic truth, that's where Waits would be found. He would continue to make statements like, "I'll always be a night owl," or, "The moon beats the hell out of the sun." And he would continue to listen, not just to the stories but to the sounds: "The night is music. I couldn't sleep on 23rd Street in New York — it was a musical traffic jam session. You can hear a melody, a horn session . . . broken glass jig jag clack whack shuffle shuffle. And a radiator with all those little Doc Severinsens playing. There's food for thought at our fingertips, and it begs to be dealt with."[16]

4

WARM BEER AND
COLD WOMEN

Waits's manager, Herb Cohen, suggested that he do a live album. One that would showcase the compelling Waits stage persona. Everyone involved was determined to avoid rehashing the first two albums, though, so they decided to use only the new ideas and songs that Tom was coming up with. Few precedents existed for them to follow, because while a concert album entirely made up of new material was no rarity in jazz, it was in rock. There were only a scattering of exceptions, like the MC5's 1969 debut album *Kick Out the Jams*, but most had come about for economic reasons as opposed to artistic ones.

Waits himself had some reservations about embarking on the live-album project, but he eventually agreed to do it. Bones Howe was enthusiastic from the outset, and he knew just how the job should be done. "I said I didn't want to go into a club. I'd seen Tom live and we could make a much better record if . . . we made a recording studio into a club. There was a room at the back of the Record Plant. It's a big recording studio, almost a soundstage. We put a little stage over in the corner. There was a booth with glass, so we didn't need to be in the room." Howe scheduled the Record Plant shows for the last two days of July 1975, and everyone got to work creating the appropriate ambiance.

"We put tables in the room and we had a guest list," says Howe. "We had beer and wine and potato chips on the tables. And we sold out four shows . . . two nights in a row. Tom got this stripper named Dwana to be the opening act." Dwana was an old-time burlesque queen whom Tom had met on one of his jaunts to the Hollywood underworld. She warmed up the crowd — which was largely made up of friends and acquaintances of Waits and crew — and everyone was primed for a drunken voyage into an

61

Edward Hopper painting or a Charles Bukowski poem. Waits didn't plan on disappointing them.

Bones had put together a live band from the session musicians who had worked on *The Heart of Saturday Night*. Mike Melvoin served as bandleader and also covered keyboards. Pete Christlieb blew tenor sax, Jim Hughart hauled the upright bass, and Bill Goodwin played drums. Melvoin recalls the scene: "Candles on the tables . . . A room full of people. The show started with a stripper, who was the classic old tassle-twirler. It was wonderful. The ambiance was great. The band was sensational. The inter-action between the band and Tom was wonderful — between the band and Tom and the audience. It was great chemistry, and I have to hand it to Bones for putting that together."

The shows did sizzle. Tom bantered fluently with members of the au-dience (the song intros are as prominent on the album as the tunes). He was the hep-cat master of ceremonies, and he regaled everyone with long, off-color stories about his experiences in a series of seedy Hollywood haunts. His connection with the audience was genuine and strong. With his tales he bridged the gap between Beat poetry and vaudeville comedy, peppering his monologue with racy puns, like, "I've been so goddamned horny, the crack of dawn ain't safe around me," and tossing out politically incorrect jokes, like, "I've been busier than a set of jumper cables in a Puerto Rican wedding." These days, Waits dismisses all that hipster speak, insisting that he sounded like a cranky old drunk back them. Maybe he did sometimes, but for every groaner there were several turns of phrase that could take your breath away. When Waits was on, nobody did it better.

Later on, says Howe, when the time came to mix the album, he and Tom "just went out and hid in a recording studio. We took the best of each of the four shows, put an album together out of it and then mixed it. We had a really, really good time doing it. The album shows that." The album's working title had been "Nighthawk Postcards from Easy Street," but they shortened it to *Nighthawks at the Diner*. Listening to the finished product, it's evident that the sessions it documents were a hoot for everyone in-volved, but, as often happens with live albums, fun in concert didn't quite translate onto vinyl.

Essentially, the problem was the songs. While *Nighthawks* does boast some solid tunes, few of them are as clever as their spoken-word intros. Too many tracks are slight, not fleshed out well enough. Too many resemble other album cuts or older Waits songs. Such shortcomings hadn't marred Waits's earlier efforts, and *Nighthawks at the Diner* became the first Tom

Waits album to fail across the board. It sold poorly, the critics were uniformly unimpressed, and even Tom's loyal fan base considered it to be a strange misstep.

Of the handful of pearls strewn across the album's messy terrain, the best is probably "Better Off Without a Wife," an aging bachelor's recital of rationalizations for staying single. Other memorable cuts are "Warm Beer and Cold Women," the touching lament of a loser who "just don't fit in," and the moody "On a Foggy Night," a leftover from the *Heart of Saturday Night* sessions. Waits once explained that "Foggy Night" was the soundtrack to a film-noir thriller he caught on the late show one night. According to Waits, George Raft and Fred McMurray fight each other to win the heart of Rosalind Russell. The film ends as McMurray drives a big old Plymouth along a foggy road with Raft stowed in the trunk and this song playing on the radio.[1]

Also included on the album was the first Tom Waits/Chuck E. Weiss collaboration; titled "Spare Parts I (A Nocturnal Emission)," it was also the first Weiss song ever to be recorded. "Big Joe and Phantom 309" was Waits's first recorded cover, a remake of a 1967 release (called "Phantom 309") by Red Sovine, a country singer who had been recording since the 1930s. Sovine was nicknamed "The Old Syrup Sopper" when he did an early radio series sponsored by Johnny Fair Syrup. The moniker was apt in more ways than one: Sovine's songs themselves were rather syrupy. His specialty was tunes about truckers — their lonely lives on the road, far from their homes and hearths and good women. Sovine died at the age of sixty-two in 1980, a few years after scoring his biggest hit with "Teddy Bear." His greatest-hits album was flogged on late-night T.V. mail-order commercials for the rest of the decade. "Phantom 309" was an odd choice for inclusion on a Tom Waits album, but Waits, of course, never shied away from the offbeat, and he did a decent job with the song.

"Eggs and Sausage (In a Cadillac with Susan Michelson)" was released as a single. It's a good contribution to the album but ultimately too reminiscent of better Waits late-night diner songs, like "The Ghosts of Saturday Night." At this point in his career, Tom's stories were becoming as vital a part of his presentation as his songs. His vivid accounts of life on the road and on the town served to complement his songs, not merely to introduce them. For example, he made his way into "Eggs and Sausage" during his 1976 show at the Boston Music Hall by saying, "I was in a little place called Stanfield, Arizona. I was only there one night. It was one of those kind of places — I spent a whole year there one night. I'll tell you about this little diner. Walked inside, elbowed up to the counter with every other loser in town and ordered me up some Eggs Overwhelming and the Chicken Catastrophe. The waitress was wearing them little rhinestone cat glasses with the little pearl thing that clips on the sweater, so I knew I'd come to the right place."[2]

Another fun but slight *Nighthawks* cut was "Emotional Weather Report," in which Tom describes his mental health in terms of the evening forecast. This and a number of other songs included on the album worked beautifully in the concert setting, but they didn't quite make the grade on your home stereo. "The idea of singing the weather report was just a silly idea that came up in the middle of hanging around in the studio while we were doing . . . *The Heart of Saturday Night*," Howe concludes. "I don't think that so much foreshadowed *Small Change* and *Foreign Affairs* as much as [it reflected] some of the things that are buried down in *The Heart of Saturday Night*. I think that *Nighthawks* is just like a playful little interlude in the middle of all that."

As had become his habit, Waits hit the road as soon as he was released from the studio. There were venues to play, towns to visit, bars to check out, hovels to sleep in. Over the three years he'd been touring, he'd established a club circuit for himself: start off in Los Angeles; hop a plane to Denver; continue on to Detroit, Chicago, Atlanta, Washington, DC, New York, Boston, Philadelphia, Pittsburgh, Minneapolis, Seattle, Portland, San Diego; head back to Los Angeles. Six shows a week — two a night, three nights a week — a day of travel between each stop. Waits would often remark to his concert audiences at around this time that he enjoyed arriving home after a tour and finding the food he'd left in the fridge transformed into some petri-dish science experiment.

It hadn't taken Waits long to realize that he'd rather headline at a small venue than open for another act in an arena. Still, some of those little clubs could be a drag. He once spent a week playing a Toronto steak house where the patrons clearly had a deeper interest in their porterhouses or rib eyes than in the entertainer before them. Such washouts were balanced by the great places, like the Cellar Door in Washington, DC, where the audience truly came to listen. There were even little cards on the tables that read "Quiet please."

Night after night, club after club, Tom was honing his act, perfecting his *Nighthawks* monologues, scatting and jiving like a hipster stand-up. He was developing some highly stylized (and somewhat exaggerated) riffs on the Life and Times of Tom Waits. It was part Charles Bukowski, part

Milton Berle. Witness this rap he did at the 1976 Boston Music Hall show: "It had all started one night in a place called Bloomington, Illinois, you know. I was hangin' around a little place called the Wilmont Hotel, staring at the animated wallpaper and the color-television test pattern. I stumbled down to a little place called the Four Corner Bar. Walked inside, passing out wolf tickets, decked out in full regalia — looking slicker than deer guts on a doorknob. I pulled up next to a shapely little miss . . . I'm talkin' about hubba hubba and ding ding ding . . . I elbowed up next to her. She took one look at me and she said, 'Lookit here. In the first place, you're so ugly you can probably make a freight train take a dirt road.' I didn't let it get me down, though. She said, 'You might as well hang it up, I'm a lesbian anyhow.' Shit . . . 'I don't mind if you're a lesbian. I know there's a whole lot of that shit goin' round nowadays. It don't bother me . . . Shit, I got relatives out in Beirut. We oughta get along real well.'"[3]

Waits's reputation as a top-quality live act was mounting. Here was an artist who could paint word pictures, and his music simmered. This led to Waits being offered his first serious television gig: he was invited to perform live on the PBS show *Soundstage*. Heightening the thrill factor for Waits was the knowledge that he would be sharing the bill with his long-time idol Mose Allison. The segment's highlight is the opening number, Waits's dramatic a capella performance of "Eggs and Sausage." Wearing a ratty black sports coat, a loose tie, and a brown beret, he sits at the counter of a real diner, cigarette in hand. Around him we glimpse tired waitresses, bored patrons, sizzling burgers. His only musical accompaniment is the snapping of his fingers and the slapping of his leg. Finishing the tune, he turns to a waitress and asks for another cup of coffee.

Big Daddy Graham, stand-up comedian and Philadelphia radio personality, remembers seeing Waits during the *Nighthawks* tour in a small Philly club. "We were going to the late show. There used to be a bar across the street from the Main Point, where I saw him countless times. We already had our tickets, but the line was so long outside we figured let's go grab a drink. When we sat down, I sat directly next to Waits, who was drinking at the bar." Big Daddy laughs. "He ran over there for a drink in between shows. Never happened to me before and never since . . . where you sit and drink with the guy you're going to see. It was pretty cool. I gave him a long set list of stuff I wanted him to do. And he pretty much did everything I asked. During the show he did 'Phantom 309' and he dedicated it to 'my new friend at the bar.'"

There is a tale dating from about this time that has made its way into

Philadelphia music lore. Whether it's the gospel truth, an exaggeration, or pure fiction, Big Daddy isn't prepared to say, "But it's a great story." It also revolves around the Main Point. Nearby there was a watering hole and restaurant called H. A. Winston's, an early incarnation of the chain bar — potted ferns, bulk-purchased antiques, and cute memorabilia strewn about. Everyone who played the Main Point — James Taylor, Pink Floyd — would stop in after their gig. The Winston's management was quite proud of this, but they could never get Waits to pay them a visit. Big Daddy explains why: "Because Waits conceived it as an un-Waits-like type of place. Which it was. It was really a thorn in their side that they couldn't get Waits up there."

Working as a dishwasher at Winston's was a guy named Artie, who had once been in a band. In the Winston's pecking order, you started out as a dishwasher, you were promoted to busboy, and, if all went well, you finally became a waiter. When the time came for Artie to hang up his dishrag, he balked. He wanted to stay in the back washing dishes. Dealing with the public didn't appeal to him. Artie had played a gig with Tom Waits somewhere along the line, and somehow Waits found out that Artie had ended up at Winston's. He decided to drop by and see Artie after one of his shows at the Main Point.

"The management and everyone goes nuts that Waits has finally showed up," says Big Daddy. "But he's not there to eat. He just wants to see Artie. And they don't like Artie. They're, like, 'Artie is in the back washing dishes.' And Waits goes back and washes dishes with Artie for, like, an hour, while Artie tells him his story. They had those glass portholes that look [through to] the back of the restaurant. People kept peeking in. What I always remember was, according to Artie, Waits came back and went, 'Hey, I see you have a Hobart there.' Hobart is the company that makes a particular kind of dishwasher. I always liked that line — 'Hey, I see you have a Hobart.' Waits apparently was familiar with the workings of a Hobart."

At about this time, Waits found himself looking down an intriguing new career path. Director Hal Ashby was making *Bound for Glory*, a film based on the autobiography of Woody Guthrie, the socialist songwriter and folksinger who, in the 1940s, penned such standards as "This Land Is Your Land" and "I Ain't Got No Home." Guthrie saw America: he rode the rails, crossed the prairies, climbed the mountains, and sang for his supper during the Great Depression. In 1952, when he was just forty, Guthrie was diagnosed with Huntington's chorea, a degenerative neurological disease, and he died in hospital fifteen years later.

Ashby entered Waits's name on the list of actors he would like to see portray Woody Guthrie — along with nearly every other folk-ish singer of note, from Bob Dylan to Loudon Wainwright III ("Dead Skunk") to Tim Hardin ("If I Were a Carpenter") to Guthrie's son Arlo ("Alice's Restaurant"). Somehow the part ended up going to a nonsinger, actor David Carradine, who was a hot property at the time due to his starring role in the martial-arts T.V. Western *Kung Fu*. Although Waits had been shut out in this instance, the notion that he could be an actor had taken root.

And he was fed up with touring. The daily grind was getting to him. Wake up in a new town, stumble out of the motel, try to find a decent cup of coffee, do a sound check, meet with some local interviewers, poke around town a bit, do a couple of shows, have a few drinks, sleep, head out to the airport — and on it went. It was getting kind of old. Add to that the fact that Waits was suddenly experiencing writer's block. It seemed inevitable. He had no time to himself. Someone was always there, pulling at his sleeve. He no longer had much opportunity to pull a stool up to the piano and let his ideas flow.

What finally pushed him over the edge was an incident that occurred at a little New Orleans club called Ballinjax. Waits was slated to appear there on a night that Bob Dylan was in town with his Rolling Thunder Revue (or, as Tom called it, Rolling Blunder Revue), a touring band made up of Dylan cronies. The revue featured one of Dylan's ex-girlfriends, folksinger Joan Baez; the former lead singer of the Byrds, Roger McGuinn, whose cover of Dylan's "Mr. Tambourine Man" was a major hit; and novelist and singer Kinky ("The Texas Jewboy") Friedman. Rolling Blunder trooped into Ballinjax on Waits's gig night, settled in, and decided to hold an impromptu jam session. "They got up there for an hour just before I was supposed to begin my set," Waits told David McGee of *Rolling Stone*. "Nobody even asked me. Before I knew it, fuckin' Roger McGuinn was up there playing guitar and singing and Joan Baez and Kinky were singing. By the time I got onstage the audience was stoked. They were all lookin' around the room and shit. I don't need this crap — it was my show."[4]

Tom needed a total change of scene, so he asked Herb Cohen to set him up some shows in Europe — a kind of working holiday. The dates were set, and Waits headed across the pond to play Ronnie Scott's, a famous London blues club. It was 1976, and as far as the British press was concerned, this new American phenomenon was a source of great interest. Here was the inheritor of the Beat tradition, a weather-beaten raconteur who'd been around. But, most importantly, Tom Waits gave great interviews.

Punk was big in London, and the ladies and gentlemen of the press had already had their fill of interviewing sneering, uncommunicative punk-scene movers and shakers. And as pleased as these journalists were with Waits, Waits was delighted with them. They constituted a whole new audience for his stories. He'd joyfully spin yarns for them about all those seedy characters he hung out with back home — like this guy Chuck E. Weiss (or "Chalky Weiss," as one British scribe recorded it), who'd sell you a rat's ass as an engagement ring.[5] Then Waits would start handing out advice, telling his interviewers where, in America, they could find a drink at any hour of the day; listing the worst places to stay in a variety of cities; and explaining how to find a reasonably priced pavement princess when you're a stranger in town. The Brits loved Waits's stories of cruising L.A. in a big old honker of a car, equipped with a six-pack of Miller High Life, singing along with Ray Charles testifying "What'd I Say?" or James Brown begging "Please, Please, Please." They could just picture him tossing his empties out the window, driving everywhere, going nowhere. The appeal was obvious. To these Europeans, who were forced to contend with confined spaces and complex social hierarchies, Waits embodied a drive-all-night, be-yourself dream of freedom.

Most of the European journalists who became so enthralled with Waits were unaware of the tradition he'd come out of. They were just too young. After all, Jack Kerouac and Lenny Bruce were already dead, Ken Kesey had entered the mainstream (the 1975 film adaption of his novel *One Flew Over the Cuckoo's Nest* swept the Academy Awards), and Allen Ginsberg and William Burroughs weren't getting any younger. But what did it matter? Tom Waits, great American storyteller and spokesman for the (somewhat romanticized) denizens of the night, was here and now and happy to oblige. He loved Britain. The pubs, the people, the attention — it was just what he needed, and he returned home rejuvenated.

By this time, Waits had pulled together enough material to make a new album, which he'd tentatively titled "Pasties and a G-String." It represented a new direction for him, and that was evident to anyone who listened to the first few seconds of the finished product: "Wasted and wounded / It ain't what the moon did / I got what I paid for now." The lyrics of the new song collection, which was finally named *Small Change*, had a dark immediacy to them, a sense of hurting that Waits hadn't really tapped before. Like his earlier recorded material, the *Small Change* songs were very well written and reflected their composer's famous sense of humor, but their lyrics had more sting.

Tom has always considered *Small Change* to be the high watermark of his early recording career. "There's probably more songs off that record that I continue to play on the road, and that endured," he told Barney Hoskyns. "Some songs you may write and record but you may never sing them again. Others you sing every night and try to figure out what they mean. 'Tom Traubert's Blues' was certainly one of those songs I continued to sing, and, in fact, close my show with."[6]

"Tom Traubert's Blues (Four Sheets to the Wind in Copenhagen)" is the album's stunning opener, and it sets the tone for what follows. It tells the story of a man who finds himself stranded and penniless in a foreign land "where no one speaks English, and everything's broken." Traubert is etched as a sympathetic character, but it's clear that he inhabits a hell of his own making. He'll never make his way home again because any cash he gets his hands on he squanders on drink. The song's chorus incorporates "Waltzing Matilda," the classic Australian ballad of aimless travel. ("Matilda" is Aussie slang for "backpack," and "waltzing matilda" means being on the road or hitchhiking.)

Bones Howe distinctly remembers when Waits wrote "Tom Traubert's Blues." Howe's phone rang in the middle of the night. It was Tom. Howe had long since become accustomed to the fact that being Tom's friend meant receiving calls from him at all hours. "He said the most wonderful thing about writing that song," Bones recalls. "He went down and hung around on skid row in L.A. because he wanted to get stimulated for writing this material. He called me up and said, 'I went down to skid row . . . I bought a pint of rye. In a brown paper bag.' I said, 'Oh really?'" Waits replied to Howe, "Yeah — hunkered down, drank the pint of rye, went home, threw up, and wrote 'Tom Traubert's Blues.'" Howe was even more struck by what Waits said to him next: "Every guy down there . . . everyone I spoke to, a woman put him there."

Howe was amazed when he first heard the song, and he's still astonished by it. "I do a lot of seminars," he says. "Occasionally I'll do something for songwriters. They all say the same thing to me. 'All the great lyrics are done.' And I say, 'I'm going to give you a lyric that you never heard before.'" Howe then says to his aspiring songwriters, "A battered old suitcase to a hotel someplace / And a wound that will never heal." This particular Tom Waits lyric Howe considers to be "brilliant." It's "the work of an extremely talented lyricist, poet, whatever you want to say. That is brilliant, brilliant work. And he never mentions the person, but you see the person."

Small Change explores a different mode with the next cut, "Step Right Up," Waits's jumpy and jivey indictment of advertising. The singer is a huckster who's selling the ultimate product, but his description of that product is so vague and rambling that you can't figure out exactly what it is — you just know you have to have it. Speaking to David McGee, Waits explained what he was up to: "I didn't take things at face value like I used to. So I dispelled some things in these songs that I had substantiated before. I'm trying to show something to myself, plus get some things off my chest. 'Step Right Up' — all that jargon we hear in the music business is just like what you hear in the restaurant or casket business. So instead of spouting my views in *Scientific American* on the vulnerability of the American public to our product-oriented society, I wrote 'Step Right Up.'"[7]

To Waits, one of the special things about *Small Change* was that it gave him the opportunity to work with a jazz drummer who'd been pounding the skins since the early forties. Shelly Manne had worked with a host of jazz greats — Coleman Hawkins, Stan Kenton, Woody Herman, Raymond Scott, Stan Getz, Les Brown, Art Blakey. He'd also recorded many highly respected albums of his own. Waits had been telling interviewers for some time that he wanted to work with Manne, that he considered Manne's backbeat on Peggy Lee's "Fever" to be close to perfection.

"The first time Tom worked with Shelly," recalls Jerry Yester, "Tom invited me down because I was going to be doing strings and he wanted me to hear the album and get into the atmosphere of it. I was there for the first take he did with Shelly Manne. And Shelly came out of the booth and said, 'Who is this guy? This is the oldest young guy — or the youngest old guy — that I've ever met in my life!' He was blown away by [Tom]."

"Pasties and a G-String (At the Two O'Clock Club)," Tom's tribute to the fine art of stripping, was Manne's best *Small Change* showcase. Of course, because this was a Tom Waits song the tribute was to the old-time burlesque cabarets, not to the impersonal chrome-and-mirror "gentleman's clubs" that prevail today. "Pasties and a G-String" honored the smoky old theaters where wild women with names like Chesty Morgan and Water-melon Rose delivered the bump and grind and twirled the tassels that dangled from their pasties to a tacky jazz backbeat, those darkened rooms where guys sat and watched, drank beer, and got "harder than Chinese algebra." Atmospherically, "Pasties and a G-String" is pure Waits; musically, it's Manne's show — no other instrument intrudes on Waits's voice and Manne's swinging and crashing drums and cymbals.

The album's title track may be the best known, and it is an awesome achievement. "Small Change (Got Rained on with His Own .38)" condenses a hard-boiled Mickey Spillane novel into a five-minute morality play. A small-time gangster named Small Change eats in a quiet neighborhood diner before making his way to the track to bet on Blue Boots in the third. As he leaves the diner he gets his ticket punched with his own piece. Waits claims that the song is based on a shooting he witnessed on 23rd Street in New York City. It is a compendium of reactions and effects: the cops joke about hookers and the cabbies, and the workers swear they know nothing; even the fire hydrants plead the fifth; someone steals Small Change's porkpie hat; no one bothers to close Small Change's eyes as his life trickles onto the linoleum and runs under the jukebox.

The listener is pulled into that dead-end diner, feeling the tension, the possibilities, the tragedy of the violent passing, the unmourned victim. Here, in the details, is everything that Waits had learned about telling a story with music. Unfortunately, a couple of those details had to be edited out. Tom was forced to change the lines, "The whores all smear on Revlon / And they look just like Jayne Meadows," when the cosmetic giant threatened legal action. And Meadows — the wife of Steve Allen, who had performed on Waits's favorite Jack Kerouac album — also had a problem with this vivid image. When the LP *Small Change* was reissued the offending passage was replaced with, "The whores all hike up their skirts / And fish for drug-store prophylactics." On the CD version of the album Waits sings the compromise lines, but the printed lyrics read: "The whores all smear on _____ / And they look just like _____ _____." Apparently Waits wasn't willing to let Revlon and Meadows off the hook so easily after all.

The moving ballad "Bad Liver and a Broken Heart (In Lowell)" is perhaps the album's best indicator of the small changes that had taken place in Waits's music and philosophy. Like "Tom Traubert's Blues," it explores the down side of the romantic image Waits had created for himself, but to even better effect. "I put a lot into 'Bad Liver and a Broken Heart,'" he says. "I tried to resolve a few things as far as this cocktail-lounge, maudlin, crying-in-your-beer image that I have. There ain't nothin' funny about a drunk. You know I was really starting to believe that there was something amusing and wonderfully American about a drunk. I ended up telling myself to cut that shit out. On top of everything else, talking about boozing substantiates the rumors that people hear about you, and people hear that I'm a drunk. So I directed that song as much to the people that listen to me and think they know me as to myself."[8]

Bones Howe knew that the songs Waits was now bringing to him were as good as anything he had ever written, so he stepped back and allowed Waits to develop his vision. "My purpose was to make the best record that I could with Tom. Tom is, and has been from the very beginning, very strong about what he wants on his records. He was not a produced artist, ever. As Albert Grossman used to say, I just delivered the baby, you know? [Tom] was the creative engine. But I did make a lot of suggestions, I think, that helped him. Tom always said that with each record I held the bar a little higher for him to jump over."

And *Small Change* was a success — critically and commercially. The album far outsold any of Waits's previous albums, particularly *Nighthawks at the Diner*. With it, Waits broke onto *Billboard*'s Top 100 Albums chart for the first time in his career. (He wouldn't manage it again until 1999, with the release of *Mule Variations*.) Suddenly Tom Waits was everywhere. He was profiled in all the music publications. Interviewers from such magazines as *Time*, *Newsweek*, and even *Vogue* lined up to talk to him. Waits remarked that his mother had never been entirely sure that a career in music was right for her son until she saw him looking back at her from the pages of *Vogue*. This was as close as Waits had ever come to being a rock star, and, given the choice between being an obscure cult artist and a cult artist with a sizable following — well, that was a decision Waits didn't need to mull over. He sat back and enjoyed what was happening to him.

Waits had toured solo for years, but now, thanks to the money and prestige that *Small Change* had brought him, he was able to put together a regular band. He called it The Nocturnal Emissions, and it featured Frank Vicari on tenor sax, Fitzgerald Jenkins on bass, and Chip White on percussion and vibes. They toured the United States extensively, and a number of those tour shows were broadcast on radio. Then they headed for Europe, where Waits had wowed the critics and consumed a few pints of ale the year before. They performed in Germany, Holland, and then Japan.

On Tom's twenty-seventh birthday, he and The Nocturnal Emissions played the Agora Ballroom in Cleveland. While Tom was doing "Pasties and a G-String" a woman slipped onstage, walked up behind him, caught his eye, and started to dance. Waits got into it, assuming that she was an audience member acting on impulse, but his shock was apparent when she started to perform a slow, sensual striptease. Shimmying out of her dress, the woman revealed her very own pasties and G-string. Waits regained his equilibrium and sang along to the stripper's bump and grind. As the song ended the woman disappeared back into the crowd and Waits joked, "Thank you, thank you. I haven't seen my mother in years."[9]

Nocturnal Emissions drummer Chip White explained to a European radio interviewer how all of this actually came about. Tom didn't know it, but that seemingly impromptu striptease was, in fact, a birthday surprise arranged for him by John Forscha, his road manager and old friend from L.A. It was an inspired gift: Waits enjoyed the spectacle so much that he had Forscha hire a local stripper at every remaining tour stop. Band members got to the point where they'd rate the girls. At the end of the tour, they tallied the points and named the Madison, Wisconsin stripper the hottest of the hot.

While the band was playing in Japan, White recalls, Tom met a very nice woman. They got along well, but there must have been some sort of language-based misunderstanding, because the woman was somehow convinced that Waits had proposed marriage to her. Unaware of having entered into any such bargain, Tom returned to the States along with the band. They were scheduled to do a gig with Jimmy Witherspoon at the Roxy on Sunset Strip not long afterward, and, in the middle of their set, there was a car crash outside on the boulevard. The electricity went out and the Roxy was plunged into darkness.

As club staff scrambled to get some candles lit, Tom's Japanese friend showed up. She'd flown all the way to Los Angeles to see her new fiancé. It soon became clear that the power wasn't about to be restored, and clubs up and down the strip emptied out onto the sidewalk. A huge block party ensued. Nightclubbers mingled with drinks in their hands, smoking and chatting. Among them stood Tom Waits, talking to his Japanese visitor, trying hard to explain that he just wasn't looking to get married.

Waits saw the *Small Change* album and tour as a turning point, not just in his music but also in his life. He told McGee, "I'm not money oriented, except to the point that I have bills to pay and I have to support a trio. I want to be respected by my peers and I want my old man to think that what I'm doing is good. For me, it's more of an internal thing. I'm just trying to do something that I think is viable, that I can be proud of, trying to create something that wasn't there before. My wants and needs are small and limited. I'm not going into real estate or buying oil wells or becoming a slumlord . . . I've got to cinch something before we get out of the seventies. I've got a lot invested in this whole thing . . . in my development as a writer . . . I don't want to be a has-been before I've even arrived.

That would be hard to live with . . . I don't want to think about it, man. Let's go get a pizza."

On a number of fronts, Waits really was creating "something that wasn't there before." For example, in 1976, six years before the advent of MTV, *Small Change* spawned what many considered to be the first music video. *The One That Got Away* was a hand-painted animated short featuring Tom pursuing a scantily clad woman of questionable virtue down a neon-hued street. The film was directed by John Lamb, who would later win an Oscar for his animation; the character design was done by Keith Newton, who went on to become a top Disney animator; and head animator for the project was David Silberman, who became the chief character designer on the T.V. series *The Simpsons*. Not only did this clip spark a revolution in the music business, but it also broke new ground in the field of animation: it was the first cartoon to be filmed live and then animated, a technique that has since become widely used.

Waits was having an impact on the vast national-television audience, as well. He warmed up while on tour in Germany by appearing on the popular show *Rockpalast*, and then, in April 1977, he did the hipper-than-hip new comedy show *Saturday Night Live*. The guest host for that segment was civil-rights activist Julian Bond, and Waits was one of two musical guests — the other was Brick, a disco-funk outfit that had scored hits with "Dazz" and "Dusic." When Waits came on he knocked them dead with "Eggs and Sausage (In a Cadillac with Susan Michelson)." (The song's title seems to have confused *Saturday Night Live* historians; in just about every book and Web site devoted to the subject, "Susan Michelson" is listed as Tom's duet partner.)[10]

Tom also guested on *Fernwood Tonight*, comedian Martin Mull's hilarious parody of T.V. talk shows. Waits had been the opening act for several of Mull's stand-up performances and the voice of a bartender on a Martin Mull comedy album, so he was pleased to take part in his old friend's latest project — and a highly successful venture it was. *Fernwood Tonight*, a spin-off of the popular soap-opera satire *Mary Hartman, Mary Hartman*, was a late-night-T.V. sensation. Mull played Barth Gimble, the smarmy host of one of the most inept local talk shows ever produced. Rounding out the *Fernwood Tonight* team were Fred Willard as Gimble's breathtakingly stupid sidekick and Frank DeVol as the show's tone-deaf bar mitzvah bandleader.

In the August 1, 1977, installment of *Fernwood Tonight* Waits plays himself — a "rock star" who literally stumbles into Fernwood after his car breaks down. As he is interviewed by Mull/Gimble, Waits demonstrates his deft comic touch. He complains about the meal he's served at the local greasy spoon called the Cup and Sup: "A buck ninety-nine for all you can stand. I didn't know whether to eat mine or give it a ride home." Offered a Sprite, he pulls out a bottle of wine and cracks, "I'd rather have a bottle in front of me than a frontal lobotomy." Finally he hits Gimble up for a loan to fix his car, "I had to leave our four-year-old for collateral." The only unfortunate aspect of Waits's *Fernwood Tonight* appearance is the way the chuckling of the studio audience (or, more likely, of the laugh track) intrudes on his heartfelt version of "The Piano Has Been Drinking (Not Me)."[11]

Don Roy King, who had caught Waits's act at Reno McSweeney's in New York City a few years earlier, was now directing *The Mike Douglas Show*, a live television broadcast out of Philadelphia. The impression that Waits had made on King that night in New York hadn't diminished, so when Douglas's head booker received a press release announcing Waits's new album King was personally interested. King was the only member of the show's staff who had ever even heard of Waits, so he filled his colleagues in, explaining that Waits played this cool character onstage, a kind of beatnik street poet. An invitation was extended. One week later, during rehearsals, King got a call from an agitated staffer: Waits hadn't shown up at the appointed hour. The car they'd sent for him had picked him up, but he then seemed to have disappeared. A search of the studio revealed that the security guard posted at the door had refused to let Waits in. Confronted with this wild-haired, unshaven, generally disheveled-looking individual with no laces in his shoes, the guard could not believe that he was a guest of the dapper Mike Douglas. The show's frantic stage manager eventually found Tom asleep in the lobby.

"Now it was my turn to panic," says King. "Tom Waits shuffled into the studio, mumbling something about South Philly, scratching a three-day beard, balancing an inch-and-a-half ash on a nonfiltered cigarette." King was freaked. "It wasn't an act! I pushed for this guy to be on our national television show, and he's going to panhandle the audience!" There was no time left to rehearse. King instructed Waits to talk to the bandleader and go over his charts. The studio audience was taking their seats. "Ten minutes later, Mike Douglas stormed into the control room. 'I just stopped at the green room to say hi to the guests and there's some homeless guy in there asleep!'"

King tried to reassure Douglas that everything was okay. The "homeless guy" was a guest, he explained, a jazz singer named Tom Waits. "It's just a role he plays. You'll love him." In his mind, King was typing up his résumé. "The first half of the show went by in a blur," he recalls. "I can't remember who the cohost was that week — Sheckey Green, Red Skelton, perhaps; maybe Joey Heatherton, Robert Goulet, Roy Clark — some seventies' popular-culture name. I can't remember any other guests either. Could have been Professor Irwin Corey, Shari Lewis, The Amazing Kreskin, I don't know. [The other guests were actress Glenda Jackson and composer Marvin Hamlisch.] But what I do remember is Tom Waits. And I'll bet every member of that staff and crew, every member of the studio and home audience remembers him, too. Tom knocked 'em dead!"

"Mike introduced him," continues King, by saying, "'A new talent on the cabaret scene, blah-blah-blah.' Something like that. And then suddenly there was Tom and all the regular rhythms of television talk skidded from four/four time into some beat only three-armed drummers could play. Mike was asking simple 'How did you get started?' kinds of prewritten questions. But Tom was answering in this otherworldly, or rather under-worldly, way. He was sputtering and wheezing and barely intelligible but genuinely poetic. Street poetic. His answers sounded like quotes from some Clifford Odets Depression[-era] play. Mike was getting nervous. I was holding my breath."

Finally Douglas asked Waits to sing a song. The control room went quiet, and on the floor technicians scurried about, trying hard to stay out of Douglas's line of vision. The floor producer lost track of the cue-card sequence. King had the sickening feeling that the show was going down in flames. "Tom got up, lurched to the performance area, and began. I glanced over at Mike's monitor. He was hooked. I saw that small, crooked smile of his, the one that meant he liked what he saw. I always believed that Mike's success was due mostly to his unselfish love of performers doing well. He didn't mind being upstaged by his guests. If they got big laughs or standing ovations he was thrilled. They'd scored on his show, and he loved it. Well, he was loving this. Tom was mesmerizing and he knew it. We all knew it."

King resorts to figurative language in conveying the impact of Waits's performance: "In three riveting minutes the painting was done. It was harsh and hard-edged and very real. But there was an abstract rush to it, too. Some steady hand had splattered reds and blacks and yellows in a way that opened up a dark and unknown world and let us in. We'd been escorted to those backstreets we fear. Those alleys we've never seen after dark. Mike jumped up at the end, rushed over to Tom. I could tell he was surprised and happy and relieved. (Not nearly as relieved as his director, however.) I seem to remember Mike putting his arm around him, probably catching his ring on the rip in Tom's jacket. Tom mumbled a thank-you, and the show went on." After that, King says, they filled their ninety-minute time slots with a parade of popular guests, "But things were never quite the same. Every camera operator, every band member, every writer on that show did Tom Waits impressions for weeks."[12]

5

FOREIGN AFFAIRS

"He talked to me about doing this other material," Bones Howe recalls. Waits was ready to record again, and he described to Howe his method for putting *Foreign Affairs* together. "He said, 'I'm going to do the demos first, and then I'm gonna let you listen to them. Then we should talk about what it should be.' I listened to the material and said, 'It's like a black-and-white movie.' That's where the cover came from. The whole idea that it was going to be a black-and-white movie. It's the way it seemed to me when we were putting it together. Whether or not it came out that way, I don't have any idea, because there's such metamorphosis when you're working on [records]. They change and change."

Broken dreams, back alleys, and whiskey bars made up the by-now-familiar terrain Waits traveled through while writing material for this new album. The delicate instrumental "Cinny's Waltz" opens *Foreign Affairs*, setting a nostalgic mood, echoing Gerry and the Pacemakers' sixties hit "Ferry 'Cross the Mersey." "Muriel," a sorrowful ballad, extends that mood a little farther into habitual sadness. In it, a man finds that since his lover has left him, the bars have been shuttered, the lights have been dimmed, the earth has gone dark. He's visited by the ghosts of their dead love — don't those apparitions know it's the end of the world?

Next up was "I Never Talk to Strangers," which Tom did as a duet with the inimitable Bette Midler. David Geffen had introduced Midler to Waits's music as part of his campaign to expose the work of lesser-known artists to the broad audience a star performer could command. On her 1976 album *Songs for the New Depression*, Midler had included a sweet, intense version of "Shiver Me Timbers," and now she was carrying the association a step further by agreeing to sing a duet with Waits. "I Never Talk to Strangers" appeared on both *Foreign Affairs* and Midler's 1977 release

Broken Blossom. The song feels like the sequel to the *Closing Time* track "I Hope That I Don't Fall in Love with You." Both are about a barfly who spots an attractive woman sitting a few stools over, but while the "I Hope That I Don't Fall" barfly fails to act, the "I Never Talk to Strangers" guy summons up enough courage to approach the object of his desires. Waits sings the man; Midler sings the woman. Each has been battered and scarred in the war of the sexes, and they circle one another warily — he tentatively sweet-talks her, she vigorously fends him off and then yields just a little. Waits's gruff patter and Midler's chiming responses dovetail exquisitely.

Foreign Affairs also includes Waits's musical tribute to his Beat Generation heroes Neal Cassady and Jack Kerouac. "Jack and Neal/California, Here I Come" depicts a wild cross-country road trip undertaken by the legendary *On the Road* buddies and a sexually adventurous nurse ("A redhead in a uniform will always get you horny"). They tear along highways and byways like race-car drivers, attempt to buy uppers from Mexican pushers, make love with their nurse while traversing the Nebraska plains, drain bottles of Mad Dog wine, moon passing cars, and perpetually run out of smokes. The song's virtuoso lyrics and jazzy melody perfectly capture the antisocial abandon of the novel it salutes. "Jack and Neal" builds to its joyous conclusion with Al Jolson's triumphant demand, "Open up your Golden Gate, California, here we come!"

Perhaps the most arresting *Foreign Affairs* cut is "Potter's Field," a spoken-word piece about a blind, alcoholic stool pigeon who tries to score some booze in exchange for his account of a gangland hit. Behind Waits's voice, drums pound, horns wail, and a short, wonderfully nuanced crime drama unfolds in the listener's mind. There is an immediacy, a catch-you-by-the-throat urgency to this track, which was the most successful of Waits's spoken-word pieces to date.

Howe remembers that Waits said of "Potter's Field," "I've written this lyric, and I don't think I want it to be a song. I think I want to recite it." Responded Howe, "If you're going to recite it and not sing it, maybe we should score it like it's a little movie." Waits thought this was a great idea. "That's how [Bob] Alcivar got involved," says Bones. "Alcivar had been doing arrangements for me and had done some scoring and stuff for T.V. movies. I said [to Tom], you'll read it and the orchestra will play and we'll do it live. We'll score it live. We did it once, and it didn't exactly work out. But we had the tape of it. We took the tape back and Bob worked with the tape. I remember he shortened some places, and Tom wanted some things to be faster and some things to be slower, and we went back in and recorded it again . . . live."

Another beautiful *Foreign Affairs* musical story is the bittersweet ballad "Burma Shave." Based loosely on an old Farley Granger film called *They Live by Night* (Granger is also mentioned in the song), the ballad tells of the singer's escape from a decaying town named Marysville. Tough as it is to leave behind the known and the familiar to head into uncharted territory, he has no choice. To stay on in this dying community is to die along with it, so he points his sedan toward an illusive destination — a nirvana called Burma Shave. Years later, Bruce Springsteen covered similar ground with the melancholy and moving "My Hometown," but he didn't quite manage to capture the sense of desperation and regret that suffuses Waits's "Burma Shave." Or, for that matter, the *Foreign Affairs* cut called "A Sight for Sore Eyes," in which an aging bar patron explains to the bartender what has become of his friends — alive or dead — who have moved on.

Foreign Affairs was a commercial flop. No one could realistically have expected Tom Waits to become a pop star, so the fate of *Foreign Affairs* wasn't particularly surprising, but it was a bit of a letdown after *Small Change*, which had sold well nationwide. The record-buying public is notoriously fickle, and Tom Waits had always been the very definition of a cult artist. He was continuing to produce strong, uncompromising material, and he knew it. He would simply absorb such disappointments and get on with it. Tailoring his work to enhance its commercial appeal was not an option he was prepared to consider.

Over the years, Tom had experienced a few brushes with the law. Nothing too serious. He told *Time* magazine in 1977 that he had been pulled over three times for driving while intoxicated (an infraction that was much less frowned upon in the late seventies than it is today) and had once been caught stealing cigarettes from parked cars. So he'd spent a little time in the iron-bar suite, but none of this had prepared him for the run-in he was about to have with the Hollywood cops.[1]

Early in the morning of May 27, 1977, Waits and Chuck E. Weiss were arrested at Duke's Coffee Shop. The police said that Waits and Weiss, accompanied by an unidentified "female companion," were disturbing the peace. Waits said that he and Weiss were put in handcuffs and held at gunpoint. The police report said that the whole thing started when Waits and Weiss defended a guy who had butted in ahead of three plainclothes cops who were standing in line at Duke's. "Suspects Weiss and Waits . . . yelled to the unknown male, 'Hey man, I've got you covered,'" the report reads.

The cops claimed that Waits and Weiss then taunted them, calling out, "You guys want to fight? Come on." Waits and Weiss walked out of the coffee shop, and when "the deputies exited the location, suspects Waits and Weiss assumed the combative stance with clenched fists, stating 'Let's go at it.'" According to those "deputies," when they informed Waits and Weiss that they were officers of the law, Chuck made a "sudden movement" as if he were reaching for a gun or some other weapon. At this point both Weiss and Waits were placed under arrest.[2]

Waits was incredulous. He insisted that the plainclothesmen were at fault, not he and Chuck. The cops had been picking fights with the patrons of Duke's. He and Weiss were minding their own business and had just gone outside to make a phone call. *Rolling Stone*'s Delores Ziebarth spoke to Herb Cohen just after the arrest, and he described to her what happened next: "the cops came running out, pulled their guns, threw Tom and Chuck to the ground and handcuffed them. They told Chuck they were arresting them for homosexual soliciting and being drunk and disorderly."[3] Years later, Tom recalled that one of the arresting officers had put a gun to his head and asked him if he had any idea how fast a bullet could penetrate a skull. When the cops bundled Tom and Chuck into their car, Tom was sure they were going to be taken to some lonely location and shot.[4] Instead, they were carted off to the station house and booked. They pleaded not guilty to all charges. "When we start taking the testimony of witnesses," Cohen added in that post-arrest interview, "the police will look pretty stupid. They are going to get a little upset. But they deserve it." Waits himself told Ziebarth that "those guys must have gotten their dialogue from watching too many reruns of *Dragnet*."[5]

At the trial, Waits — whom *Rolling Stone* accused of being "uncharacteristically well groomed"[6] — responded to the charge that he had uttered profanities at police during the showdown at Duke's, admitting that he'd "growled a little under my breath. It was somewhere between a harrumph and a Bronx Cheer."[7] These strange proceedings lasted three days. Waits's lawyer, Terry Steinhart, called to the stand eight eyewitnesses who corroborated Waits's and Weiss's stories and confirmed that the police report was largely fabricated. They also described the abuse that Waits and Weiss had suffered at the hands of the deputies. One of these witnesses was Mike Ruiz, a member of a rock band called Milk N' Cookies. Ruiz told the jury that the cops had put Waits in a headlock and rammed him into a phone booth. District attorney Ronald Lewis asked Ruiz to help him reenact this particular moment, with Ruiz acting as Waits and Lewis himself playing the cop. Ruiz retorted, "No, you be Waits and I'll be the cop." The court-room erupted and Judge Andrew J. Weisz yelled for order.[8]

The jury was unanimous: Waits and Weiss were found not guilty. The two immediately filed suit against Los Angeles County for false arrest, false imprisonment, assault and battery, intentional infliction of emotional distress, malicious prosecution, and defamation of character. Each requested $100,000 in general damages and reimbursement of attorney's fees and court costs. The lawsuits dragged on for almost five years. Weiss and Waits again emerged victorious, but they were ultimately obliged to settle for a mere $7,500 apiece. Speaking to Steve Pond of *Rolling Stone* in 1982, Waits was clearly relieved that the whole ordeal was behind him. Still, he never regretted taking action: "It was insulting and embarrassing, so I felt it was my duty to make sure the record reflected the truth of the matter."[9]

Waits was back on the road again, and he was sensing that things had changed. He'd begun to play a lot of college-campus gigs, and they weren't working for him. A lecture hall filled with rich daddy's girls and hair-sprayed disco boys sporting coke-spoon jewelry wasn't exactly the definition of Waits's dream venue — he knew beyond a doubt that kids like these would never understand what he was singing about.[10]

Tom's travel routines were changing, too. His custom of checking into the worst hotels available had, of necessity, fallen by the wayside. The Nocturnal Emissions didn't share his adventurous lodging preferences.[11] The tours just seemed to drag on and on, and Waits often seemed listless and tired onstage. The exuberance that drove his *Nighthawks at the Diner*–era shows had evaporated, and he was relieved when all the tour commitments had been fulfilled and he could return to the old Tropicana.

Life on the road also seems to have undermined Waits's love life. He was never in one place long enough to focus on it. He did meet women he liked from time to time, but nothing ever seemed to work out. Itinerant lifestyle aside, Tom attributed his lack of success with the ladies to a basic image problem. One of his most famous quotes from the seventies was, "I've never met anyone who made it with a chick because they owned a Tom Waits album. I've got all three, and it's never helped me."[12]

By late 1977, Chuck E. Weiss was making some extra bucks between gigs by working in the Troubadour kitchen. One night a guy named Ivan Ulz was playing the Troub, and he introduced Chuck E. to his companion, a local waitress named Rickie Lee Jones. Ivan had asked Rickie Lee to come by and do a couple of songs with him — an Ulz tune called "You Almost

Look Chinese" and a song that Jones had penned herself called "Easy Money." It had come to her as she was sitting in a Venice Beach coffeehouse called Suzanne's (now long gone) during the summer of 1976. The song was the first, and at that point the only, thing she'd ever written. Rickie Lee and Chuck hit it off, and, another night at the Troubadour, Chuck introduced Rickie Lee to Tom. The three started hanging out together.[13]

Rickie Lee Jones had come to Hollywood to escape from home and find herself, as have countless other restless kids over the years. She had first run away in 1969, at the age of fourteen, with a girlfriend. The pair had stolen a Pontiac GTO in their hometown of Phoenix, Arizona, and headed for San Diego. They were caught the next day, but Rickie Lee hit the road again later, eventually making her way to L.A. in 1973. Jones didn't succumb to the young-girl-gets-devoured-by-wicked-city syndrome: she didn't hit a wall; she didn't get dragged into drugs or prostitution. Managing to keep her head slightly above water, she toiled as a waitress at a greasy spoon. Sometimes things got tough. Chuck E. said that at one point Rickie Lee was so broke that she had to sleep under the Hollywood sign. Rickie Lee herself recalled being fired from her job at a sleazy Italian restaurant near Echo Park, going home to find that the guitar player she was living with had split, taken the car, and skipped out on the rent.[14]

Waits told Timothy White of *Billboard* that the first time he saw Rickie Lee she reminded him of Jayne Mansfield. It's not surprising. The fifties' blond bombshell was a kind of low-rent Marilyn Monroe whose sex-kitten va-va-va-voom act had enticed legions of male moviegoers. But Mansfield was a tragic figure, too. As beautiful as Monroe and even bustier, but not as talented an actress, she was never taken seriously in Hollywood. Toward the end of her career Mansfield was reduced to taking small roles in such puerile fare as *Las Vegas Hillbillies*. Mansfield died in 1967, in a car accident. She was just thirty-four. The story goes that she was on her way to see a lover and that she was decapitated in the crash, but these are just mythical embellishments. With or without the mythic dimensions, Jayne Mansfield was an incarnation of the ideal so many Tom Waits heroines were striving for — that, or the fantasy lover of his cockeyed male dreamers. Waits's table dancers or tragic whores would view the life of a Hollywood sex bomb as the absolute limit: what could beat getting paid for your beauty and adored for it, too? It's a classic setup for crushing disappointments and even tragic outcomes.

Tom was instantly smitten with Rickie Lee, describing his initial reaction to her as "primitive." They embarked on a rocky romance. Sometimes they were lovers. Sometimes they were bar buddies. Rickie Lee loved the shady nightspots and dark corners of Hollywood as much as Tom did; Tom liked "Easy Money" and encouraged Rickie Lee to pursue her singing and songwriting. He was also impressed by her performing style, telling Timothy White that she came across to the audience like a "sexy white spade" — a glowing compliment in Waits's book.[15]

At the time, Waits would sometimes reduce the dynamic of their relationship to a very basic formula: she was drinking a lot then; he was, too; so they drank with each other. He'd add that one of the best ways to really get to know a woman is to get plastered with her. One of his favorite memories of their time together was the night that Rickie Lee showed up at his window and yelled to him, insisting that he come out and paint the town with her because she was wearing a brand-new pair of high-heeled shoes! He didn't have to be asked twice. They eventually found themselves staggering along Santa Monica Boulevard, smashed, with Rickie Lee barely able to stay on top of her heels. Waits really respected that kind of behavior in a woman.[16]

Part of Rickie Lee's powerful appeal was that she was always up for whatever Tom and Chuck could suggest. If they wanted to steal those cheesy ceramic jockeys from the lawns of Beverly Hills mansions, she was game. Rickie Lee was equally willing to hop a freight car. She had no fear. Once Waits invited Rickie Lee and Chuck E. to a high-powered music-industry party, and as soon as they entered Rickie Lee sat down with an avocado placed strategically between her legs. This embarrassed Tom a little, but he loved her moxie. When the trio finally realized that they were social outcasts at this soiree, they lathered their palms with chip dip and started shaking hands with people.[17]

Sometimes Tom's fascination with Rickie Lee turned to fear for her well-being. She was so much more streetwise than he was. She'd been living on her own for years; she'd experimented freely with drugs and withstood many hard knocks. If she could sometimes seem like a wise old goddess surveying life on Earth, then on other occasions, to paraphrase the immortal words of Bob Dylan, she could break like a little girl. Chuck E. described her as, by turns, tough and soft, nurturing and playful.[18]

While he was still caught up in his adventure with Rickie Lee, Waits prepared to record his next album. His momentum still hadn't abated:

he'd record an album, tour on the strength of it, and then head right back into the studio to record another one. Waits told Mikal Gilmore of *Rolling Stone* that *Blue Valentine* was "contemporary urban blues, sort of like the music of Ray Charles or Jimmy Witherspoon." What instigated the album was the realization that "you can get away with murder if you sing the blues. I heard a Roosevelt Sykes album not long ago that had a seven-minute song on it called, 'I'm a Nut.' For seven minutes, he sang, 'I'm a nut . . . I'm a nut . . . I'm a nut.' So I sat down and wrote a song called 'The Lunch-room Closed Down, The Newsstand Folded Up and the Rib Joint's Gone Out of Business.' But I've got a lot of sophisticated stuff on there, too."[19]

Unfortunately, that tune with the promising title never saw the light of day. Nor did another that Waits told Gilmore he'd written for the album. It was called "Conversation in a Car between Two Suspects After Having Knocked Over Yonkers Race Track with Three-and-a-Half Million Dollars, Riding in a '62 Nova, Headed in the Direction of East St. Louis." Explained Waits, "Titles can be very important. If you can turn one into your opening stanza, it can save you some work."[20] Even if evocatively titled tunes such as the two Waits mentioned didn't make the final cut, *Blue Valentine*'s song list is studded with gems like these: "A Sweet Little Bullet from a Pretty Blue Gun," "Red Shoes by the Drugstore," and "Christmas Card from a Hooker in Minneapolis."

Blue Valentine, Waits went on to remark, would display a tougher edge than his previous efforts had. "I'm playing the electric guitar for the first time, and shit, I know three chords, just like every other guitar player. But really, there's more blood in this record, probably more detective-type stories. It just comes from living in Los Angeles, hanging out where I hang out. I kind of feel like a private eye sometimes. I'm just trying to give some dignity to some of the things I see, without being patronizing or maudlin about it."[21]

There was blood, there was an infusion of the dignity Waits was so uniquely capable of perceiving in the battered and broken lives around him, and there was a new kind of energy fueled by Rickie Lee Jones. *Blue Valentine* reflected Waits's relationship with Rickie Lee in several ways. There was the album's artwork. Rickie Lee is the mysterious back-cover blond lying across the car parked outside the open-all-night gas station; her back is to the camera as Tom leans in for a passionate kiss. And *Blue Valentine* opens with a tribute, of sorts, to Rickie Lee. Waits liked to serenade her when the mood struck with songs from *West Side Story*. Rickie Lee loved it, so Tom decided to include a tune from the Romeo and

Juliet–themed tale of gang warfare in fifties'-era New York City on his latest release. He chose the showstopper "Somewhere," the song Maria sings to Tony as he lies bleeding to death from a gunshot wound.

Waits's version of the song — written by Leonard Bernstein and Stephen Sondheim — is as powerful as those versions performed within the context of the tragic musical. His voice cracked and ravaged, he transforms the song into a prayer for absolution. Somewhere, "There's a place for us / A time and a place for us . . ."

The next track, "Red Shoes by the Drugstore," has a lustful, jittery jungle pulse to it. The song skitters through the listener's consciousness. Frustration and neediness come welling out of the narrator, communicating through Waits's sly vocals, as he watches a good-time gal waiting on her man at a soda counter, wondering where he is, unaware that he is fast becoming a statistic in a botched robbery. "Christmas Card from a Hooker in Minneapolis," constructed on Waits's recital of a note from a prostitute to an old boyfriend named Charlie, follows. She insists that her life is coming together — she's going to have a baby, and she's finally got a nice place to live, on Ninth, above a dirty bookstore. She's met a nice jazz musician who is gonna take care of her and her baby, even though it's not his. She's off the bottle. She's off the dope. She's finally happy. But she eventually has to confess to Charlie that this is all just wishful thinking. "I don't have a husband / He don't play trombone." The hooker's back in jail and needs money to pay for a lawyer.

"Kentucky Avenue" is a bittersweet childhood memoir in which Waits recalls his boyhood home and his old pal Kipper. Two dead-end boys, one of whom is stuck in a wheelchair, look for adventure in their hometown. They smoke Luckies, watch the fire truck going about its business, avoid mean old Mrs. Storm, and dream about the local fourth-grade hottie, Hilda (who plays strip poker and even lets Joey Navinski French-kiss her). The memories compound and Waits sings his longing to set his wheelchair-bound friend free so that they can ride the rails together to New Orleans. "All these things are real," says Bones Howe. "'Kentucky Avenue' still brings tears to my eyes. I fought him for those cellos, by the way. In the end, he relented. He just said okay. Because I think there's another version of him doing it just sitting at a piano. It doesn't have the power. To me, it doesn't have the emotional feel."

"Whistlin' Past the Graveyard" accelerates the beat, the bluesy, bragging rant of a hooligan who stumbles into town on a freight car and sticks around long enough to stir up a little ruckus and get into a fight before blowing out of town. The hooligan's taunts are propelled outward in stutters and jerks, but he eventually concedes that his life's a hard and lonely one. "Romeo Is Bleeding," another of Waits's clever, jazzy crime stories, rounds out the proceedings. A guy who sticks a shiv into the local sheriff is fatally shot in the chest — a familiar Waits image, with echoes of *West Side Story* — and he feels his lifeblood seeping into his shoes.

The album closes with the glum, subdued title track. A criminal has been forced to enter the witness-protection program and move far away from his Philadelphia home. It kills him that he has had to abandon the woman he loves. As he struggles to forget, to assume his new, manufactured identity, he receives a card from her. Out of the blue. He has no idea how she's managed to find him — all he knows is that if he gives into temptation and contacts her, he'll die. So he sits and drinks and tries to obliterate the memory of what he has sacrificed, but the bad dreams and the good recollections just won't go away.

Intent on evolving musically and never falling back on established formulas, Waits made a momentous decision. After recording two *Blue Valentine* tracks — "Romeo Is Bleeding" and "Wrong Side of the Road" — he cut his ties with The Nocturnal Emissions and brought some strong collaborators into the project. One of them was former Mother of Invention and Jean-Luc Ponty keyboardist George Duke (who used the alias Da Willie Conga while working with Tom). Duke was about to become a well-known jazz/R&B performer and producer, scoring a big hit with the ballad "Sweet Baby" as part of a band he formed with bassist Stanley Clarke called The Clarke/Duke Project. As well, Waits put together a new touring band made up of veteran New Orleans musicians. He was stimulated by the prospect of working with old pros like Herbert Hardesty, Fats Domino's longtime horn player; percussionist Big John Thomassie, who'd worked with Dr. John and Freddie King; and guitarist Arthur Richards.

Waits also took a chance on a young bassist named Greg Cohen, who would eventually become one of his closest collaborators and a pillar of his band for years to come. At twenty-five, Cohen was only a few years out of Sonoma College and the California School of the Arts. A mutual friend told Waits about him, and Waits called to offer him the chance to try out for the band. "Waits auditioned us all at once," Cohen told journalist George Kanzler, "so he couldn't really tell how well each of us played, individually. He ended up hiring the whole band. At the time, I was playing with a lounge band in Los Angeles, doing the schlocky pop tunes of the day, so Tom rescued me from all that."[22]

When Kanzler asked Waits to describe what he saw in Cohen, the answer he received was predictably interesting and over the top. The truth is in here somewhere: "Greg plays everything from dinosaur music to dinner music, from steakhouse to Stravinsky. He is a Renaissance man and a road hog. He will always be the most indispensable member of the band. He is an irreplaceable obstetrician in the birthing room of the recording studio. He knows arranging, conducting, composing, bow-making and electricity."[23]

With a new band standing solidly behind him, Waits was ready to spice up his live act. His stage presentation became much more theatrical as he combined sets, props, lighting, and special effects to achieve a heightened visceral thrill. The club circuit was rapidly becoming a memory. Waits had a lifelike gas-station set constructed — complete with gas pumps and spare tires — to give an even more spartan and urgent feel to "Burma Shave," which he was doing live as a medley with George Gershwin's "Summertime." While performing the crime drama "Small Change," Waits would stand beneath a streetlamp; as the number concluded a shower of glittering confetti would come down and Waits would open an umbrella. Reminisces Bones Howe, "That gig that he did at the James Doolittle Theater on Vine Street [in Hollywood] . . . Herb booked him in there for a week. That was when he had the umbrella and the sparkles came down and stuff like that. It was really, really wonderful. In the time I was with him, that was the best. That was the way he should have been shown. He should have been onstage, like a performer. Like a one-man show, in a way. That was really the best that I think he ever was . . . at least the best that I ever saw."

Waits's acting career was finally jump-started when he became friendly with a former Philadelphia boxer named Sylvester Stallone. Sly had been bouncing around Hollywood for years, waiting for that elusive big break, taking a series of bit parts in B movies and doing odd jobs to stay afloat. Early on, he'd even been desperate enough to do a porn film. When it became obvious that he was just spinning his wheels, he took charge of the situation and wrote a script with a starring role for himself. *Rocky* tells the story of a Philly club fighter who gets a shot at the big time when he becomes involved in a publicity stunt: the heavyweight champion of the world fights an unknown contender.

The script was a strong one, and it generated a lot of interest within the film industry, but Stallone refused all offers because none of the potential purchasers would allow him to play the title role. He ultimately sold the script to United Artists at a significantly reduced price with the studio's assurances that he would star. *Rocky* was shot on a shoestring budget. The critics raved, moviegoers were moved and inspired by this timeless tale of an underdog who triumphs over the odds, and *Rocky* won the Oscar for Best Picture of 1977. Riding high, Stallone got the green light to work on a new project, also based on a script he'd penned himself. *Paradise Alley* was about life and times in a tough Italian neighborhood, and it marked Stallone's directing debut.

Bones Howe remembers that Sly and Tom "got to be friends somehow or other. Maybe Sly saw him at the Troubadour or met him through somebody. I have no idea. He was suddenly there. But it wasn't unusual, because Tom had a way of accumulating people. Chuck E. Weiss. Rickie Lee Jones. People just sort of appeared all of a sudden." Stallone offered Waits the small role of Mumbles and asked him to record some songs for the *Paradise Alley* soundtrack album. Tom jumped at the chance to act, and the part was perfect for testing his wings. Mumbles, a piano player at a neighborhood saloon, wasn't exactly a stretch for him.

Howe recalls that in the end he and Tom only contributed a couple of songs to the film's soundtrack — "Bill Conti was really upset because he wanted to do all the source music himself. He and Sly were very close, but Sly wanted Waits in that movie." Conti, a jazz musician, had scored *Rocky* and he was thrilled when the movie's rousing, horn-based theme rose to the top of the pop charts. Of the five tracks that Waits and Howe recorded for *Paradise Alley*, only two made it into the soundtrack: "(Meet Me In) Paradise Alley," a pretty piano ballad in which one of Waits's barfly lovers wards off desperation in the local taproom; and "Annie's Back in Town," a sad love tune with just a touch of *West Side Story* grit.

The other tracks that Waits and Howe had laid down for Stallone were a new version of the *Small Change* song "Bad Liver and a Broken Heart" (which incorporated the old standard "As Time Goes By" into its intro and outro) and two different versions of a song called "With a Suitcase." Neither version of the latter song was ever released. One was done with a rhythm section. The other — the "street" band version in which, says Howe, "we were banging on bass drums and all that kind of stuff" — reflected Waits's growing interest in experimental tones and instrumentation.

Paradise Alley was released to scathing reviews, and it flopped at the box office. Tom, however, didn't experience the acute disappointment that Stallone must have felt. After all, the project had allowed him to become an actor, and he'd thoroughly enjoyed himself. And soon another interesting opportunity presented itself. Tom was asked to write the text for *Vegas,* a book of art reproductions featuring the paintings of Guy Peellaert, who had recently published another art book called *Rock Dreams*. Excited about this new undertaking, Waits told *Rolling Stone*'s Mikal Gilmore all about it. He described *Vegas* as, "a set of emotional profiles and portraits of old heroes, like Marlene Dietrich, Jimmy Durante, Bugsy Siegel, Milton Berle, and Lenny Bruce." Waits dabbled happily in his various projects and remained convinced that none of this was interfering with his songwriting. "Well, y'know, ya have to keep busy," he remarked. "After all, a dog never pissed on a moving car, know what I mean?"[24]

With Tom's encouragement, Rickie Lee Jones had begun performing from time to time. One night in 1978, she played a gig at a little club in Hollywood, and in the audience was Lowell George, leader of the Southern rock ensemble Little Feat.

George had founded Little Feat in 1969 and now, nearly ten years later, he was bored with the enterprise. He wanted to do some solo work. Stifled by band life, by Little Feat's improvisational-jazz leanings, by his own towering reputation, by audiences that just wanted to hear retreads of "Dixie Chicken," George was determined to break out of his old musical groove and try his hand at some different genres and styles. He hadn't actually disbanded Little Feat yet, but all signs pointed in that direction. George didn't seem in any hurry to head back into the recording studio with his bandmates.[25]

In fact, George had been plugging away at a solo album, *Thanks I'll Eat It Here*. He'd wanted to use this title for an earlier Little Feat album, but his suggestion was vetoed and the safer, more blurb-friendly *Sailin' Shoes* had been selected instead. On *Thanks I'll Eat It Here* George planned to concentrate more intensely on his singing and create something that sounded completely unlike anything he had done with Little Feat.

There were, however, two problems inhibiting Lowell George's solo project. One was that George was a perfectionist. He'd record a song over and over again in his quest to achieve just the right feel. Tracks were tweaked, instrumental parts were trashed, and vocals were redone. The second problem was cocaine. George, and many of the people he hired to work with him on the album, had frittered away most of the recording budget, and quantities of George's own cash, on Bolivian marching powder. With a hopped-up perfectionist at the helm, the album's release date receded into the mists of the future. George had been working on *Thanks I'll Eat It Here* since 1976, and the end still wasn't in sight.

Watching Rickie Lee that night in 1978, George was captivated by

"Easy Money," her hipster story ballad. He had to have it on his album. It was to be one of the two *Thanks I'll Eat It Here* songs that George didn't write — the other was a remake of soul siren Ann Peebles' 1973 hit "I Can't Stand the Rain." George told Lenny Waronker, an executive and producer at his label, Warner Brothers, about Rickie Lee Jones. Waronker, who knew a good thing when he saw it, checked her out and signed her to a recording contract. At the same time, permission for Lowell George to record "Easy Money" was obtained, and George got down to work. He committed "Easy Money" to tape with uncharacteristic speed and efficiency because he was worried that Rickie Lee would release her own version before his album came out.

Jones won that race hands down. She made her debut album, *Rickie Lee Jones*, and Warner Brothers released it in March of 1979. It was a resounding success. By the time *Thanks I'll Eat It Here* was released, later that year, George's health was failing. He was a heavy man with drug and alcohol addictions, and he'd been hospitalized with hepatitis and extreme back pain. Just weeks after his labor-of-love solo album hit the record stores, the thirty-four-year-old guitarist/songwriter/singer died of a massive heart attack while on a press tour.[26]

Witnessing *Rickie Lee Jones* become a smash hit, many music-industry insiders shook their shaggy heads in disbelief. This was the late seventies. The music scene was littered with arena rock bands like Toto and Styx, pissed-off punks like The Sex Pistols and The Clash, and disco units like Chic and (at this point, anyway) The Bee Gees. Rickie Lee's debut was a jazzy, delicate, funky-bebop symphony, and it stood out on the *Billboard* charts like a sore thumb.

What had actually propelled *Rickie Lee Jones* to the top of those charts was an earthy tribute to good friend Chuck E. Weiss, called "Chuck E.'s in Love," inspired by a remark that Waits had once made. One night Jones was with Waits in his room at the Tropicana when the phone rang. It was Chuck E. calling from Denver to say that he'd just met a distant cousin and was quite taken with her. Tom and Chuck talked for a while, and when Tom hung up he looked over at Rickie Lee and said, "Chuck E.'s in love."[27] The line caught Rickie Lee's fancy and she constructed a song out of it. It wasn't the first song ever written about Chuck E. Weiss; Waits had sung about his buddy in the *Nighthawks at the Diner* tune "Nighthawk Postcards (From Easy Street)," and Chuck E. was also mentioned in two *Small Change* songs — "Jitterbug Boy (Sharing a Curbstone with Chuck E.

Weiss, Robert Marchese, Paul Body and the Mug and Artie)" and "I Wish I Was in New Orleans (In the Ninth Ward)."

The single "Chuck E.'s in Love" was a good-time finger-popper about the boho nightlife to be found in pool halls, diners, and clubs. It was unlike anything else in radio rotation at the time, and it became one of the biggest hits of the year. Tom didn't contribute directly to *Rickie Lee Jones*, but the album bore many traces of the trademark Tom Waits musical sensibility, and the delicate musical photographs "On Saturday Afternoons in 1963" and "The Last Chance Texaco" featured the type of hard-luck romanticism that was so dear to Tom's heart. The jazzy swing of "Danny's All-Star Joint" and "Young Blood" further enlivened the collection.

Rickie Lee's sudden success meant a packed schedule and increased strain on her already-tenuous relationship with Tom. The two finally admitted that they wanted different things from life and stopped seeing each other. Since the breakup, Rickie Lee has generally been reluctant to discuss their relationship. Still, in one interview with Timothy White of *Billboard*, she did tarnish the carefully constructed Waits persona to some extent by insisting that in the long run what Tom really wanted was to lead a normal suburban existence with all the standard features — loving wife, kids, pets, Little League games, PTA meetings. Her remarks would prove prophetic.

When Waits finally became fed up with the fact that the Tropicana Hotel had become an amusement park for rock stars, he pulled up stakes and moved out. He said that the last straw was when they painted the swimming pool black.[28] "When I started making albums and touring," he told Dave Zimmer of *Bam* in 1982, "certain things started happening. People started sending me letters, telling me I was top drawer. And when I put my address and telephone number on the back of [*Small Change*], strangers started looking for my place and calling me on the phone. So while I gained a certain amount of professional success, my personal life began to shrink to the point that I became like a kind of geek." At the Tropicana he'd begun to feel imprisoned. "When you can't go back and live in the world you come from, and you can't live in the world you're in, you get in your little sports car and drive ninety miles an hour down a dead-end street. There was always the danger of getting sucked down . . . I felt I'd painted myself in a corner. I'd fallen in with a bad crowd and needed a new landscape, a new story."[29]

So Waits went off into a new landscape and didn't tell many people where he was going. He became very hard to find. He moved into a little house on Crenshaw Street in Los Angeles — and Crenshaw, as Waits pointed out, is one very long street. The Tropicana was finally torn down and replaced with a huge art-deco gay hotel, which producer Mary Aloe describes as "a Dr. Seuss version of a Ramada. You go there and it looks like Whoville." The motel's neighbor, Duke's Coffee Shop, moved up into the heart of Sunset Strip.

When reminiscing about the old Tropicana, Waits betrays a certain nostalgia. He told the listening audience of the Los Angeles radio show *Morning Becomes Eclectic*: "It wasn't that bad. It doesn't seem that long ago. I guess my life's different now. When I moved into the Tropicana it was nine dollars a night, and it was one of those out-of-the-way places — about a block away from the Alta Cienega, which is another one of those 'murder motels' — but it's changed a lot. That bowling alley that used to be there changed hands four or five times and I think they're selling slacks there now. If you live in Los Angeles, things change so rapidly. Places that you used to go . . . if you leave town for two or three months, chances are they'll tear down the gas station or the donut shop or the cleaners where you go. The hotel is gone, so I guess it kind of stimulates your imagination about it once you tear down the place where it all happened. The stories get taller as the building gets shorter."[30]

Waits continued to tour with his new, theatrical show, and it met with raves. He even arranged his props and backdrops on the set of the PBS concert series *Austin City Limits*, much to the delight of the live studio audience. But for the first time since the inauguration of his recording career Waits let a year go by without releasing an album; 1979 came and went with no sign of a Tom Waits record. *Blue Valentine* had gone over well with the critics, but it hadn't sold well in the United States. Neither had his previous album. It now seemed that Waits's popularity as a major recording artist was on the wane — at home, at least; he could take solace in the fact that he was getting bigger internationally. During his 1979 tour he traveled to Australia for the very first time.

Through it all, however, Waits's confusion over his work, and his life in general, was deepening. His retreat to the little house on Crenshaw had helped in the short term, but what he needed, he soon realized, was a dramatic change of scenery. In order to begin the process of recharging he was going to have to put some serious distance between himself and his familiar California milieu. So Tom Waits decided to move to New York City. Manhattan would challenge him, wake him up, shake him up. Tom, of course, put a lighter spin on the decision. He told everyone that New York was a great town for shoes — that's why he was going, dammit! And it had a whole new set of bars for him to experience. So off he went, checking into the legendary Chelsea Hotel on arrival.

On *VH1 Storytellers*, Waits recalled sitting alone in his room at the Chelsea one night, trying to watch *The Ox-Bow Incident*. When the movie was less than half over the door opened and a strange couple, engaged in an argument, came in and sat down. Waits perched on the bed, watching them fight and missing his movie. It turned out that the two had stayed in the room before and had kept the key so they could get back in. Waits pointed out that they couldn't stay and that they were interrupting his evening's entertainment. It became apparent that the only way to get rid of the pair was to give them money for another room, so Tom slipped the guy a fifty-dollar bill. He was taken aback when the man came back with the change.[31] Soon afterward, Tom left the Chelsea and moved into a small flat he'd rented nearby. He even became a member of the McBurney YMCA because he wanted to get himself into good physical shape. His life as a New Yorker had begun.

Bones Howe believes that the real reason Tom chose Manhattan as his new base of operations had nothing to do with scenery changes or shoes or a quest for fresh watering holes. He admits, "You know, Tom did go to New York and try to work with another producer. I was aware of that. He did some demos and stuff. He came back and we talked a lot about what he wanted to do. It was between *Blue Valentine* and *Heartattack and Vine*." While in New York, Waits attempted to come to a meeting of the minds with Jack Nitzche and several other producers, but it just wasn't happening for him. None of it — neither the producers nor the city itself. New York, New York may be a wonderful town, where the Bronx is up and the Battery down, but Tom Waits was feeling a little lost.

He realized that it was time to give it up the day he found himself running through Chelsea trying not to spill his drink on his way to a workout at the Y. In fact, he more than once compared his time in the Big Apple to a prison term. "It was thirty below," he told Dave Zimmer. "I was paying six hundred dollars a month for a miserable little apartment and I spent three hundred on locks for my doors, because I was constantly worried about burglars. One of my neighbors was this Yugoslavian lady who wore black pajamas and sticks on her back. I was rescued from this situation by Francis."[32]

6

THIS ONE'S FROM
THE HEART

In the spring of 1980, Waits's New York City adventure was terminated when he learned that director Francis Ford Coppola wanted him to score his latest film. It was to be the first movie Coppola had made since releasing *Apocalypse Now*, in which he'd taken *Heart of Darkness* — Joseph Conrad's voyage into the Belgian Congo and the dark recesses of the human soul — and transformed it into a stunning, surreal take on the Vietnam War. Coppola was by now powerful enough within the industry (he also had *The Godfather* and *The Conversation* on his résumé) to be heading up his own studio, American Zoetrope Pictures, which had recently taken over the premises of historic Hollywood General Studios. Coppola was a player.

Apocalypse Now came out in 1979. It had been a hellish picture to make. Shot on location in the Philippines, the production was plagued by a ballooning budget, schedule overruns, and the megatantrums thrown by Marlon Brando, who was being paid millions for a cameo role. Things got so taxing, physically and mentally, that star Martin Sheen suffered both a heart attack and a nervous breakdown. (Coming to terms with the ordeal that nearly broke her husband, Eleanor Coppola made a fascinating documentary based on the project called *Hearts of Darkness: A Filmmaker's Journey*, which was released in 1992.)

Emerging from the pressure cooker that was *Apocalypse Now*, Coppola was ready to plunge into something a little simpler and lighter. Also, despite the fact that *Apocalypse Now* had rocked the film community and won critical raves, it was not an immediate commercial success. The costs of making the film had been staggering, and this coupled with the relatively poor box-office revenues it was generating amounted to a significant financial blow for Coppola. He needed a commercial hit in order to refill the coffers of Zoetrope, his fledgling dream factory.

Coppola was banking on *One from the Heart*, a romantic trifle about Hank (Frederic Forrest) and Frannie (Teri Garr), a couple whose relationship has run out of steam. They drift apart and wind up in the arms of exotic new partners (played by Nastassja Kinski and Raul Julia). This lover's waltz is set against the frenetic, glowing backdrop of the Las Vegas Strip. Coppola, yet another notorious perfectionist, resolved to recreate Las Vegas on a studio soundstage — the hotels, the shops, the streets, the cityscape ablaze with a million twinkling lights were all constructed, at a horrendous cost, on-site at Zoetrope, and the results were astonishing.

Shortly after, he'd discovered Waits's music for himself. Coppola was given a copy of the Bette Midler/Tom Waits duet "I Never Talk to Strangers" from *Foreign Affairs*. "He liked the relationship between the singers," Waits told Dave Zimmer. "That was the impetus for him contacting me and asking me if I was interested in writing music for his film."[1]

Coppola did not conceive of *One from the Heart* as a traditional Hollywood musical; none of the film's stars would actually sing (except for Kinski, who performed the tune "Little Boy Blue" in a fantasy sequence). But Coppola strongly believed that his movie should have a kind of running lyrical explanation — almost like a Greek chorus — to move the story forward. It would be interesting, he thought, if Waits could write songs that expressed the feelings of Forrest's character and for Midler to sing the inner voice of Garr. "I Never Talk to Strangers," Waits told Steve Pond of *Rolling Stone*, provided Coppola with "the thread of what he wanted for this score, which was a lounge operetta: piano, bass, drums and musical commentary."[2]

This idea captured Waits's interest, though looking back he acknowledges that the timing was off. He had already begun to tire of the cocktail-lounge dimension of his music, and he was eager to experiment with a new set of sounds. The piano and strings that had sweetened so many of his songs was now getting on his nerves — he claimed he was starting to sound like Perry Como. He wanted his songs to have a more earthy, visceral, lived-in sound. So in his contributions to *One from the Heart* he combined the best of the two approaches, blending the old-school melancholy of "Old Boyfriends" and "Broken Bicycles" with the stark experimental impulse that had driven "You Can't Unring a Bell." "When we were working on *One from the Heart* there was a lot of banging on tire irons," Bones Howe recalls. "What I call Tom's junkyard music was really coming."

"I think by the time Francis called and asked me to write those songs, I had really decided I was gonna move away from the whole lounge thing," says Waits. "He said he wanted a lounge operetta, and I was thinking, well, you're about a couple of years too late. All that was coming to a close for me. So I had to go and kind of bring all that back. It was like growing up and hitting the roof. I kept growing and kept banging into the roof. Because you have this image that other people have of you, based on what you've put out there so far and how they define you and what they want from you. It's difficult when you try to make some kind of turn or change in the weather for yourself. You also have to bring with you the perceptions of your audience."[3]

Zoetrope sent out feelers, Coppola and Waits came to terms creatively, and soon Waits was saying farewell to New York and catching a flight back to Hollywood. Waits's own version of how he hooked up with Coppola goes like this: "I met him in a bar. I gave him a ride home. He started borrowing money from me. And I said, 'Look, I'll see what I can do to help you.'"[4] Seriously though, Waits had always been intrigued by the medium of film and, despite his reservations about revisiting familiar musical sites, he jumped at the chance to score an entire movie.

He'd contributed a few songs to Stallone's *Paradise Alley*; Robert Altman had used some Tom Waits music in his 1978 film *A Wedding*; in 1980 esteemed European director Nicolas Roeg had chosen an older Waits tune, "Invitation to the Blues," for the soundtrack of his art-house flick *Bad Timing (A Sensual Obsession)*. And not long before getting the Coppola offer Waits had agreed to write the theme song for an indie film called *On the Nickel*. (An alternate version of the theme showed up on Waits's next studio album, *Heartattack and Vine*.) The film documented the experience of the bums who inhabit a skid-row area in downtown Los Angeles. Veteran character actor Ralph Waite (best known as Pa on the seventies T.V. family drama *The Waltons*) not only starred in the film, but also wrote and produced it. *On the Nickel* was Ralph Waite's labor of love, and the story it told — of a street survivor who goes back into the trenches to save a gutter-bound friend — piqued Tom's interest.[5] But no matter how much pleasure Waits derived from contributing bits and pieces to all these projects, nothing could match *One from the Heart* — quite simply, because Coppola had put the entire score into Waits's hands.

As a bonus, Tom was given a cameo role in *One from the Heart*, as a street musician who plays trumpet out on the strip. (The way Bones Howe describes it is that "Tom wanted to be in the movie, so Francis [stuck] him in a cameo somewhere.") Waits has since acted in four Coppola films, and the two men have become close friends (Waits even sang at the wedding of Coppola's director daughter Sofia and fellow director Spike Jonze). Says Coppola, "I am extremely fond of Tom Waits . . . as a wonderful person and friend, and great composer and performer. He is truly one of a kind. The score he wrote for *One from the Heart* is as fresh and imaginative now as it was twenty years ago. Also, Tom is a fine actor and a pleasure to work with."

As "fresh and imaginative" as the finished product turned out to be, the score was a major undertaking for Tom. Poised to begin his score-writing odyssey, he knew that he would need a guide and a support. Bones Howe, who had an intimate understanding of Waits's music and style of working, was obviously the man for the job. He was also willing to take it on.

With that settled, Waits and Howe embarked on the project. Waits became a nine-to-five worker. He trekked to American Zoetrope every day, and there he occupied a cluttered little office furnished with a couch, a piano, and a tape recorder. His window overlooked Santa Monica Boulevard and he had an inspiring view of a Gulf station — which he said made him feel like he was at the shore.[6] Waits imagined his new existence was like that of the people who had toiled in the famous New York songwriting factories. "I'd always admired the Tin Pan Alley writers, guys writing in brick buildings and hearing stuff like, 'Well, we need an opening song now, because we'll be opening in Poughkeepsie in two weeks. Come on, write something, then we'll run it up the flagpole and see if anybody salutes.' That kind of writing routine always looked attractive to me. I don't know how successful I was with it in *One from the Heart*, because it was new for me, and I had to strain and stretch."[7]

Waits was successful with it. *One from the Heart* contains some of his most effective and affecting songs, but the stretching and straining involved was considerable. For a man who was accustomed to recording an album in about a week or two, the experience of working on a single project for an extended period was an eye-opener. Waits labored over the *One from the Heart* score for nearly two years.

Then there were the inevitable bumps in the road. The first was Bette Midler. The official word was that Midler would not participate in Coppola's project due to "scheduling conflicts," but that entertainment-industry catchphrase conveys only a grain of truth. When Bones Howe floated the suggestion to Midler's people, he discovered that the Divine Miss M. had some serious reservations. She was working on a concert film called *Divine Madness*, and she'd recently acted in her first film, *The Rose*, in which she played a boozing, pill-popping, self-destructive rock diva, loosely based on

Janis Joplin. It was an impressive debut, the film had been well received, and Midler also had a smash single with *The Rose*'s title track. Her second film would be *Jinxed*, a failed attempt at pitch-black romantic comedy, costarring Ken Wahl and Rip Torn, that would effectively stop Midler's acting career dead in its tracks for about four years. At this point, however, she sensed that she was riding her wave of success straight to the top, and she was a busy, focused woman.

"We went through all sorts of gyrations because [Coppola] wanted Bette to be there," Howe maintains. "I called Bette's manager and he said, 'Bette doesn't want to sing in a movie that she's not acting in . . .' [I said], 'But she's going to be the voice of the movie. The same voices are going to be through the whole movie. It's a great opportunity for her. She's going to be working with Francis Ford Coppola.' He said, 'She's a bigger name in film than Francis is.' I said, 'Jerry, if you believe that, she shouldn't do the movie.' That was the end of it."

In the meantime, Tom Waits had fallen in love. Her name was Kathleen Brennan, and Tom, intent on both protecting their privacy and spinning a good yarn, offered many riffs on how they'd met. Kathleen was living in a convent, planning to become a nun. Her superiors had allowed her to leave the sanctuary to attend a New Year's Eve party, and there she met Waits. Kathleen gave up God for him. Other times, Tom suggested that Kathleen was an Irish freedom fighter who was enlisting him to the cause. He'd also hint that she'd been a member of the Ringling Brothers, Barnum and Bailey Circus. The truth is that Kathleen Brennan was a script analyst in the Zoetrope story department. She and Waits had been introduced at a party thrown by Art Fein, a fixture in the L.A. music scene and a close friend of Chuck E. Weiss.

"We met on New Year's Eve at a party in Hollywood," said Waits, in a more down-to-earth moment, during a 1998 radio interview. "I was leaving the next day. I was moving to New York City and I was never coming back here to the Los Angeles area ever again. That was what I said. But I'd said that before. So we met on New Year's and then I left. I was gone for about four months and then I got a call to do *One from the Heart*. I came back and I got a little office with a piano in it and I was writing songs and Kathleen was working at Zoetrope. She was a story analyst. Somebody told her to go down and knock on my door and she did and I opened the door and there she was and that was it. That was it for me. Love at first sight. Love at second sight."[8]

Kathleen and Tom quickly became inseparable. She saw the genius in him and wanted to help him develop it. She also saw that he wasn't taking care of himself. Soon Waits was looking better groomed; he also quit smoking and cut down on his alcohol consumption. (To one interviewer he announced that he now drank wine exclusively — Carlo Rossi was his personal favorite.[9]) Kathleen, it appeared, was the impetus Tom needed to clean up his act.

In the summer of 1980, Waits took a short hiatus from his *One from the Heart* job to record an album. "I took a break . . . and got in a humbug over my whole thing with the picture there," he admits. "For a brief spell, I moved out of my office at Zoetrope and went and wrote a record."[10] Waits named the new album *Heartattack and Vine*, explaining that he came up with the title while sitting in a bar at the corner of Hollywood and Vine. In walked a middle-aged woman clad in a bedraggled fur. She had on far too much makeup, but Tom could still see that she was a bit flushed. He watched as she approached the barkeep and told him that she thought she was having a heart attack. He ordered her to take it outside — he didn't want any trouble in his place. And out of this cold message an album title was born.[11]

Forsaking his view of the Gulf station over at Zoetrope, Waits moved into the RCA Building on Ivar and Sunset in Hollywood. He actually took up residence in a studio, and everyone began wondering if he'd taken leave of his senses, but he insisted that he needed the booth close at hand. It would push him to write fast. In Studio B of Filmways/Heider Sound at RCA, Waits bedded down on a couch and was relieved when it became clear that he wasn't going to be hassled by the security guards or dusted by the janitors. He was happy to soak up the vibe of the studio where The Rolling Stones and Ray Charles had once laid down tracks. (Not to mention, Tom liked to add, The Monkees.)

When the *Heartattack and Vine* marathon got up to speed, Waits would write a song at night, hand it off to Bones Howe the next morning, record it during a session that would begin at about two o'clock in the afternoon, and start working on his next composition. Tom's mission was to complete a new song every night so that when the band arrived, there would be something for them to work on. He was highly energized. The music was pouring out of him. His relationship with the members of his band was rock solid. And his rapport with Bones Howe was stronger than ever, because Bones's willingness to work against the deadlines Tom was imposing clearly demonstrated his commitment to Tom's work. All in all,

Tom felt that this was a great way to work, and he joked that next time it would be even better —he'd cage the band up with him.[12]

The album's title track is the most blatantly funky song Waits had ever written. "Heartattack and Vine" is infectious. It has a wild cockiness to it, and its smart-ass lyrics contain some funny and yet surprisingly profound observations, like, "Well I bet she's still a virgin / But it's only twenty-five til nine"; "Don't you know there ain't / no devil, there's just God when he's drunk."

"In Shades" is an old-fashioned-sounding R&B instrumental (initially named "Breakfast in Jail") that evokes Harlem's Cotton Club in its heyday or the establishment the singer frequents in "Pasties and a G-String." The next song, "Saving All My Love for You," is a vow of faithfulness that Tom had originally intended to include on *Foreign Affairs*. "Downtown," a rollicking, bluesy barrelhouse romp, is one of those magical first takes. Tom and the band got it right on the first practice take; although they went ahead and tried a few more, those efforts lacked spontaneity. Waits was particularly taken with Ronnie Barron's organ, which he described as "amphetamine."[13]

The centerpiece of *Heartattack and Vine* is a subtle little love song for Kathleen. In "Jersey Girl" (Kathleen spent much of her childhood in New Jersey), a guy walks along on his way to see his baby. Waits thought it had a Drifters feel to it and laughed that he'd never imagined he was capable of pulling off a song with "sha-la-la" in it.[14] Bruce Springsteen picked up on the song, and for years it was a staple of his concert repertoire, much to Tom's amusement. The Boss and Waits actually performed the song together live in L.A. during the early eighties. "There are T-shirts with 'Jersey Girl' [on them]," Waits marveled when speaking to Elliott Murphy. "It always reminds me of a social group. Is this like a gang or what?"[15]

Waits has referred to "'Til the Money Runs Out" as an old-time mambo, but the song is something much more intriguing and subversive than that. It's fueled by what is probably the most straightforward rock vibe that Waits had ever recorded, and it also features an early stab at the falsetto vocals that Waits would experiment with periodically in the coming years. The song rides on a jagged percussion track laid down by Big John Thomassie and a strange, squealing organ riff, courtesy of Ronnie Barron. Musically, it is both accessible and slightly disorienting. The listener is drawn into a dense narrative about Chinamen on Telegraph Canyon Road and hoodlums swinging from the rafters, before being dismissed with a taunting "Bye-bye baby, baby bye-bye." "'Til the Money Runs Out" is not just another strong Tom Waits song; when it was first released it amounted to a musical declaration. Waits was on the move again and the evolution of his sound was accelerating.

Heartattack and Vine also contains the sad and delicate "On the Nickel"; then there's "Mr. Siegel," a sleazy blues romp Waits says was inspired by gangster Bugsy Siegel. The beautiful "Ruby's Arms," in which the singer slips away from his lover forever as the sun rises, closes the proceedings on a tender note.

Waits had invited Jerry Yester to arrange and conduct "Jersey Girl" and "Ruby's Arms," and he later remarked that Yester's arrangement for the latter just blew him away — he loved the fact that the brass choir sounded so much like a Salvation Army band.[16] It would be the last time Yester and Waits ever worked together. "Right after *Heartattack and Vine* — or like a year after — I moved to Hawaii," Yester recalls. "And he moved up North. And I haven't seen him since. I've talked to him on the phone, but I haven't seen him since then — except in the movies . . ."

By now, the standard reaction to a new Tom Waits album was critical approval and public indifference. *Heartattack and Vine* didn't disrupt the pattern. The critics trotted out their superlatives, but the album got little-to-no radio airplay and the sales figures were disappointing. It seemed as though Waits was diving into some challenging and perilous new waters, and even his staunchest supporters were, for the most part, reluctant to follow him there. *Heartattack and Vine* did fare better commercially than either *Foreign Affairs* or *Blue Valentine*, but that wasn't saying much.

For the first time in his career Tom Waits did not hit the road after finishing an album. Instead, he went back to Zoetrope to fulfill his obligation to Coppola. Reinstalled in his little office, he quickly learned that such transitions can be tough. "When I resumed my work on *One from the Heart*," he said to Zimmer, "it was a little difficult for me to resume writing music that wasn't a little gnarled and driving — the kind of stuff I was writing for *Heartattack and Vine*. But Francis wanted the 'cocktail landscape.' So for me, as a composer, it was like trying to be an actor and having to try on different gloves."[17]

Furthermore, Howe confides, Tom "was a little befuddled by Francis, because [Tom] would call me up and say, 'Aw, I've written this great song. It's called 'Pickin' Up After You.' I would go in . . . and sit down with him at the piano and he'd play and sing me this song. I'd say, 'That's great.' We'd book a studio and record it. We'd take it to Francis and Francis would go, 'Oh, okay, that's nice. What else are you writing?' Tom was constantly grinding out stuff. There's tons of material that didn't get used in the picture."

So, on the one hand, Waits was under real pressure to produce, but on the other, he had the director's trust. Coppola was convinced that Waits understood what he was trying to do with *One from the Heart*, and the guidelines he staked out for him were anything but strict. Waits actually quotes Coppola as saying, "Anything you write that deals with the subjects of love, romance, jealousy, breakups can find its way into the film."[18] Coppola even constructed certain scenes with a given song in mind, so that Waits's music became integral to the project — it wasn't merely background or atmospheric. The male and female singers would fill a crucial role, providing revealing commentary on the experiences of the film's small community of characters.

"There was never any gospel script. There was a blueprint, a skeleton," Waits continued. "And right out front, Francis explained that the story would be changing as the production unfolded. Before I started writing anything, I met Francis in Las Vegas. In a hotel room, he took down all the paintings from the walls and stretched up butcher paper like a mural. Then he sketched out sequences of events and would spot, in very cryptic notations, where he wanted music. It was helpful. I was able to get an idea of the film's peaks and valleys."[19]

Waits and Howe would have "musical summit meetings" with Coppola at the director's Napa Valley home. As Waits hunkered down at the piano, Coppola would articulate his ideas, describing the series of little dramas that coalesced to form the whole story. The musical dialogue began to take shape, and the brainstorming continued. It was a cooperative exercise all the way through. Coppola had enough respect for Waits's talent to avoid telling him what to do. He did, however, push him to be as prolific as possible — Coppola wanted a large pool of ideas to pick and choose from.[20]

Diligently filling that pool, Waits maintained the day-job rhythm he'd established for himself before the *Heartattack and Vine* hiatus. He seemed to enjoy the normalcy of it all. "I'd get up in the morning," he later remarked, "have a cup of coffee, read the paper, get in my station wagon and then drive to work along with millions of other Americans." At Zoetrope, he'd get down to it in his spartan little office located in the story department. He'd launch into a stream of consciousness, taping or taking note of everything. He'd tinker with a melody, throw out some words, splice things together, blend ideas. "If one line didn't work in a song, I might stick it in somewhere else," he explains. "I never threw anything away. Because I never knew, when I was writing, what Francis might end up using. What, a year and a half ago, might have been a scratch track, could have conceivably been used in the final cut of the film."[21]

Since Tom had begun scoring *One from the Heart* before shooting commenced, he was working at Zoetrope during the set-building stage. He claims that he liked to hear the distant racket of hammers and drills as he went about his business. It was an inspiration to him, but it was also a goad: the project was moving steadily forward. With progress being made on all fronts, a festive, carnival-like atmosphere developed — carpenters, designers, actors, composers met, mingled, interacted. Then, when shooting was about to begin, Coppola gathered together the entire cast and crew to listen to the songs Waits had written so far.[22]

They were still, however, lacking a vital component. *One from the Heart*'s female voice had yet to be recruited. Midler wasn't an option, so Waits and Howe put their heads together. They got nowhere. It was Kathleen who put forward the surprising suggestion of Crystal Gayle, the younger sister of country-music legend Loretta Lynn. Crystal Gayle herself had recently hit the country big time, and her songs "Don't It Make My Brown Eyes Blue," "Talking in Your Sleep," and "Half the Way" had rocketed to the top of the pop and country charts. Her voice was undeniably gorgeous, but her polished, country-lite offerings were completely at odds with the jazzy urban squalor of Waits's compositions, particularly the gin-soaked Vegas blues pieces he was coming up with for *One from the Heart*. This didn't faze Kathleen. She'd recently heard Crystal's rendition of the Julie London standard "Cry Me a River," and she was impressed with the strength and purity of the young singer's voice.

During a meeting at Zoetrope, Bones and Tom were sweating the female-voice issue when Kathleen asked if they'd ever heard Crystal Gayle's "Cry Me a River." They hadn't, so Bones sent an assistant out to buy a copy. "Tom and I listened to it, and it was a great suggestion," Howe recalls. "I called down to William Morris in Nashville and got in touch with her manager, who was also her husband." He learned that Crystal Gayle was going to be in Hollywood the very next week to appear on *The Tonight Show*. Over a large lunch served with wine at Coppola's bungalow on the Zoetrope lot, Crystal Gayle, her husband, Howe, Waits, and Coppola discussed *One from the Heart*. Howe says that the two visitors from Nashville were totally seduced by the charismatic director. Crystal Gayle agreed to work on the soundtrack. Tom would send her songs to learn, and she'd travel to Hollywood periodically to record them. "She sang them exactly the way he wanted," says Howe. "She never changed a word, changed a note, changed anything."

Tom told Zimmer that "Crystal Gayle had worked out real well. She was nice and easy to work with."[23] Although it was a challenge for Waits to write for a female voice, some of the songs that he penned for the film were heartbreakingly beautiful. "Once Upon a Town/The Wages of Love," a smoky medley of Crystal Gayle/Tom Waits duets, sets everything in motion. It's followed by "Is There Any Way Out of This Dream?" — a simply ravishing piano ballad in which the singer reflects upon the ways in which her life has fallen short of her expectations. Crystal Gayle's honeyed vocals, through the medium of Tom's music and lyrics, capture the vague discontent that suffuses the movie.

"'Is There Any Way Out of This Dream?' and 'Take Me Home' were written for Crystal to sing," Waits explains. "'Old Boyfriends' was originally for me, then for her, then it turned into a duet. [Crystal Gayle's solo version was used on the soundtrack album.] 'Picking Up After You' and 'This One's from the Heart' were written as duets. I found that it was hard writing for a woman. There are certain words they're uncomfortable with. I can get away with a certain vernacular, while a woman singing it would have trouble. I had to change things around, put everything onto her words. It was tough. I felt like I was writing lines for an actress."

The film's core story is set out in the duet "Picking Up After You," which is as trenchant a breakup song as Waits has ever recorded. It is essentially a full-length musical argument. Each singer casts blame, identifies the other's unbearable habits, vents anger, yet the melody all of this is couched in is so sweet and tender that the potential for healing seems to exist even as the rift widens.

In "Old Boyfriends," Crystal's longing vocals make romantic disappointment palpable. The song is a reflection on former lovers who "look you up when they're in town, to see if they can still cut you down." Waits originally wrote it for himself, but sung by a woman it takes on more power. The songs that Waits did sing himself were just as redolent of emotional pain. "Broken Bicycles" uses busted-up bikes left outside to rust as a symbol for love grown cold. Tom has said that the tune "was an orphan for a while, until Francis shot a separate scene with Freddie [Forrest] in the junkyard, despondent. We tried that song against the scene; it worked and stayed in the film."[24]

Waits also sang "I Beg Your Pardon," a humbled lover's plea for reconciliation. Wearing his heart on his sleeve, he begs his woman to take him back, offering to give her "Boardwalk and Park Place and all of my hotels." The pace of the ballad-heavy soundtrack then picks up with the jazzy "Little Boy Blue." Waits sings this hopping tune on the album, though it was performed (half-spoken) in the film by Nastassja Kinski. "That was originally a song I was singing," said Waits. "Just another song in the movie. Then they cut it, sliced it up, and adapted it for [Kinski] to sing."[25] "Little Boy Blue" was the only number in *One from the Heart* that wasn't performed by Waits and/or Crystal Gayle, with the notable exception of "Used Carlotta." Waits had been toying with the idea of doing a piece like this for several years — an instrumental suite for car horns and motors. It was used as part of a fantasy sequence in which Forrest shows Kinski around the salvage yard where he works. In a bid to impress her, he conducts an orchestra of smashed autos. It's not surprising that this piece didn't make it onto the soundtrack album.

On the spooky, percussion-laden "You Can't Unring a Bell," Waits indulges his new infatuation with offbeat instrumentation. Next up is, arguably, Waits's most beautiful love song ever: "This One's from the Heart." To a muted sax and piano accompaniment, Tom and Crystal muse on the splendor and the suffering their relationship encompasses; they know that without each other life is mundane and colorless and needs to be tempered by the occasional stiff drink.

Tom and Crystal's voices melded beautifully, sandpaper and honey, but that didn't stop Tom from worrying. "Toward the end, Tom started getting cold feet," says Howe. "Saying, 'Well, you know, [Crystal's] really vanilla and all.' I said, 'Tom, you know something? Everybody knows what great lyrics you write. But nobody knows the great melodies you write because you just don't do them justice. You have somebody who really sings those melodies so you can hear them.'" Howe believes that Crystal Gayle's "best contribution was that she sang those songs exactly the way Tom taught them to her. We would go into the studio and he would sit with her on the piano and work the songs out. She would learn them and he would tell her exactly how he wanted to phrase the words. Tom had total control of the way they were performed."

The last session Waits and Gayle had together was, in Howe's estimation, the most incredible one of all. They posed for the album-cover photos, and then they performed two duets, the centerpieces of the score: one was the angry lover's spat, "Picking Up After You"; and the other was "This One's from the Heart."

Yet the perfect session came very close to being scuttled. While in L.A., Crystal learned that her mother had become gravely ill. She called Howe to say that she was too upset to come to the studio. "The rap on Crystal Gayle in those days was she had this beautiful voice but no soul," Howe recalls. "I thought she sounded really vulnerable and figured if I could get her to the studio now, I might really get something." He urged her to reconsider, saying that working might prove therapeutic for her — at the very least it would keep her mind off her mother's condition, a situation she couldn't control. "She came into the studio, and she and Tom sang those duets together that day. They sat at the piano together and sang those duets. It was such a wonderful, wonderful day in the studio."

During that final session, Crystal also recorded the redemption piece of the score, a beam of sunlight that penetrates the dark, smoky atmosphere. Said Waits, "Toward the end of shooting, Francis said, 'Everything's so sad, we need something with hope in it.' That's when 'Take Me Home' came about. The musical idea came early on, but the words were some of the last ones I wrote. I tried to sing it and it sounded real soppy, so I gave it to Crystal. I sat down at the piano, played it three or four times for her, then she cut it. I liked the way she did it."[26] The soothing "Take Me Home" is a gentle call for reconciliation, an acknowledgment that no one is perfect and that only through the eyes of love do our flaws become invisible. In this touching moment the musical story comes full circle.

Bones Howe had negotiated a one-off deal with CBS Records to release the *One from the Heart* soundtrack, but the idea didn't sit well with Tom. Bones remembers that Tom called him and said, "'I don't want to give them the soundtrack album.' I said, 'Why?' He said, 'I think it's too commercial Hollywood. I think what I should do is I should just sit at the piano and just sing all those songs. The soundtrack album should just be me singing the songs from *One from the Heart* by myself at the piano.' I said, 'Well, Tom, that's not what CBS bought.' So Tom went to Francis, and Francis said, 'No, I don't think that's what we should do. We should put all the sound effects into the soundtrack album from the place where they are in the movie. The soundtrack album should be like a little audio minimovie.' So it turned into this huge brouhaha about all that, and finally CBS just kind of threw up their hands and said, 'Well you guys just figure out what you're going to do.'"

Soon enough, though, the decision was made for them. Coppola had set up a New York preview screening for *One from the Heart*, and the critics in attendance gave it a big thumbs down. The word was that Francis Ford Coppola had followed up *Apocalypse Now*, a modern masterpiece, with a stinker. The love story was confusing, the characters were cyphers, and the happy ending felt tacked on. *One from the Heart* was rushed back to Zoetrope for some hasty surgery, but the damage was done. By the time it was released, *One from the Heart* was doomed to failure. Says Howe, "Then, of course, the guy from CBS called me and said I'm not going to put out a soundtrack album from a stiff movie. So there that soundtrack album sat for six or eight months."

During that interval, Elektra/Asylum released an odds-and-ends Tom Waits collection. *Bounced Checks* was an assortment of established songs — they couldn't really be called hits — from earlier albums, among them "Tom Traubert's Blues," "Heartattack and Vine," and "Burma Shave." Mixed in with these were a few alternate versions and live recordings — of "Jersey Girl," "Whistlin' Past the Graveyard," and "The Piano Has Been Drinking (Not Me)." A bluesy track called "Mr. Henry" was the only previously unreleased song on the album. *Bounced Checks* was, essentially, the product of a record company becoming impatient for new material.

One from the Heart turned out to be a bomb of epic proportions and was soon being mentioned in the same sentence as the previous year's epic failure — Michael Cimino's *Heaven's Gate*. While *Heaven's Gate* nearly sank Columbia Pictures, *One from the Heart* actually did torpedo American Zoetrope. Coppola was forced to give up the lot, thereby sacrificing his dream of presiding over a mecca for independent filmmaking. What made this defeat even more bitter was the fact that *One from the Heart* didn't deserve such a blanket condemnation. The quirky romantic drama had a current of truth to it, a lived-in feel that so many Hollywood romances never even approach. Plus, the cinematography and the art direction combined to give the film a remarkable visual impact.

While the film itself was almost universally panned, few had a bad word to say about the soundtrack. Many felt that what Waits had achieved was truly amazing. "Picking Up After You" and "This One's from the Heart" were rightly heralded as small masterpieces. Critics and music execs alike praised the score — the only problem was that only those who bought a ticket to see the movie could hear it and few, apparently, were willing to go that far.

About eight months after the film had fallen on its face, Bones Howe finally saw an opportunity to deliver the music directly to the people. When he discovered that *One from the Heart* was about to be released in Europe, he quickly got in touch with Coppola's attorney, who had worked out the original contract with CBS, and said to him, "Francis Ford Coppola in Europe is like Truffaut is here. He's a God. You call [CBS] and you tell them that [*One from the Heart*] is going to come out in Europe. If the foreign division of CBS finds out that there's a soundtrack album in the can and they're not going to release it, there's going to be a lot of heat."

So the attorney put in a call to CBS and asked them if, given the circumstances, they were going to release the *One from the Heart* soundtrack in Europe. The answer was, "We don't know," so Howe announced that he would contact CBS in England and tell them all about it. "And it's amazing," he says. "It worked! You know, you just kind of dream these stupid things up and figure, well, if this is the show-business game, I'll play the show-business game. But fear really works . . . They said, 'Well, how do we do this?' I said, 'You have a Tom Waits and Crystal Gayle album. That in itself should be worth something to you.' That's what they did. They just flipped the covers, put the front on the back and the back on the front. Called it *Tom Waits and Crystal Gayle Sing Music from One from the Heart*."

The album came out, and when the 1982 Oscar nominees were announced, Waits was among them. "We lost [the Academy Award for best score] to *Victor/Victoria*, as I remember," says Howe. Henry Mancini's faux-jazz score for Blake Edwards' cross-dressing comedy bagged the coveted statuette; but Waits had gotten some major exposure. Its effects, however, were short-lived. While the *One from the Heart* soundtrack was released on CD in 1989, it was never widely available for any length of time. It was a crying shame that such stellar work was allowed to sink so rapidly into obscurity. Finally in 2004 the soundtrack was returned to the stores, complete with a couple of never-released bonus tracks.

Waits emerged from the extended *One from the Heart* adventure a little older, a little wiser, and very eager to move on. At times during that undertaking, he'd hit a wall. "I wasn't used to concentrating on one project for so long," he explained — "to the point where you start eating your own flesh." Kathleen coaxed him through his periods of writer's block, and he refreshed himself by doing a few shows back East and in Australia.[27] He also accepted a cameo role in the big-budget 1981 horror flick *The Wolfen*; Waits portrayed a drunk and distracted piano player who plows through a ragged rendition of "Jitterbug Boy." And in 1982 he was thrilled to contribute to *Poetry in Motion*, a documentary on the Beats directed by Ron Mann and starring the likes of William Burroughs, Charles Bukowski, John Cage, and Allen Ginsberg.

Then Tom married Kathleen. The powerful Tom Waits sense of style dictated that the wedding take place in an all-night chapel that was listed in the Yellow Pages — Tom was pleased to discover that Marriage Chapels came right before Massage Parlors. Kitsch, of course, ruled the day. Waits told Elliott Murphy, "We got married in Watts, at the Always and Forever Wedding Chapel, twenty-four-hour service on Manchester Boulevard." He then added, quite soberly, "She's my true love."[28] (Love must have been in the air during the "Always and Forever" nuptials of Tom and Kathleen: bassist Greg Cohen met Kathleen's sister Marguerite, an artist and a potter, at the ceremony, and they were wed a couple of years later.)[29]

As a married man, Tom had a new set of responsibilities, and it was time to take a hard look at certain things he'd been taking for granted — personal finances, for one. Having pulled together and recorded a respectable body of work over the years, and having toured hard, Waits fully expected the figures to show that he was riding well within the comfort range. They didn't. In fact, as Tom and Kathleen discovered, Tom barely had any money at all. Like so many other entertainers, Waits had become a victim of his own shortage of business savvy. The contract he'd signed, in all innocence, with manager Herb Cohen ten years earlier had bound him to earning much less than most other artists of his stature, and, even worse, it gave Cohen the rights to all of his songs. Not only did Waits receive no income from them, but he also had very little control over their commercial use. Tom and Kathleen knew what they had to do. They took over all of Tom's business affairs, severing their ties with Cohen. Over the years, they've launched a series of lawsuits against Cohen in a bid to ensure that the Tom Waits catalog is treated with respect.

The next aspect of his life that Tom subjected to scrutiny was his approach to recording. He'd obtained a professional divorce from Cohen, and now he wanted to let go of Bones Howe for good. He was ready to produce his own work. Seven Tom Waits albums had been bolstered by Howe's talents, and now Tom needed to find out if he could do it on his own. "When you're working with the same producer," he told Barney Hoskyns, "and you're kind of collaborating on the records, it's a little harder to go your own way. You kind of wanna take everybody with you. For me, eventually I just wanted to make a clean break. Those records [*Blue Valentine*, *Heartattack and Vine*, and *One from the Heart*] I did with Bones, and I was kind of rebelling against this established way of recording that I'd developed with him. I don't know if I'd call it particularly unhappy, but I was at the end of a cycle there."[30]

Howe himself had seen the writing on the wall. He and Waits were clearly pulling in different directions. "After we did *One from the Heart* and the soundtrack album came out," he recalls, "Tom and I sat down and had a glass of wine at Martoni's. He said, 'I'm trying to write the next record. The problem that I'm having is, I know you so well and everything that I write, I keep thinking to myself, I wonder if Bones is going to like this? Or, I can't write this tune because I don't think you'll like it.' I told him, 'Tom, I shouldn't have any influence on what you create. Yeah, we do know each other really well, and of course you know the things that I like.' He said, 'I really want to get away from composing on the piano, because I feel like I'm writing the same song over and over again.'"

While assuring Tom that he was in no such rut, Bones did concede that if he truly felt that way, there was no "more rational reason for two people to stop working together than this. So, we sort of shook hands and said, 'Okay, that's it.' I just told him, 'Look, if you ever want to make another record with me, you know the kind of records I'll make. Call me, and wherever I am, whatever I'm doing, I'll stop it and make a record with you.' Because that was really, really fun. I miss doing that with him. I've never found anybody I've enjoyed doing that with as much as Tom."

So, over an amicable glass of wine, a long and fruitful partnership was dismantled. Howe adds that Kathleen played a role in the demise of the relationship, as well. "She really separated him from everybody in his past. And, frankly, it was time for that for Tom. Kathleen has been very good for him. He was never as wild as many people have said, but he was living in a motel and not really taking that good care of himself. It really was time. She separated him from everybody. Unfortunately, I was in the cut. I was from the past."

7

SWORDFISHTROMBONES

"I'm no longer a bachelor. I'm very happily married. I've also gotten rid of my ex-manager, and a lot of the flesh peddlers and professional vermin I'd thrown in with. My wife and I are taking care of all my affairs now. But I am looking for a new manager." Speaking to Dave Zimmer of *Bam* in 1982, Tom was flying high. Marriage, it seemed, had liberated him. With a smile he concluded, "I believe in happy endings. More now than I ever have."[1]

Heading into 1983, he was further energized by the fact that he was working on a new project. The ideas for his next album were flying fast and thick — he was even toying with the notion of making it a full-length video album and calling it *Flesh Peddlers*, in honor of his newfound independence. That independence was, after all, already having a powerful effect on Waits's art. It was inducing him to take chances that he had been afraid to take before. The warning of others, self-doubt, commercial considerations — all of these things now seemed to carry less weight. Kathleen had convinced Tom that he didn't need to find someone to replace Bones Howe. He could produce himself, taking full control over the finished work, because he knew his own music better than anyone else.

So the new Tom Waits album, entitled *Swordfishtrombones*, would be a Tom Waits production right down the line; with a little help from his friends and some esoteric creative influences, he'd conceive it, write it, arrange it, produce it, and consult on the artwork. He told Zimmer, "I used to think that after I was done writing and singing, I'd already done all that I was supposed to do. I left the rest in someone else's hands. I didn't want to deal with the rest of the production. Now I'll get more involved."[2] The prospect was scary — Tom was entering a steep learning curve — but it was also exhilarating.

Howe, then, would have no successor, but neither would Herb Cohen, the man Waits considered responsible for the sorry state of his personal finances. "I thought I was a millionaire," said Tom, "and it turned out that I had, like, twenty bucks."[3] He and Kathleen would take on the task of managing his career. It was an arduous task, involving mind-numbing forays into the universe of rights and residuals and several energy-sucking court battles, but at least it was under their control. There would be no more nasty surprises at the bank.

Setting in to work on his new project, *Swordfishtrombones*, Tom was thinking about Captain Beefheart. Known as Don Van Vliet to his mother and to the IRS, Beefheart was a high-school chum of Waits's former touring partner (and recurring nightmare) Frank Zappa; both hailed from Glendale, California. As a child, Beefheart had been a musical prodigy and a gifted sculptor. He and Zappa had played together in a few R&B cover bands before putting together a short-lived unit called The Soots. Zappa eventually left Glendale and made his way to Los Angeles, where he formed The Mothers of Invention. Van Vliet took the stage name Captain Beefheart from a Soots song and founded his own group, Captain Beefheart and the Magic Band.

That's when the fascinating Captain Beefheart odyssey began. Too obstinately off-the-wall to ever achieve much popular acceptance, Captain Beefheart and the Magic Band set about inventing a brand-new sound, melding the twelve-bar blues with avant-garde jazz and a touch of classical. With his gruff voice and multi-octave range, Beefheart gained a reputation for being one of the most soulful white singers of all time, and he and his Magic Band (which went through many personnel changes over the years) released a string of eclectic and brilliant albums. But while they were so strenuously pushing the musical envelope they were attracting only a very small following. Captain Beefheart himself was undeterred by this lack of endorsement. In fact, he was rumored to have been rather miffed when his single "Mirror Man" became a fluke hit in England. He'd become bored with it all just a few years before Waits recorded *Swordfishtrombones*, and moved to the Mojave Desert to concentrate full time on painting.[4]

Swordfishtrombones was going to be, among other things, something of a tribute to Captain Beefheart. Waits was burned out on his own trademark sound. He wanted to experiment more extensively with the blues, to create a calliope swirl of sound. New outfits, new moods, new noises — Tom would try it on and see how it fit. *Swordfishtrombones* would feature some obvious Captain Beefheart echoes and manifest an original, risk-taking musical viewpoint. "I felt like one of those guys playing the organ in a hotel lobby," Waits told David Fricke of *Rolling Stone*. "I'd bring the music in like a carpet, and I'd walk on it."[5]

One major difference that *Swordfishtrombones* would feature was the banishment of the saxophone. For the first time in his career, the saxophone was not used on a Tom Waits album. Waits had almost needed an intervention to kick the habit. It was easier for him to quit smoking. But he struggled mightily against the impulse — motivated by the suspicion that his material had developed a velvety, Italian-crooner aspect — and won. Into the saxophone void Waits poured all manner of offbeat and obscure sounds. Among the instruments he used to make them were metal aunglongs, marimba, bass drum with rice, bass boo bams, brake drum, bell plate, harmonium, freedom bell, bagpipes, parade drum, dabuki drum, African talking drum, and glass harmonica. Experimental percussion was clearly the order of the day, and most of that magic was performed by respected percussionist Victor Feldman.

While Waits had played around with the drums on previous recordings, particularly on Shelly Manne's songs, he rarely went further than layering on a snare drum or cymbals. "Until that point, I'd been paranoid about percussion," he told the *Morning Becomes Eclectic* audience in 1988. "I'd been terrified of drums for some reason. I started becoming a bit more adventuresome . . . trying to bring things up and out . . . that I couldn't reach before. You get to an impasse. You kind of have to take a hammer to it — so I did."[6]

Much of Waits's infatuation with various forms of sensual instrumentation came via Harry Partch. A groundbreaking composer whose career spanned several decades, beginning in the thirties and ending with his death in 1974, Partch played the harmonium. He also exploited "found" sounds. In his hands, household items and assorted pieces of junk became the tools for creating a collage of sound. Partch's project was nothing less than a reappraisal of the way we make and hear music. He broke down the octave into forty-three notes rather than twelve, unheard of in formal or classical music theory, thereby sparking heated debate among music theorists. Partch invented a series of instruments to suit his sonic experiments — the Ptolemy, the Chromelodeon I, and the Old and New Chromelodeon II — using them in the process of recording such revolutionary works as *Bewitched*, *Revelation in the Courthouse Park*, and *Bitter Music*.[7]

Waits was in awe of the iconoclastic Partch and his awe was evident when he spoke to *Playboy*.

PLAYBOY: Who was Harry Partch, and what did he mean to you?

WAITS: He was an innovator. He built all his own instruments and took the American hobo experience and designed instruments from ideas he gathered traveling around the United States in the thirties and the forties. He used a pump organ and industrial water bottles, created enormous marimbas. He died in the early seventies, but the Harry Partch Ensemble still performs at festivals. It's a little arrogant to say I see a relationship between his stuff and mine. I'm very crude, but I use things we hear around us all the time, built and found instruments. Things that aren't normally considered instruments: dragging a chair across the floor or hitting the side of a locker real hard with a two-by-four, a freedom bell, a brake drum with a major imperfection, a police bullhorn. It's more interesting. You know I don't like straight lines. The problem is that most instruments are square and music is always round.[8]

Joining Captain Beefheart and Harry Partch as a *Swordfishtrombones* influence was an old friend of Waits's by the name of Francis Thumm. The two had known each other since their San Diego days; Thumm is still a music teacher at a public school there. The arrangements for several songs on the new album were Waits/Thumm collaborations, and it was Thumm, in fact, who first brought Partch's music to Waits's attention. Thumm, in the Partch tradition, would occasionally play an offbeat instrument of his own — the gramolodium.

It's not surprising, then — given what went into its formulation — that *Swordfishtrombones* turned out to be utterly unlike anything that Waits, or anyone, had ever created. And Waits was understandably proud. "We'd done something on our own," he explained. "It just felt more honest. I was trying to find music that felt more like the people that were in the songs, rather than everybody being kind of dressed up in the same outfit. The people in my earlier songs might have had unique things to say and have come from diverse backgrounds, but they all looked the same."[9]

When the people at Elektra finally got to hear tapes of a few *Swordfishtrombones* songs they were dumbfounded. Wasn't this music awfully out there? What were all these weird instruments? How were they going to market this stuff? When the label insisted that Waits start again from scratch bearing in mind the concept of accessibility, Waits refused. This, he countered, was his best work yet. He finished the album. Elektra was thrown into a quandary: Waits was one of its prestige artists, but he'd never sold all that well for the company. Finally, Waits ended the impasse by asking to be released from his contract, and Elektra was by then quite willing to oblige.

Shopping for a new label, both Tom and Kathleen were confident that they had an important piece of musical property to offer. The head of Island Records thought so, too. "Chris Blackwell loved the album and said, 'We'll put it out,'" Waits told radio interviewer Chris Douridas. "So that's what happened. He was very in tune with it. Blackwell has great ears, you know? Because he likes what I did, so I guess that means he has great ears."[10]

Island, an artist-driven label, was the ideal home for Waits. Blackwell was known for allowing the members of his stable great freedom to explore their musical visions. Growing up in Jamaica, he'd become enraptured with Rastafarian music, philosophy, and culture. The story goes that a boat the teenage Blackwell was sailing ran aground on a reef and he was forced to swim to the distant shore. Emerging from the sea, he collapsed from exhaustion. Some Rastafarians found him and took him to their camp, where they nursed him back to health, fed him, and shared their philosophies with him — a rare privilege for a white person.[11]

Blackwell's fascination with Rasta music — ska, rock steady, and reggae — deepened as the years passed, and in 1959 he founded Island Records with the mandate to bring Jamaican music to a larger audience. Most of the label's early offerings Blackwell produced himself; he also handled distribution and even performed on many recordings. Then, in 1962, Blackwell moved Island to London. A novelty ska number, "My Boy Lollipop" by Millie Small, vaulted the label out of obscurity in 1964, and then another Island reggae act put Blackwell's enterprise on the map forever. Bob Marley and the Wailers are, to this day, the definitive reggae group. Marley died of cancer in 1981, but his legacy lives on, and while he was at the helm of The Wailers the classics just kept coming: "I Shot the Sheriff," "Jammin'," "Get Up, Stand Up," "No Woman, No Cry."

In England, Blackwell rapidly became known for having exceptional taste, taking real chances with his artists, and branching into new styles. Soon Island nurtured such acts as superstar Irish rockers U2, the innovative new-romantic outfit Roxy Music, and psychedelic pioneers Traffic. The label also took on rock acts like Free and The Spencer Davis Group, as well as the venerable English folk-rock group Fairport Convention. But Blackwell didn't forget his roots — just about every reggae act that ever mattered, including Marley, Jimmy Cliff, Black Uhuru, Desmond Dekker and the Aces, Toots and the Maytals, and Sly and Robbie, recorded for Island at one time or another.

By the eighties, the label was having a lot of success with U2 as well as the middle-of-the-road rockers Robert Palmer and Steve Winwood (who had been with Island for years as a member of both The Spencer Davis Group and Traffic before going solo in 1981). The curse of Island Records had begun to manifest itself by this point: with the notable exception of U2, whenever an Island act achieved major commercial success, it would attempt to maximize its earning potential by signing with a larger label. But maybe the curse was actually on the artists, because Palmer and Winwood, for example, never did as well again after they left Blackwell's stable.

Tom Waits would remain unencumbered by this particular form of bad luck — or bad decision making. All he cared about was that he'd found a label that trusted him, and there he would stay. Having learned from past experience, he negotiated a fair contract with Island: he'd now enjoy complete creative control and be paid more generously for his work. He would own the rights to every song he wrote. As far as Blackwell was concerned, Waits had a strong musical vision, and that was good enough for him.

When Island released *Swordfishtrombones* in September 1983, the reviews were ecstatic — the best Waits had ever received. The album had an otherworldly, slightly skewed feel that struck a chord in many people but was difficult to capture in words. (Perhaps crooner Tony Bennett put it best, once remarking that *Swordfishtrombones* sounded like "a guy in an ash can sending messages.")[12] Even Waits himself was compelled to reflect, after the fact, upon the nature of his new sound and in doing so he recognized an interesting irony: "My life was getting more settled. I was staying out of the bars. But my work was becoming more scary."[13]

"Underground," the album's first track, is the result of Waits's desire to compose a piece that sounded like a group of mutant dwarfs performing a Russian march, stomping on a wooden floor, and banging on pipes. Yet this only hints at the eccentricity of the track. Here, on Waits's tribute to the Manhattan hobos who live in tunnels, his voice can only be described as a series of strangled yelps. The next song, "Shore Leave," reels things in a bit; it's a minor blues frame garlanded with weird sound effects and a screeching falsetto. "Dave the Butcher," an instrumental, feels like the soundtrack to a silent film playing in some bizarre alternate universe.

The first song on *Swordfishtrombones* that betrays a backward glance is Tom's second musical love letter to Kathleen. Like "Jersey Girl," "Johnsburg, Illinois" takes a former home of Kathleen's as its lyrical springboard. Kathleen was born in Johnsburg and lived on a farm there before moving with her family to New Jersey. The song is short — a single verse clocking in at a minute and a half — but that just adds to its poignant immediacy. It is one of Waits's most intimate piano ballads, a quiet pledge of devotion to the woman he can't live without. Waits has said that he wanted to make his profession of love quickly, the way a man does when showing someone a wallet photo of his wife before slipping it back into his pocket.[14]

With "16 Shells From a Thirty-Ought-Six," the album returns to the realm of experimental instrumentation. This blues is augmented with an array of clangs and thumps — Waits's conception of what a chain gang working beside a highway would sound like. The first time Kathleen heard "Town with No Cheer," the lyrics touched her profoundly, and she remarked to Tom that he must have been very much in love with the woman he had been writing about. He explained that the song isn't about a woman at all: it's the story of a man who can't get any liquor. While on tour in Australia, Waits had read a newspaper article about a little town whose one saloon had gone out of business and been boarded up. He had clipped the story, figuring that one day he might write something about it.[15]

The album's first side closes with the single "In the Neighborhood," in which Waits tries to evoke a Salvation Army band clanging out an old drinking song. The song conjures an image of a crazed, Fellini-esque marching band tramping down a dirt road (carrying a glockenspiel, apparently) and occasionally stopping to raise their glasses in a toast. It resembles "A Sight for Sore Eyes" from *Foreign Affairs*, but the new instrumentation gives it a more offbeat, jittery vibe.

Perhaps the most important song on *Swordfishtrombones* is "Frank's Wild Years." At least it was for Waits — to a certain degree, the song would influence his musical creation for the next five years. "Frank's Wild Years" is a tragic monologue, although it does contain a substantial streak of twisted, black humor. In it, Waits annihilates the hallowed American conviction that if you put your shoulder to the wheel then nothing can stop you from having it all — a lovely wife, a stimulating job, a side-by-side refrigerator, a self-cleaning oven, and "a little Chihuahua named Carlos." Performing the song as a spoken-word jazz piece, Waits explodes the idyll before we can believe in it and describes how one night Frank goes home, douses the place with gasoline, and sits in his car laughing as his old life burns down.

The song closes with the bitter punch line, "Never could stand that dog."

But Waits was anxious to ensure that no one construed "Frank's Wild Years" as pure tragedy. "I didn't want to give the impression that [Frank's wife] went up in smoke through the chimney," he told Barney Hoskyns of *New Musical Express*. "No, she was at the beauty parlor. The dog may have gone." When asked what he was trying to accomplish with "Frank's Wild Years," Waits paraphrased a Charles Bukowski story he'd once read, saying that it isn't the big things that destroy a man's psyche — it's the little nagging ones. It's your shoelace breaking when you haven't got the time to replace it that will drive you wild, not some major catastrophe.

If Waits's music was becoming more expansive, then his storytelling was becoming more intimate. Accounts of grand passion, like "Small Change," were being eclipsed by subtle, devastating little tales, like "Soldier's Things." In the latter, a man finds a little box of war mementos and medals in a pawnshop. An individual's experience of battle — sweat, blood, fear — has been reduced to a handful of odds and ends, tossed into a cardboard box, and sold for a dollar apiece. Is this what dying for your country amounts to? In its own quiet way, "Soldier's Things" is a more devastating indictment of war than such better-known protest anthems as Jefferson Airplane's "Volunteers," Country Joe and The Fish's "I Feel like I'm Fixing to Die Rag," and Bruce Springsteen's "Born in the U.S.A."

In October 1983, about the time that *Swordfishtrombones* came out, Tom and Kathleen's first child was born — a girl named Kellesimone. "I didn't wanna be the guy who woke when he was sixty-five, and said, 'Gee, I forgot to have kids,'" said Waits. "I mean, somebody took the time to have us, right?"[16]

The name that Waits had really wanted to give his daughter was Wilder. It seemed to suit a daydream image he had of her as an adult so perfectly: she'd be flying down Freeway 405 in a big old white convertible, her red hair flying in the wind, as old-time soul tunes came pumping out of the car radio.[17] No frail ballerina types for Tom Waits. His baby would grow up to be a hell-raiser, a heartbreaker, a beauty with a brain and the guts to use it, a thorn in the side of the establishment. In short, a woman just like Kathleen.

Fatherhood gave Waits a whole new appreciation of the advantages that come with being just another face in the crowd. His anonymity would surely enhance Kellesimone's comfort and safety, and it also afforded him the luxury (and the artistic necessity) of observing the world around him in relative peace. "I like to go to places where I can be anonymous and just sit," he said to Hoskyns. "That's what writers want — to be invisible. Sometimes when your face gets recognizable, then there are places that you can't go. So I think you have to retain a certain amount of that for the sake of the intrinsic value of what it is that you do so you can go places, be a fly on the wall."[18] Waits was, in fact, in an ideal position: he could run to the supermarket to pick up diapers for Kellesimone without being recognized and waylaid; but his professional reputation was such that he continued to be offered stimulating projects. Of course Waits was occasionally recognized on the street, but it never became overwhelming.

Again, the release of a new album had little effect on the situation. The reviews for *Swordfishtrombones* were phenomenal, the sales were sluggish (in the U.S., that is — the album was a hit in Europe), and Waits's right to privacy remained uncompromised. Waits, who had never longed to see his face on a lunch box or a kung fu–grip action figure, could live with it.

Due to the quality of his music and film credentials, Waits was able to recruit a Hollywood heavyweight to direct his second music video. Haskell Wexler was the award-winning cinematographer of *American Graffiti*, *One Flew Over the Cuckoo's Nest*, and many others. He had also won raves for his 1969 directing debut, a docudrama about a jaded T.V. newsman called *Medium Cool*. Turning his talented gaze on Tom Waits, Wexler translated the street-band feel of "In the Neighborhood" into a series of visual images by casting Waits as the leader of a motley group of mummers. The medium of the music video was exploding at this point thanks to an upstart cable channel called MTV, Music Television, which had been on the air for less than a year. But because the video for "In the Neighborhood" didn't conform to the rapidly set standard — Duran Duran's "Hungry like the Wolf," Michael Jackson's "Billie Jean," and David Bowie's "Let's Dance" were the station's current choice clips — Wexler's little film received next to no attention.

At about this time, Rickie Lee Jones recorded one of Waits's early unreleased songs, "Rainbow Sleeves." Her emotional delivery on the cut was heartbreaking, and it enriched her 1983 EP *Girl at Her Volcano*. The song was also included on the soundtrack to Martin Scorsese's film *The King of Comedy*. In 1981, she had released the album *Pirates* — the follow-up to her self-titled debut — and its first single was "A Lucky Guy," the confession of a woman who is holding on to a man who, "When he talks about me / He don't look this way." The song was loosely based on her relationship with Waits. Rickie Lee could sing eloquently about the pain of their separation, even though she was reluctant to talk about it.

On the acting front, things were more straightforward for Waits. The work was coming in; he could make his contribution and go home at the end of the day. For the most part, this was courtesy of Francis Ford Coppola. After *One from the Heart* crashed on take off, Coppola had decided to do a couple of small, intimate films based on the teen novels of S. E. Hinton. He offered Waits small parts in the two films, both of which were released in 1983. The first was *The Outsiders*, a sentimental drama about gang life set in the fifties, which turned out to be a vehicle for introducing members of the so-called Hollywood Brat Pack, and a future superstar or two, to the world. The cast included Rob Lowe, Emilio Estevez, Ralph Macchio, C. Thomas Howell, Leif Garrett, Diane Lane, Patrick Swayze, Matt Dillon, and Tom Cruise. Into this dynamic ensemble Coppola inserted Tom, of whom he'd grown very fond. He referred to him as "a prince of melancholia" and gave him the cameo role of Buck Merrill. When the time came to cast *Rumble Fish*, Coppola rewarded Tom with a bigger role. The director's second run at bringing a Hinton novel to the screen presented a darker vision of teen rebellion than the tragic but fundamentally uplifting *Outsiders*. *Rumble Fish* also starred Dillon and Lane; Mickey Rourke and Dennis Hopper added their eccentric energies to the mix; and Tom Waits turned in a credible performance as Benny, the local pool-hall owner.

The following year, 1984, Waits not only did a cameo in the well-received Robert Duvall vehicle *The Stone Boy*, but he was also available to help Coppola. The director was returning to more ambitious, risky, big-budget filmmaking with *The Cotton Club*, a tale of crime and passion set during the Roaring Twenties at Harlem's most famous hot spot. Richard Gere, Diane Lane, James Remar, Gregory Hines, and Lonette McKee headed the cast, and Tom Waits backed them up as Herman Stark, the club's manager. Waits had to admit that the roles he was getting weren't exactly straining his acting muscles — no one, it seemed, was interested in having him play an emergency-room doctor or a hardened defense attorney or a man of the cloth. Still, he had some fun with Stark, an elegant character who sports a tux, smokes a fat stogie, and constantly exudes a cold menace.[19]

The switch from music to acting "was like going from bootlegging to watch repair," Waits told *Rolling Stone*'s David Sheff. "*Rumble Fish* was like a fractured teenage opium dream. Francis had all the actors out in the morning, on a vacant lot, doing tai chi chuan. Then there was *The Outsiders*. I had one line: 'What is it you boys want?' I still have it down if they need me to go back and recreate the scene for any reason. For *The Cotton Club*, I was in a tuxedo for like two and a half months."[20]

The Cotton Club took longer to complete than anyone expected, and Tom had begun to feel the itch to create something new. He and Kathleen had hatched the idea of staging a musical, starring Tom, based on the character of Frank from "Frank's Wild Years," and they started building on it. The prospect of collaborating on such a project excited them both. The play would have a long gestation, but finally, after many rewrites and idea shifts, it opened in Chicago in 1986.

In order to give their theatrical piece a fighting chance, Tom and Kathleen realized that they'd have to make a couple of sacrifices. The first was giving up the opportunity to tour with *Swordfishtrombones*. The second was giving up their home. The heart of American theater beats in New York City, not Los Angeles, so Tom, Kathleen, and Kellesimone packed up and relocated to the Big Apple.

Tom was ready to give New York another chance, even though he considered it "a hard city." He told Hoskyns, "You have to be on your toes. A cab driver actually said to me, 'I love New York.' He said, 'If you can make it here, you can make it anywhere, just like Frank said.' I just fell out." Soon, however, Tom was having his usual odd, funny, scary encounters with the city's inhabitants — a sure sign that he was settling in. A woman approached him at a newsstand and said, "'Excuse me, sir, is this the place where the clocks are?' And I said, 'This is the place where the clocks are.' She asked me who I was. I said, 'Father Time.' She said, 'Dad!' and she opened her arms."[21]

Continuing in this vein, Waits talked about midtown gridlock — an incomprehensible phenomenon to the average out-of-towner — and opined, "It's hard to live with dignity because it's not a very civilized place. You have to be a little off center; if you don't bend with it, it will snap you because [the city] itself is off. It's not round and it's going around and every time it comes around it's in a different place. So if you try to walk a straight line it'll knock you over. But then you get a Romanian cab driver who is playing Romanian music full blast in his cab. And there's a picture of Malcolm X on the dashboard and he's wearing a Budweiser hat and he has different shoes on — a tennis shoe and an Oxford . . . and he tells you about a club in Queens. It's insane. It's thrilling, addicting . . . It requires a special training."

The Waits family needed a home, a refuge from the turmoil of city life, so Tom and Kathleen went hunting. They found a burned-out loft off

West 14th Street in Little Spain, not far from Union Square. The place was centrally located, within a block of the Babalu Bar and Grill, the Salvation Army Diner, and Courmey's Restaurant (which Tom considered amazingly clean for New York). Furnishing their new digs was a task Tom attacked with the same fervor he'd demonstrated when searching out new kinds of musical instruments. He claimed to have picked up everything that finally went into the loft's decor on the streets — New York, he insisted, was truly wonderful.[22]

Throughout the resettlement process, music was never far from his thoughts. "There's construction sounds here all the time," he explained to Hoskyns. "So I started taping a lot of stuff. How that will integrate into what I'm doing, I'm not certain. But I started taping the sounds of machinery a lot and I play it back at night, 'cause you miss it, you know. When it gets quiet and you're relaxed . . . so I play it back at full volume so I can re-experience the sounds of the day. There's, like, a pile driver outside of my window. You know what a pile driver is? It's all what you get used to."

New York's intellectual and artistic currents had Waits enthralled. His best creative tool had long been his vocabulary, and the city served up a daily buffet of words. Everywhere he went, words, phrases, and ideas — spoken, yelled, written, flashing in neon — came at him. In bars, in restaurants, and in SoHo galleries, on piers at the waterfront. Where slaughterhouses rubbed shoulders with modeling agencies, where movie houses gave way to sex-paraphernalia shops, where sweatshops alternated with gyms and diners and cavernous antique/junk marts. "It's all the contrasts," he said to Elliott Murphy. "There are distinctive lines of demarcation, but for the most part, it's like an aquarium. It's almost overwhelming. Words are every-where. All you have to do is look out the window and there's a thousand words."[23]

Instinctively, Waits went on soaking it up and channeling it into his art. He remarked that "Musically, the density is interesting. The types of things you hear while you're here . . . if you remember them and put them together it's real international — if you're listening. I usually enjoy things that I misinterpret. When you hear music through a wall. You've missed a couple of beats and the words aren't what they are but you hear them and you think that's what it is. That happens a lot in New York cause you're hearing everything filtered through things — it's like being on a party line. You have to have a lot of money to live here."[24]

When asked if he was happy in Manhattan, Waits replied, "I don't know. It's such a transient thing anyway . . . happy. I [could] go out in the street and drop my trousers and start singing 'Fly Me to the Moon' and no one would notice. I can shave my head, put on a dress, and pee in the beer glass . . . I was looking for a place that repairs chairs, an upholstery place . . . There was a place that sold nothing but buttons — just buttons, millions of buttons of all sizes. Next to that was a place for sewing machine repair and then I saw a mountain of nothing but silverware in the window — a mountain of silverware. It's not logical. But all of that can be stimulating if you can allow it." Waits also told David Letterman that living in New York was like being aboard a sinking ship while the ocean is on fire.[25]

In September 1985, Tom and Kathleen had their second child, a son. Tom had his heart set on naming the kid Senator Waits, figuring he'd have a leg up if he ever decided to go into politics. Kathleen, her husband alleged, vetoed the idea — she wanted to name her baby boy Representative Waits. In order to avert a war between the Houses, the two reached a compromise: Casey Xavier Waits.[26]

One night Tom went to a party held in honor of painter Jean-Michel Basquiat, toast of the SoHo art scene. Basquiat, a Brooklyn kid who'd been discovered applying graffiti to various Manhattan surfaces, was the type of do-it-yourself artist Waits could respect. His work was passionate and original, but Basquiat's rise was tragically meteoric. He would die of a drug overdose at twenty-seven. (In 1996, artist Julian Schnabel made *Basquiat*, a film about the painter starring Jeffrey Wright, Dennis Hopper, Gary Oldman, and David Bowie; in it, Waits's song "Tom Traubert's Blues" plays a prominent role.)

At that party for Basquiat, which was held in a SoHo bar, Waits met independent filmmaker Jim Jarmusch. Jarmusch had recently released his first film, *Stranger than Paradise*, and it had become an art-house phenomenon. He was a big fan of *Swordfishtrombones*, so he went over to introduce himself to Waits. They connected immediately, and before the night was over, they'd hit three other watering holes together. Jarmusch, a maverick in his own right, was drawn to Waits's quirky individualism. He recalls visiting Waits in his 14th Street loft; there he witnessed Kellesimone painting pictures on the walls while Tom painted pinstripes onto a suit.[27] It was inevitable that Jarmusch and Waits become friends and collaborators.

Waits's next album, *Rain Dogs*, emitted a New York vibe. It was only natural. "Any place you move is going to have some effect," Waits told Hoskyns. "I was exposed to a kind of melange of sounds [in New York], because I went to clubs more. It's rather oppressive, I think. I'd . . . go down to the Westbeth Building [in Greenwich Village], where I shared a room with [jazz musician] John Lurie and his brother Evan. We'd go down there at night and write songs. It was quiet at night. I'd work 'til late and come home. The thing when you have kids is that you can stay up 'til five in the morning, but you still gonna get up and have to feed them."[28]

Through John Lurie, Waits met a guitarist named Mark Ribot, a member of Lurie's avant-garde jazz group The Lounge Lizards. Waits recruited Ribot to work on *Rain Dogs*, and they hit it off so well that he invited Ribot on tour, as well. In contributing to the album, Ribot joined forces with two high-profile strummers. The first was the former Hall and Oates guitarist and longtime *Saturday Night Live* bandleader G. E. Smith. The second was the legendary Keith Richards. When the heavily committed Rolling Stone agreed to play on the songs "Big Black Mariah," "Union Square," and "Blind Love," Waits was thrilled. Not only was Richards a brilliant guitarist, but he was also one of the few musicians whose reputation for hard living had outstripped Waits's own. (Waits himself has claimed that he tried to party with Richards but couldn't keep up.) So entrenched was Waits's admiration for Richards that he'd been known to say, when searching for a way to explain to his band what type of guitar sound he was going for, "It's a Keith Richards thing." Now he'd have the genuine article there with him in the studio.

It really was a coup to get Richards. He rarely did guest work. "He's the best," Waits enthused. "He's like a tree frog, an orangutan. When he plays, he looks like he's been dangled from a wire that comes up through the back of his neck, and he can lean at a forty-five-degree angle and not fall over. You think he has special shoes. But maybe it's just the music that's keeping him up."[29] In more sedate language, Richards expressed his own appreciation of Waits: "I'm really interested in his work and it's fun to sit around and write songs with him."[30] In 1986, Waits returned Richards' favor by singing on "Sleep Tonight," a track from the Stones album *Dirty Work*.

The name *Rain Dogs* is a reference to New York's army of homeless people. When dogs are out in heavy rain, they become disoriented because the scents that guide them are washed away. Unable to find their way home, they cower in doorways or slink along back alleys. Waits envisioned the homeless this way — they'd lost their bearings and were condemned to wander through hostile terrain. Pleased with the metaphoric resonance of this title, Waits also liked its manly feel. For him it brought to mind "some kind of war movie starring Ernest Borgnine, Lee Marvin, and Rod Steiger as Solomon the watchmaker."[31]

Rain Dogs would be a vehicle for experimentation even more radical than the experimentation that had yielded *Swordfishtrombones*. "Yeah, it's more rhythmic, much more rhythmic," Waits remarked. "I still want to use a percussionist rather than a drum machine. This is gonna be even more oddball than *Swordfishtrombones*. I mean oddball for me. One man's ceiling is another man's floor. The thing is you have ideas — the hardest thing is bringing them out and making them as clear on the outside as they were to you . . . For me, there are things that I imagine and that thrill me that I want to hear that I'm going to try to accomplish in the studio. Sometimes you only get halfway there. The way that I'm constructing songs is different now than the way I used to, it's more like collage really. I'll take bits — I'll put that there and this here and I'll nail that to the side and then we'll paint it yellow and put a hat on it. It's more construction."[32]

With "Singapore," the first *Rain Dogs* cut, Waits cranked up the "mutant dwarf orchestra" sound he'd been working with on *Swordfishtrombones*. The song almost defies description: it's a deranged sea-shanty road tune. "In the land of the blind / the one-eyed man is king . . ." Waits couldn't remember who he'd lifted that line from — he thought it was George Orwell, but it could have been *Mary Poppins*. For all its dissonance and rough edges, "Singapore" is strangely compelling, a glimpse of a world few people will ever experience. So is "Cemetery Polka," a peek at the family's internal workings; or, as Waits described it to Mark Rowland, "The way we talk behind each other's backs: 'You know what happened to Uncle Vernon?' The kind of wickedness nobody outside your family could say."[33]

The German music-hall feel of such *Rain Dogs* tracks as "Singapore," "Cemetery Polka," and "Tango 'Til They're Sore" prompted a lot of people to conclude that Waits had been influenced by Bertold Brecht and Kurt Weill. "That macabre, dissonant style," says Waits — "see, when I hear Weill I hear a lot of anger in those songs. I remember the first time that I heard that Peggy Lee tune 'Is That All There Is?' I identified with that. 'Is that all there is? If that's all there is, then let's keep dancing.' So you just find different things that you feel your voice is suited to. I didn't really know that much about Kurt Weill until people started saying, 'Hey, he must be listening to a lot of Kurt Weill.' I thought, I better go find out who this guy is. I started listening to *The Happy End*, and *Threepenny Opera* and *Mahagonny* and all that really expressionistic music."[34] In fact, Waits became so fond of Weill's work that he recorded a version of "What Keeps Mankind Alive?" for the Kurt Weill tribute album *Lost in the Stars*, which was produced by avant-gardist (and former *Saturday Night Live* musical director) Hal Willner.

After these three edgy songs, *Rain Dogs* shifts gears with "Jockey Full of Bourbon." To a Tex-Mex swing-rumba beat, the song barrels through ranchero-jazz territory, evoking the tunes Waits's father used to play on the car radio as they drove down to Mexico together. "Tango 'Til They're Sore" is about a guy who falls out of a window at a New Year's Eve party and is somehow saved by the fact that he has confetti in his hair. "Big Black Mariah," which coasts along a rock-steady Keith Richards guitar line, is pure voodoo New Orleans as it tells a little tale involving a Black Mariah — a type of paddy wagon that is often used as a hearse.

And *Rain Dogs* is enriched by even more forms of musical exploration. The instrumental "Midtown" could easily pass as the theme for a fifties cop show. "Blind Love" was probably the first country song Waits had written since *Closing Time*. While he admitted that he wasn't a great country-music fan, he did say that with "Blind Love" he was striving to reproduce the same roadhouse feel that fueled certain Merle Haggard classics. "Anywhere I Lay My Head" sounds like a New Orleans funeral march — the kind of piece that a Dixieland combo would offer up as it accompanied a casket to its burial site, winding its way through the narrow streets of the French Quarter.

More traditional Waits compositions find their place on *Rain Dogs*, too, including a couple of his most beautiful love songs. "Hang Down Your Head," Tom and Kathleen's first official songwriting collaboration, is a lovely, unaffected folk-rock ballad. "Time" might have been one of Waits's most gorgeous piano ballads except that in his fever of instrumental experimentation he chose to play it on acoustic guitar, accordion, and bass.

The spoken-jazz piece "9th & Hennepin" was named for the Minneapolis street corner where Tom once stumbled onto a pimp war. It was a typical Tom Waits off-kilter and somewhat-out-of-sync-with-the-times experience: he was in a doughnut shop when three twelve-year-old pimps wearing fur coats pulled knives and other assorted pieces of silverware on each other. Although set in Minnesota, the song has an unmistakable New York feel.

"Downtown Train," which became *Rain Dogs*' first single, is an unusually accessible Waits composition, and it is fueled by some quirky guitar work by G. E. Smith. Video director Jean Baptiste Mondino (red hot at the time thanks to his moody take on Don Henley's "Boys of Summer"), was hired to make the "Downtown Train" video, and boxer Jake LaMotta (subject of the Martin Scorsese film *Raging Bull*) was cast as Waits's irate Italian neighbor. Despite its accessibility, the song features some of Waits's best lyrics; and its array of offbeat touches reveal it to be the work of a cockeyed genius.

Rain Dogs shows Waits stretching and testing his art like never before, but it triggered the usual dynamic: critics loved it (Robert Palmer of the *New York Times* named it best album of 1985), but sales were poor. Waits, as ever, took it in stride. And he gave no sign of being tempted to compromise. "What do you mean by success?" he said to Mark Rowland. "My record sales have dropped off considerably in the United States [but] I do sell a lot of records in Europe. It's hard to gauge something you don't have real contact with. We have no real spiritual leadership, so we look to merchandising. The most deprived, underprivileged neighborhoods in the world understand business. Guns, ammo, narcotics . . . But yes, *sales have dropped off considerably in the last few years* . . . and I want to talk to somebody about it. I used to play Iowa. I haven't been to Iowa in some time."[35]

8

FRANK'S WILD YEARS

By 1986, Waits was ready to launch into *Frank's Wild Years*, the musical. But before he submerged himself completely in that project he had another movie role to do. It was to be his biggest yet, and he planned to take full advantage of the opportunity. Since their first meeting, Tom and Jim Jarmusch had been talking about working on a project together, and now Jarmusch was offering Waits a starring role in his next film, a jailbreak drama called *Down by Law*. Jarmusch also wanted two of his songs, "Jockey Full of Bourbon" and "Tango 'Til They're Sore," for the film's soundtrack.

Tom and Kathleen's New York minute was coming to an end. Their initial attraction to the frenetic metropolis was wearing thin, and now it was becoming apparent to them that midtown Manhattan was not an ideal environment for child rearing. Jarmusch provided them with the impetus to leave it all behind by setting *Down by Law* in New Orleans and arranging for the film to be shot on location there. The Waits clan packed up and headed south.

In the film, Waits plays Zach, a New Orleans DJ who gets drunk after losing his job and his girlfriend and agrees to deliver a car for a local con man. When a body is found in the car's trunk, Zach is framed for murder. Joining Zach in jail is Jack, portrayed by Waits's friend John Lurie, a sweet-tempered pimp who is himself framed when a local stool pigeon sets him up to meet a new girl — who turns out to be about twelve years old. Completing this trio of cell mates is an Italian tourist, played by comedian Roberto Benigni (who so ecstatically accepted the Best Actor Oscar in 1999 for *Life Is Beautiful*). Benigni's character, Bob, barely speaks English (he insists to his cell mates, "I ham a good egg"), and he has actually committed the crime he is accused of — he killed a man to defend the honor of a woman.

"It was good working with those people," Waits told radio interviewer Dierdre O'Donohue. "Bob Benigni, who's a big comic in Italy . . . played Bob. Outside of the Pope, there's nobody bigger in Italy than Bob Benigni. He really was a joy to work with . . . He made his name as an outsider. He would speak at rallies and say the unspeakable. He used to make jokes about the Pope and the Vatican and he got a big name. He referred to the Pope, the equivalent of calling him 'Pope, babe.' It created quite a stir in Vatican City."[1]

After weeks of mutual distrust and fighting, the three convicts develop a grudging respect for each other. They start planning a breakout, and they finally pull it off, escaping into the Louisiana bayou. *Down by Law* is essentially an arty variation on an old film standard, but the rapport between the convicts along with mostly ad-libbed dialogue add layers of interest. Waits's portrayal of Zach was a tour de force, and he clearly reveled in it. For the first time in his career, he met the challenge of creating a fully rounded, feature-length character, and he did it with skill and subtlety.

He based his character on a DJ he'd listened to as a teen in National City. He was called Lonely Lee "Baby" Sims, and the station he worked for promoted his show by begging listeners to come and visit the man at work so he wouldn't be so alone. Eventually, Lee "Baby" moved on, disappearing from Waits's radio and entering his memory bank. When Waits took on the character of DJ Zach, something stirred up that old memory, and he decided to give Zach the professional name of Lee "Baby" Sims.

The problem was that Waits had made a false assumption. He figured that Sims had vanished from the scene long ago, that he was no longer "real." But, as Waits found out, "Lee 'Baby' Sims is one of the best-paid disc jockeys in the Western Hemisphere." Tom told O'Donohue, "I think he lives in Hawaii. I think he was trying to sue us after *Down by Law* came out. He didn't like being portrayed as a ne'er-do-well. There was no offense made or intended, honestly . . . I had no idea that since I'm a kid he became this big sensation and he's a giant in the broadcasting world." He added, "No offense, Lee 'Baby' — it's all done with love and affection . . . Don't sue me."[2]

When *Down by Law* wrapped, Waits played a small role in a low-budget feature called *Candy Mountain*, directed by the innovative Robert Frank, who had revealed to the world the internal workings of The Rolling Stones with his astonishing documentary *Cocksucker Blues*. *Candy Mountain* featured an array of musicians in acting roles — aside from Waits there was Dr. John, Leon Redbone, David Johansen (aka Buster Poindexter), Rita

MacNeil, and Joe Strummer. The film was well reviewed, but it was never widely distributed, and relatively few people saw it.

It was time for Tom and Kathleen to get back to their pet project, *Frank's Wild Years*, a musical based on the *Swordfishtrombones* tale of the suburbanite who torches his split-level home. Kathleen would write most of the dialogue and Tom would write most of the music and lyrics. They would concoct the thing from scratch. But they were still lacking several crucial components. They needed money, a director, and a producer who could pull the whole thing together. So Tom and Kathleen entered the fray. It was difficult not to get discouraged. Schedules couldn't be juggled and space couldn't be secured. The mainstream New York theater world started to seem impenetrable. Its scions had lived so well so long off such crowd-pleasing fare as the old-fashioned roof-raiser musical (*Oklahoma, My Fair Lady*) and the theme-park-ride extravaganza (*Cats, Miss Saigon, The Phantom of the Opera*) that they tended to regard newcomers and their untested ideas with a cool eye. As Waits put it, "the ritual around it is very well established. When you come in here from some other place, there's not always a place to sit down right away. So you wait for a table."[3]

The wait seemed as though it might be indefinite. *Frank's Wild Years* was one tough sell in this milieu. It featured no dancing girls, no big set pieces, no hummable showstoppers. Its musical numbers served to illumi-nate — *Threepenny Opera*–style — a gritty story involving thieves and murderers. Waits joked with Hoskyns about it, saying, "I would describe [the play] as a cross between *Eraserhead* and *It's a Wonderful Life* — because it seems to carry both sides. It's bent and misshapen and tawdry and warm. Something for the whole family."[4]

But Waits would not let go of Frank. The character continued to intrigue him. He'd begun by envisioning Frank's act of arson, encapsulat-ing it in that one-minute-and-fifty-second piece of jazzspeak, and only then did he begin to wonder what had prompted it. What had driven Frank to light that fire? The more Waits pondered Frank, the more Frank took on a vivid life of his own. It occurred to Waits that Frank could embody an artistic breakthrough for him. Here was a character capable of encom-passing a range of seminal Waits ideas and presenting them through music, storytelling, acting. With Frank, the sky was Waits's limit.

Describing his play to Barney Hoskyns as early as 1985, Waits was clearly excited by it. His tenses shifted, his recounting of the story sequence was elliptical, but his creative energy was pumping: "There's like five prin-cipal characters in it. Just to simplify the whole thing, it's a story about failed dreams. It's about an accordion player from a small town called Rainville, who goes off to seek his fame and fortune and ends up hoisted with his own petard, as they say . . . Frank's been altered a little bit. He burns his house down and he leaves it all behind and he goes off to be an entertainer in Las Vegas. He becomes a spokesman for an all-night clothing store, after winning a talent contest. He won a lot of money at the crap tables. He got rolled by a cigarette girl, and he was despondent and penniless and found an accordion in the trash. One thing led to another and before you know it he's on stage. And his parents ran a funeral parlor when he was a kid. He played the accordion. His mother did the hair and makeup for the 'passengers' and he played 'Amazing Grace' during the ceremonies. So he had already started a career in show business as a child so this is sort of a chance to get back in the business, back on the boards."[5]

The whole thing actually unfolds like this. As *Frank's Wild Years* opens, Frank lies, dejected and freezing, on a park bench in East St. Louis. It starts to snow. Thinking he's going to die of the cold, he looks skyward and yells, "Remember me? I ordered the blond, the Firebird . . . Somebody's made a terrible mistake." This initiates a series of hallucinations and memories. Frank is seemingly rescued and taken to his favorite bar in Rainville, his hometown. He entertains with his story of traveling to Las Vegas to make it big in show business. For a single, white-hot moment, his song "Innocent When You Dream," makes him famous. Then, tragically incapable of building on his good fortune, he gambles away most of his earnings and is relieved of the rest by a cheap floozy he meets. Eventually, he is reduced to hawking suits for a local clothing store. He turns his song into a jingle called "In a Suit of Your Dreams." As the play ends, Frank huddles on the same East St. Louis park bench, buffetted by fate and by the elements, enduring another lost and lonely night.

Tom and Kathleen were still knocking on locked doors in New York City when something opened up in Chicago. The Steppenwolf Theater, a renowned actor's studio, had got wind of the project. And Steppenwolf was very interested. "It was a long journey to get to where we finally put the whole thing on in Chicago with Steppenwolf," says Waits. "We really landed in the right place after a lot of dead ends. I was really glad to be there . . . They're a good theater group. Kind of garage-band-style theater . . . three chords, turn it up real loud. It worked."[6]

Terry Kinney was set to direct *Frank's Wild Years*, but just a few weeks before it was scheduled to open, Kinney resigned (or was fired) over creative differences with Waits. Steppenwolf's head was actor Gary Sinise (who would later win an Oscar nomination for his supporting role in *Forrest Gump* and turn in strong performances in *Apollo 13*, *Mission to Mars*, *Ransom*, and *Of Mice and Men*). Sinise stepped into the breach and became *Frank*'s director. There was some talk of retooling the production — building new stage sets — but by this point both time and money were in short supply. Waits remained calm. He told O'Donohue he felt that such turmoil was "normal. Sometimes the spark comes from a conflict of ideas. It's just wood and lights and people walking around until you somehow bang up against something, and something breaks, and something sparks, and something catches and then it has a life. Until then it's just on the page."[7]

The cast included Steppenwolf regulars Gary Cole, Moira Harris, Vince Viverito, Randall Arney, and Tom Irwin. Waits's touring band played Frank's band, and Teller (of Penn and Teller) worked up some magic tricks for Frank to perform. Frank, of course, was played by his creator, and Waits carried the production solidly on his shoulders. But the play remained in a state of flux; they tinkered with it constantly, even during its run. The reviews were decent, but there were no raves. *Frank's Wild Years* played Chicago's Briar Street Theater for three months.

Looking back, Waits has mixed feelings about the undertaking. "Well, you have to be a little foolish to do something because a play takes a lot of energy — emotionally, financially," he told Hoskyns in 1999. "And the other thing is that it only lives when you're in it. But Steppenwolf was the right way to go."[8]

When *Frank's Wild Years* closed, the Waits family found themselves faced with another move. Now the itinerant lifestyle was getting old, and Tom and Kathleen were becoming very attracted to the notion of putting down roots someplace private. Privacy was integral to the kind of comfort and stability Tom and Kathleen were seeking for themselves and their kids. "Yeah, I'm private," Waits said at about this time. "Someday I'll be a lieutenant, but right now I'm just a private . . . Half of you is saying 'Notice me.' The other half is saying 'Leave me alone.' It's a bit ambiguous. You want people to recognize what you do. At the same time you don't want to have to do it all the time every day."[9]

On the work front, however, Waits's next order of business was to record his *Frank's Wild Years* album, so that meant relocating to not-so-private Los Angeles, at least temporarily. Speaking to Mark Rowland, Waits could only speculate about future living arrangements. "I don't know where I'm living. Citizen of the world. I live for adventure and to hear the lamentations of the women . . . I've uprooted a lot. It's like being a traveling salesman. There's a certain gypsy quality, and I'm used to it. I find it easy to write under difficult circumstances and I can capture what's going on. I'm moving toward needing a compound, though. An estate. In the meantime I'm operating out of a storefront here in the Los Angeles area."[10]

Waits's first priority in recording *Frank's Wild Years* was to ensure that the album worked as a piece of music and wasn't just a recorded souvenir of the play. This wouldn't be too difficult. In the studio he could give free rein to his imagination; the possibilities were limited in the theater setting for technical reasons and because it was imperative that the audience fully understood the songs, which moved the story forward.

So Waits entered the studio and pushed, pulled, sculpted, and battered his songs into shapes that more closely resembled the structures in his head. He sang several songs through a bullhorn. He used lots of "pawn-shop instruments," including a Farfisa organ and an accordion. He even asked his musicians, most of whom were multi-instrumentalists, to play instruments they weren't used to. The drummer blew a horn, the guitarist played keyboards, and Waits perceived a new vigor and impulsiveness in their performances. Waits trusted the members of his band. Many of them had contributed to *Rain Dogs* and worked on the play, and he had faith that they could make the leap into the unknown with him.

For his entire career, Waits had issued his records on vinyl. Compact-disc technology had been making its imprint on the music world for about a year before *Rain Dogs* was released, but it hadn't radically altered the landscape. In the two years after *Rain Dogs* came out, though, the compact disc had caught up to vinyl, both in sound quality and in popularity, and it was now squeezing the life out of the LP.

The CD was lauded for its pristine quality. Waits wasn't particularly interested in pristine. He considered it uncomfortably close to sterile. He responded to music that felt lived in, that sounded like dirt was being shaken out of its grooves. In fact, many of Waits's earlier albums sound better on vinyl — the occasional hissing and popping add a desirable grittiness to the musical tale. So why did he record *Frank's Wild Years* on compact disc? Mainly because the new technology could do more to showcase the divergent instrumentation that he found so fascinating, and because, when it came right down to it, the new technology could boost the energy level of his sound.

The slightly woozy dreamworld of *Frank's Wild Years* comes into sharp focus with the album's first cut. "Hang On St. Christopher," a driving rocker, is thrown off its axis by North African horn lines that intrude pointedly on the melody — they actually chase the melody like a police cruiser after a speeder, a beat behind. Waits's already offbeat vocals have a tinny, echoing ring here; he's singing through a police bullhorn. The melody swerves, careens, rushes on like a car with no brakes descending a mountain, like a frantic, lost traveler in need of St. Christopher's intervention.

Waits was pleased with the distorting effect of the bullhorn, which he used on several other tunes, too. It lent a certain menace to his vocals and imbued the proceedings with a somewhat unnatural, dreamlike quality. "It was your MP5 Fanon transistorized bullhorn with the public address loudspeaker in it, available down there at Radio Shack," Waits told the *Morning Becomes Eclectic* audience. "For about $29.95 you can pick one of those up. I've tried for a long time to get the same effect through other means — singing into cups and pipes and trumpet mutes and singing in my hands. Just trying to get my voice to sound like at the bottom of a pool. Just to tamper with the qualities it already has, to bend it a little bit, 'cause I get sick and tired of the way I sound." He claimed that he was trying to make his voice "skinnier, so it would fit in the song. 'Cause I was going to plant all these things around it and sometimes it flattens out and it gets too thick and I can't put anything else in there. So it changes the size of my voice so that I can put more in the song. That's kind of the theory around it anyway. Biff Dawes, my engineer, got me a bullhorn for my birthday and I haven't been without it since. And it's real good around the house when you want to get somebody's attention."[11]

Waits's falsetto gets a workout in "Temptation," a percussive number that explores the weaknesses of the flesh — "A little *Pagliacci*" is the way that Waits himself describes it.[12] In the play, the song is performed when a man on a billboard advertisement for Las Vegas comes to life and urges Frank to give Sin City a whirl. Removed from that context, the tune is still a wonderful admission of human frailty. Sex, alcohol, drugs, and money beckon; man responds; these forces build him up and they tear him down. He sees the error of his ways but he is powerless to stop himself.

The prettiest and certainly the most devastating song on *Frank's Wild Years* is "Innocent When You Dream." It actually appears twice on the album, once as a barroom ballad played on a pump organ, and again as a replica of a tune you might find on an old 78 recording, complete with crackles and pops. Waits says the song — a drinking-man's anthem about life's unfairness and the escape that only sleep can provide — is a tip of the hat to Irish tenor John McCormack, to whose music Waits had been introduced by Kathleen's father.[13]

The other *Frank's Wild Years* song that is presented in two radically different versions is "Straight to the Top." There is a rumba version and a truly astounding Vegas version, in which Waits does an uncanny imitation of Frank Sinatra. "A friend of mine was in the car with his mother and he put on 'Straight to the Top,'" remarks Waits. "She looked over at him and said, 'I didn't know that Sinatra had a new album out.' And she was dead serious. I'm not bragging — just somehow she thought that was Frank, and I thought, 'Well, that's pretty good, I guess.'"[14]

Waits kept up the Ol' Blue Eyes shtick with "I'll Take New York." "There is kind of a little Sinatra influence on this," he explains. "Kind of the flip side of 'New York, New York.' This is when everything starts to melt. This is going down on the Titanic. I saw Frank Sinatra just a couple of nights ago at the Greek Theater. It was a good show, but this is — I don't know how to describe it. Somebody told me I sound a little bit like Jerry Lewis. I didn't know whether that was a compliment or not. This is kind of the darker side of Times Square."[15]

"Way Down in the Hole" is a preacher's spiel of a song. "Get behind me, Satan, get behind me!" Over a funky Ralph Carney sax break, Waits plots to keep his personal devil under control. "This is kind of a gospel number, I guess," he admits. "It kind of happened in the studio real spontaneously. That doesn't happen every time, but somehow it happened on this. We needed a gospel number, so this is all about fear of the Devil and all that — ghosts and the like. You know what they say . . . if a ghost ever starts to inhabit you, they tell you to pee your pants. It's the most reliable way to deal with having a spirit."[16]

The album hits a down note with the desolate duo "Cold Cold Ground" and "Train Song." The first of these, in particular, dishes up a big helping of life's disappointments and cruelties. No matter what we do, no matter how good or how sinful we have been, we will all end up in the same place. A sobering thought.

Waits spun two video clips out of *Frank's Wild Years*. The video for "Temptation" is standard fare — Tom tricked out in a lounge-lizard outfit and pencil-thin mustache, lip-synching the lyrics as fireworks explode around him. The "Blow Wind Blow" clip is more arresting. In it, Waits sits with a woman made up to look like a mannequin. She appears to be singing the song. The director, Chris Blum, has explained that the mannequin idea evolved from Tom's unwillingness to lip-synch this song. The clip is a hypnotic piece of filmmaking. It was shot in black and white, and a vivid touch of red is used in each shot to signal passion and pain. As Blum joked, it's black and white and red all over.[17]

While speaking to O'Donohue on *Morning Becomes Eclectic*, Waits said of the "Blow Wind Blow" video, "Kathleen and I put together the ideas for it. It was done up there at the Chi Chi Club . . . in [San Francisco's] North Beach. Miss Kiko's Chi Chi Club right there on Broadway next to Big Al's. I worked with a girl named Val Diamond, who played a doll. She drew eyeballs on the outside of her eyelids and wore a Spanish dress and I unscrewed one of her legs and pulled a bottle out of it. It's got some entertainment value."[18]

Frank's Wild Years is a unique piece of work. It bears no relation to the mainstream music of its time. It was released in 1987, and that year's megahit was Bon Jovi's "You Give Love a Bad Name." Wang Chung's "Everybody Have Fun Tonight" and Aerosmith's "Dude (Looks like a Lady)" were also dominating the airwaves. By comparison, the songs of *Frank's Wild Years* sound like emanations from a distant planet. Waits was offering the record-buying public something impressionistic, evocative, twisted, disturbing, and totally seductive. He was attempting to share his personal vision with the world. Of course, most people didn't get it, and sales were typically lethargic.

But this didn't mean that Waits had become disenfranchised from the musical collective. He remained intrigued by the work of a number of his fellow musicians, even if their styles were vastly different from his own. The power punk of The Replacements — whose sound had developed from the raw, snotty, indie *Sorry Ma, Forgot to Take Out the Trash* (1981) to the more polished but no less powerful *Pleased to Meet Me* (1987) — got Waits going. He loved the sloppy energy of the band's live show. Lead singer Paul Westerberg would regularly stop dead in the middle of a song, announce "That sucks!" and launch into a different one.

Waits also admired the range that The Replacements displayed: they could go from power pop, like "Alex Chilton" (a tribute to the former Big Star and Box Tops bandleader), to melancholy balladry, like "Swingin' Party," to exercises in sarcasm, like "Waitress in the Sky." And "Here Comes a Regular," their song about barflies, is as sad and touching as any tune that Waits had written on the subject. Waits often talked about The Replacements when being interviewed. It turned out that the members of the band were fans of his, too, and Waits recorded "Date to Church" with them. It became the B-side to The Replacements' 1989 hit "I'll Be You."

Waits was also fond of The Pogues, a band that had successfully merged traditional Irish folk music with punk rock. Lead singer Shane MacGowan's booze-ravaged voice bore a certain resemblance to Waits's own. MacGowan was a pub crawler of Waitsian proportions and could often be found doffing a pint of Courage, his hair an electrified tangle and a nearly toothless grin on his face. The band's original name was Pogue Mahone, which is Gaelic for "kiss my arse." MacGowan and his crew demonstrated their innate understanding of the working man, and The Pogues had a penchant for telling short stories of the hard life in song, much like Waits.

Songs like "The Sick Bed of Cuchulainn" and "Turkish Song of the Damned" established The Pogues' reputation as chroniclers of modern Irish life. The band had an international hit with "Fairytale of New York" (with Kirsty MacColl) — quite probably the most depressing Christmas song ever written — which tells the tale of an elderly couple who spend Christmas Eve in a New York City drunk tank. Waits once told *Creem* magazine that he loved Shane's voice but thought that he really ought to get his teeth fixed.[19]

Waits's attraction to The Pogues and The Replacements, circa 1987, made a certain amount of sense — the themes and the attitudes that vitalized their music overlapped here and there with his own. Another Waits favorite, however, was a much less likely candidate. "Prince is really state of the art and he still kicks my ass," Waits told *Musician*'s Mark Rowland. "Prince is rare, a rare exotic bird . . . To be that popular and that uncompromising, it's like Superman walking through a wall."[20] Musically, Waits and the funky Prince may have been worlds apart, but Waits could still appreciate the intricate structures of Prince's songs and the delicate balance of the religious and the profane in his lyrics. At that point in history, Prince may have ruled the music world, but he consistently refused to do what was expected of him. Prince was a leader, a pathfinder, a creator of new sounds who scorned the idea of imitating popular formulas. And he sold a lot of records.

On that score, Waits no longer had any illusions. He knew that he'd never achieve mass popularity the way Prince had done. He wasn't even expecting to crack radio playlists with *Frank's Wild Years*. Like *Swordfishtrombones* and *Rain Dogs* before it, *Frank's Wild Years* was an embarrassment of riches waiting to be shared by anyone bold enough to pick it up. It contained eighteen songs, well over an hour of music. "More for your entertainment dollar!" Waits crowed to Rowland. "That's what we say down at Waits and Associates. Go ahead. Shop around. Compare our prices. Come on back down."[21]

With the release of *Frank's Wild Years*, the *Frank* trilogy — three albums' worth of tunes inspired by carnival music and German art songs — was complete. Waits was again ready to head off in a new direction. In his last three albums he had mined a rich vein of sound, but Waits was determined to prevent that sound from growing stale. The same impulse had prompted him to abandon his earlier lounge sound as soon as it lost its fresh edge. New musical challenges were on his agenda, although he had to admit that he wasn't yet sure what they were. He mused that his next undertaking could be "a little more . . . hermaphroditic. But I'm a real procrastinator. I wait till something is impossible to ignore before I act on it."[22]

Expanding on this theme to *Playboy*, Waits confessed that he was willing to kick start the process.

> PLAYBOY: You've remarked that *Frank's Wild Years* is the end of a musical period for you . . . Have you turned a corner? Is this album your last experimentation with the scavenger of songwriting?
>
> WAITS: I don't know if I turned a corner, but I opened a door. I kind of found a new scan. I threw rocks at the window. I'm not as frightened by technology maybe as I used to be. On the past three albums, I was exploring the hydrodynamics of my own peculiarities. I don't know what the next one will be. Harder, maybe louder. Things are now a little more psychedelic for me, and they're more ethnic. I'm looking toward that part of music that comes from my memories, hearing Los Tres Aces at the Continental Club with my dad when I was a kid.[23]

Waits backed up the release of *Frank's Wild Years* with a tour. It was a chore. He was no longer a resilient kid who could play dive after dive and return home relatively unscathed. He had evolved into a family man who could be worn down by the perpetual motion and the daily scrutiny. On the road, when things were working smoothly it could be great, but when hassles arose it could suddenly be like serving a prison sentence. "It's tedious. It's loaded with problems," Waits told *Morning Becomes Eclectic* listeners. "It's tragic. It's problematic from day to day. You try to work out the kinks along the way. It's like diamond cutting in the back of a pickup truck. You never know what you're gonna get. You're dealing with a lot of variables that are constantly changing, which is both the thrill and the hell of it. It's like a narcotic. It's very time-consuming. It's very expensive and it takes its toll, but I love it when I look back on it after it's over."[24]

Still, in the annual *Rolling Stone* Critics Poll, the *Frank's Wild Years* tour was judged the best of 1987. Given Waits's attitude, the honor was a tribute to his professionalism. His set list was drawn mainly from the previous three albums, though he also slid in a couple of older songs — "Ruby's Arms" and "Red Shoes by the Drugstore." A stage-set overhaul contributed to the dynamic. Waits informed the *Morning Becomes Eclectic* audience that the staging of his show was in transition. He was working on "lights and all that, trying to make it look good. It's gonna be a little bit different. I'm trying to get it to look like a Cuban Chinese restaurant up there on stage. I'm working out the kinks now."[25]

The *Frank's Wild Years* tour was Waits's most complex yet, both musically and technically. Props, masks, costume changes, pyrotechnics, special effects all came into play. Having mounted *Frank's Wild Years*, the musical, Waits had an even greater appreciation of the theatricality of a concert. He'd stand on the stage, lean into his mike, and perform a jerky, knee-knocking stomp, something between a religious testimonial and an epileptic seizure. He'd use props and even characters to bring a song into focus. Particularly intriguing was a lounge-lizard character — complete with pencil-thin mustache, white sports jacket, and killer shades — who'd sit at the piano cracking wise and spewing clichés — "you're a great audience! Thank you!"

Even the tour lighting was bold, different. Some numbers were lit by a swinging mechanic's lamp, which produced an eerie, unsettled atmosphere. For several other songs, Waits would hold that hook light in his hand, and it would be the only source of light on the stage. At one point, feathers would flutter down from above.

Waits rearranged the songs on the tour set list, as well, freely dissecting and reassembling them. Some tunes, like "Gun Street Girl" and "Telephone Call from Istanbul," were almost unrecognizable from their studio versions. On occasion, Waits would also revisit his cover-band days and do a smoking version of James Brown's "Papa's Got a Brand New Bag." The *Frank's Wild Years* tour was long, very successful, and, as far as Waits was concerned, enough. Reaching the end of that trek, he would drop out of the tour circuit for over a decade.

Over the years, Waits had grown very comfortable in the studio. He'd become adept at translating his private musical vision into a consumer

product. But he'd never seriously entertained the idea of producing someone else. His style was too personal, too quirky for that. Then Marianne
Faithfull came along. The British pop star of the sixties was best known
for her chiming schoolgirl rendition of a song written by (then boyfriend)
Mick Jagger and Keith Richards, "As Tears Go By." It became a hit nearly a
year before The Rolling Stones' version did. But the times were fast and
intense and Faithfull was caught up in the rush. By the late seventies, she
was strung out on heroin and living on the streets of London. Then, in
1979, Chris Blackwell intervened, offering Faithfull the chance to record.
To the surprise of many, she didn't blow it. Instead, she delivered *Broken
English*, a heartbreaking and brutally frank album that — together with Patti
Smith's *Horses* and Kate Bush's *The Kick Inside* — signaled the advent of
female alternative music. Of course, recovery is never that simple: Faithfull
hadn't completely conquered her demons, and when she traveled to New
York to perform the album's title track on *Saturday Night Live*, she freaked
under the pressure and snorted some cocaine. It was a bad batch, and it
wreaked havoc with her voice. One of the sadder moments in television
history is Faithfull struggling to keep up with the band as her voice cracks
and fades in and out. It took a few years for Faithfull to kick her habit
once and for all, and then she was ready to record again.

Waits had met Marianne Faithfull when they were both working on
producer Hal Willner's *Lost in the Stars* tribute to Kurt Weill (Faithfull's
contribution was "The Ballad of the Soldier's Wife"). Waits was attracted
to Faithfull's style; her voice, much like his own, had been ravaged by hard
living and had evolved into a raspy croak. The two became phone friends,
holding transatlantic musical debates. The idea of working together naturally came up. And, for the first time, Waits felt that he could produce the
work of another artist.

He offered to produce Faithfull's next album, a concept piece that he
wanted to call *Storeyville*, after New Orleans's historic red-light district.
Waits pictured Faithfull portraying an aging hooker who tells her story in
song, a kind of Prostitute's Revenge. In her autobiography, Faithfull admits
to having had mixed feelings about the concept. "It's always curious the
way people see me, which is always in a much more sexual light than
I see myself. Much as I'd love to believe the sexpot image of me, I don't
really see myself as an unrepentant hooker belting out blues from the
bordello."[26]

This conceptualizing underscores one of Waits's central songwriting
blind spots. So many of his women characters are sketched in broad

madonna/whore strokes, untouchable porcelain dolls or alcohol-addicted broken spirits. While these stereotypes began to break down somewhat when Kathleen entered Tom's life, they still have a tendency to creep into his creations. As it turned out, however, Marianne Faithfull would not be cast as the unrepentant hooker of Tom Waits's imaginings. The *Storeyville* album wasn't destined to be.

"A project like this requires weeks and weeks of sitting around listening to old records," Faithfull remarks, "and the person you usually end up working with is the one who has the time. Tom wanted to do it, but he was busy having a life: getting married, having children, making records."[27] Waits's schedule was too hectic, and the window of opportunity to pull off such an ambitious project simply couldn't be found. Instead, Tom and Kathleen wrote a song for Faithfull's next album. It was called "Strange Weather," and it took the form of a Brechtian lament that showcased Faithfull's Marlene Dietrich–like vocals to great effect. Hal Willner produced the album, named for the Waits/Brennan composition, and the song quickly became a standard in Faithfull's repertoire. Tom started performing it in concert himself, something he'd never done before with a song he'd written for someone else.

Waits also took part in Willner's next project, *Stay Awake*, a tribute to Disney movie music. Willner had corralled a diverse group of artists to perform on the album: Michael Stipe, Natalie Merchant, Bill Frisell, Bonnie Raitt, Aaron Neville, The Replacements, Suzanne Vega, Los Lobos, NRBQ, Sinéad O'Connor, Sun Ra, Harry Nilsson, James Taylor, and Ringo Starr. As Waits put it, Willner's "getting a lot of odd characters to record their favorite Disney songs."[28] As one of those "odd characters," Waits contributed an astonishingly twisted version of "Heigh Ho (The Dwarfs' Marching Song)" from *Snow White*. Instead of whistling while they worked, Waits's Seven Dwarfs produced a sound reminiscent of a chain gang consigned to Hell. He took great pleasure in the fact that the people at Disney were deeply disturbed by this.

Yet another welcome invitation was extended to Waits at about this time. He was asked to join a supergroup that would perform on a television comeback special featuring Roy Orbison. Launching his career in the 1950s, Orbison issued a string of up-tempo rockabilly tunes — like "Ooby Dooby" and "Dream Baby" — but such heart-wrenching offerings as "It's Over," "Crying," "Blue Bayou," and "In Dreams" catapulted him to stardom. He was flying high in 1964 with his biggest hit ever, "Pretty Woman," when he was felled by a double whammy. The first blow was the result of a bad decision. He left his small record label, Monument, where he had been top dog, and signed with the conglomerate Warner Brothers, where he became lost in the shuffle, a low-priority package. The second blow was beyond anyone's control. The Beatles took America by storm and suddenly Orbison was an anachronism. His hits became smaller and more scarce. His life degenerated into a series of tragedies and disappointments.

Orbison's star would not rise again until the eighties. In 1986, David Lynch used "In Dreams" during a hallucinogenic scene in his instant cult classic *Blue Velvet*, and, just like that, Roy Orbison was hip again. Then Orbison scored a minor hit with a remake of "Crying," performed with k.d. lang, which was included on the soundtrack of the movie *Hiding Out*.

Then came the television special to which Waits was asked to contribute, *A Black and White Night*. This would be Orbison's big chance to solidify his resurrection. A group of the biggest names in rock, dubbed The Coconut Grove Band, would be on hand to lend Orbison some powerful support. This outfit included Elvis Costello, who had written a song for Orbison and was set to play organ, harmonica, and guitar. Coconut Grove's other guitarists included Bruce Springsteen, James Burton (of Elvis Presley's band), J. D. Souther, and Waits's pal T-Bone Burnett. Waits contributed guitar work, too, although he also put in some time at the organ. The backing vocalists included Jackson Browne, k.d. lang, Bonnie Raitt, and Jennifer Warnes.

A Black and White Night (shot, of course, in black and white) had the desired effect. Orbison's career surged ahead over the next two years. With George Harrison, Bob Dylan, Tom Petty, and Jeff Lynne, Orbison formed The Traveling Wilburys. The band released an album in 1988 that soared to number three on the charts and spawned the hit singles "Handle with Care" and "End of the Line." Sadly, just weeks before he was due to release *Mystery Girl*, his first solo album in almost ten years, Orbison died of a massive heart attack.

Waits's parallel career as an actor was not growing stagnant as a result of all this musical activity. When director Hector Babenco's film adaptation of William Kennedy's Pulitzer Prize–winning novel *Ironweed* premiered in 1987, filmgoers were treated to the spectacle of Tom Waits playing opposite Hollywood icons Jack Nicholson and Meryl Streep. As Babenco, who was still riding a wave of adulation for his film *Kiss of the Spider Woman*, got down to casting his take on Kennedy's dreary Depression-era tale of two skid-row alcoholics, he somehow thought of Waits. "I play a character called Rudy," Waits explained at the time. "I get hit in the head in the train yard with a big stick on a raid. I die in the emergency ward at the end from a hemorrhage or internal bleeding, brain damage, and exhaustion. It's all about . . . alcohol, baptism, and redemption . . . It was a good experience for me. I got a chance to work with great people. Well, in this one I was forced to drink against my will. Everybody was told, ''Cause it's part of the story . . .' So there was a lot of drinking going on."[29]

As Rudy, Waits demonstrated that he could hold his own in the company of top-grade acting talent. He was no longer just a diverting cameo. Rudy's story was a vital thread in the *Ironweed* narrative, and Waits's screen presence was riveting. Waits modestly claimed that he'd actually picked up a few pointers from his costars. He told David Letterman that Meryl Streep should be declared "a national monument."[30] And when *Playboy* asked him what he'd taken away from the experience, Waits again expressed his admiration.

> PLAYBOY: In *Ironweed*, you worked with Jack Nicholson and Meryl Streep. What did you learn from them?
>
> WAITS: Nicholson's a consummate storyteller. He's like a great bard. He says he knows about beauty parlors and train yards and everything in between. You can learn a lot from just watching him open a window or tie his shoes. It's great to be privy to those things. I watched everything. I watched them build characters from pieces of things in people they have known. It's like they build a doll from Grandmother's mouth and Aunt Betty's walk and Ethel Merman's posture, then they push their own truthful feelings through that exterior. They're great at it.[31]

Despite its unrelentingly grim subject matter, *Ironweed* is a strong and captivating piece of work. Playing Rudy was a valuable exercise for Tom, both a learning experience and a means of increasing his cachet as an actor. It also indirectly enriched his composing. Asked whether his film acting was having an influence on his music, he replied, "I'm getting a bit more courage about putting some optical illusions in the songs as I become more aware of visualization of music. I start with an idea that's visual and then kind of score it. I get ideas from that all the time."[32]

Ever since he and Kathleen had created their play, Waits had wanted to make a movie of *Frank's Wild Years*. When it became apparent that this plan just wasn't coming together, he shifted his focus to another, more feasible, film project. He would make a movie that was neither a film version of the play nor a concert film but an imaginative marriage of the two. It would be called *Big Time*. Waits would portray Frank and several other characters in a series of short sketches interspersed with scenes from highly theatrical concert performances filmed at the Warfield Theater in San Francisco and the Wiltern in Los Angeles. Chris Blum, who'd done the "Blow Wind Blow" video, would direct *Big Time*.

"What we tried to avoid is having a concert film that felt like a stuffed bird," Waits explained to David Sheff of *Rolling Stone*. "I tried to film it like a Mexican cockfight instead of air-conditioned concert footage. Some of it felt like it was shot through a safari rifle. You forget about the camera, which is what I was trying to do. But when you see yourself in concert, it rarely looks like the way you feel when you're up there. I thought I was much taller. I thought I looked like Robert Wagner . . . If we had more money, we would have done the Rangoon gladiator sequences. And the shot of the audience holding up their matches and all that. We could have gotten the underwater ballet sequences, but it really would have been a different film, I think . . . Now that it's completed, I would not have had my underwear coming out of the back of my pants like I did, but there's always something you want to change after it's over."[33]

Clearly, *Big Time* was not your typical rock-concert movie. It was no pallid souvenir of a special occasion; it was the vibrant occasion itself. It ranks right up there with the handful of concert movies that have managed to transcend the genre's constraints: The Talking Heads' *Stop Making Sense*, The Band's *Last Waltz*, and the Stones' *Gimme Shelter*. *Big Time* is visually and aurally stunning and often quite funny. It strikes a wonderful balance between fantasy and real life, whimsy and seriousness.

As a bonus, Waits thought, his latest undertaking would give him a break from the public aspect of his work. He'd miscalculated. He told the *Morning Becomes Eclectic* audience, "The idea . . . was you put the film out there, the film can go on the road, and I can stay home. That was the idea, but then I end up having to go out and do interviews. [*Big Time* is] getting mixed reviews. I guess that's what they call it — mixed reviews. One reviewer said, 'Piano teachers will be shocked,' which is one of my favorite reviews. Another guy said it looked like it was filmed in the stomach of a very sick animal. Now those were the good reviews. I recommend it."[34]

9

THE LARGE PRINT GIVETH, AND THE SMALL PRINT TAKETH AWAY

Tom Waits abides by a number of moral principles. This one is close to the top of his list: no musician should be an adman — a pitchman, a huckster. Musicians weren't put on this Earth to sell you a complete car paint job for just $29.99. Let someone else move the beer, the antiperspirant, the corn chips off the shelves.

Waits has always been exceptionally outspoken on the subject of musicians peddling their songs to Wall Street, but he's bucked the trend. In today's music world, few artists will resist the double allure of money and exposure. Even the most respected musicians now drink freely from the Devil's cup. Eric Clapton sang that "After Midnight" he's gonna let it all hang out and chug a frosty Michelob. And you couldn't see Sting in concert if you used an American Express card: Sting only accepts Visa. The stage sets for the last few Rolling Stones' tours have been billboard extravaganzas. Dylan's "The Times They Are A-Changin'" has been used to shill for a bank.

Tom Waits isn't having any of that crap. He expressed his frustration at what was going on to Mark Rowland of *Musician* back in 1987, and his sarcasm was lethal: "It's amazing, when I look at those artists. I find it unbelievable that they finally broke into the fascinating and lucrative world of advertising after years on the road, making albums, and living in crummy apartments. Finally advertising opened up and gave them a chance for what they really wanted to do, which was salute and support a major American product, and have that name blinking over their head as they sing. I think it's wonderful what advertising has done, giving them these opportunities to be spokesmen for Chevrolet, Pepsi, etc."[1]

Given that the ad industry is notoriously voracious for novelty and fresh content, it's little wonder that Tom Waits, the great resister, was approached to sell his talents. "I get it all the time," he continued to Rowland, "and they offer people a whole lot of money. Unfortunately, I don't want to get on the bandwagon. You know, when a guy is singing to me about toilet paper — you may need the money but, I mean, rob a 7-11! Do something with dignity and save us all the trouble of peeing on your grave. I don't want to rail at length here, but it's like a fistula to me. If you subscribe to your own credibility, to the point where you do your own work, and then somebody puts decals all over it, it no longer carries the same weight . . . I really am against the people who allow their music to be nothing more than a jingle for jeans or Bud. But, I say, 'Good, okay, now we know who you are.' 'Cause it's always money. There have been tours endorsed, encouraged, and financed by Miller, and I say, 'Why don't you just get an office at Miller? Start really workin' for the guy.' I just hate it."[2]

Waits's song "Step Right Up" on *Small Change* is a parody of hucksterism, couched in the same angry language Waits used when he spoke to interviewers about art peddling. The mystery product that the song's persona is hustling does everything and nothing. It'll shine your car. Get rid of embarrassing stains. Lie to your wife. Pay off your credit cards. Walk the dog and pick up the kids at school. Make you six foot five, blond, and beautiful. Do your taxes. Return your tapes to the video store. And then, when you're done with it, it'll turn into a six-pack of beer and a pizza. Who in the world could take "Step Right Up" seriously as a sales pitch? Well, Frito-Lay did.

The snack-food giant actually hit on the notion that "Step Right Up" would make the perfect jingle to introduce their newest corn-chip flavor, Salsa Rio Doritos. A hot and spicy song for a hot and spicy chip. They couldn't use their old corporate spokescartoon, the Frito Bandito; he'd been forced to retire during the seventies when a Mexican group protested that he was nothing but a racist stereotype. So, since they couldn't have their Bandito, the Frito-Lay people wanted the next best thing: Tom Waits.

Representatives from Frito-Lay and its advertising agency, Tracy-Locke, approached Tom with the idea. Tom, of course, turned them down flat. This did not come as a surprise to David Brenner, Tracy-Locke's executive producer, because he'd once asked Waits to do a Diet Coke commercial. "You never heard anybody say no so fast in your life," Brenner later remarked.[3] Tracy-Locke and Frito-Lay should have taken no for an answer and left it at that, but they remained smitten with the Tom Waits concept. They resolved to find a way of moving ahead that wouldn't require Waits's approval. It didn't take them long to decide that they could simply bypass the recalcitrant musician. If he refused them access to the real thing, they'd do an "homage." They'd come up with a song that sounded vaguely like "Step Right Up" and that extolled the virtues of their new chip. They'd hire someone to sing it in the signature Waits style.

A team of copywriters put together an ad that transmitted the feel of the song, Frito-Lay gave it a thumbs-up, and Tracy-Locke started to audition gravel-voiced singers. Stephen Carter was one of the hopefuls. The Dallas-based singer had been recommended to Tracy-Locke by a sound engineer who was working on the ad. A big Tom Waits fan, Carter had been covering several Waits songs for years with his band, Schwanz LaFanz ("Whistlin' Past the Graveyard" was a particular favorite). Over time, Carter had learned to do an uncanny Waits impersonation — at his audition, the Tracy-Locke people "did a double take."[4] They were amazed at how much Carter sounded like his idol.

In fact, Carter was so good that the ad's musical director told him not to count on being hired. His vocal resemblance to Waits could trigger legal headaches. That same year, Bette Midler had sued the Ford Motor Company for $400,000 when it hired one of her backing vocalists to imitate her in a television ad. The case led to the establishment of the *Lanham Act*, which states that it is illegal to misappropriate a famous entertainer's vocal style. However, Tracy-Locke and Frito-Lay just couldn't let go of their winning idea. They hired the talented Stephen Carter and proceeded with caution, convinced that they were in the clear. After all, Ford had used one of Midler's songs; they were using an original jingle that was a "tribute" to Waits.[5]

When it came time to record the jingle, they had Carter do two versions. The first, which Carter was led to believe would be the one used in the ad, evoked the spirit and the sound of Tom Waits, but it wasn't overt imitation. The second version was pure impersonation. Listening to Carter sing — "It's buffo, boffo, bravo, gung ho, tallyho, but never mellow / Try 'em, buy 'em, get 'em, got 'em!" — you'd have trouble believing that this wasn't Tom Waits selling his soul.

On the eve of the Salsa Rio Doritos campaign launch, Robert Grossman, Tracy-Locke's managing vice president, conferred with the firm's attorney, who informed him that there was still a risk of legal action in light of the Midler/Ford case. However, based on Grossman's description of the ad, the lawyer thought that the risk was slim because a musical style cannot be legally protected. Tracy-Locke, in turn, explained the situation to Frito-Lay and presented the snack manufacturer with both versions of the jingle.

When the campaign hit the airwaves in September of 1988, consumers were bombarded with the second version — the impersonation.[6]

Waits himself first heard the commercial when he was at Los Angeles radio station KCRW to do an interview. Sitting in an office waiting to go on, he realized that he was being subjected to what he would afterward call a "corn-chip sermon" delivered Waits-style. At first he was floored. And then, the more he thought about it, the more enraged he became.[7] He would later testify that his anger "grew and grew over a period of a couple of days." His position on the issues involved was well known, and now he was being made to look like a hypocrite. "It embarrassed me," he said. "I had to call my friends [and tell them] that if they hear this thing, please be informed this is not me. I was on the phone for days. I also had people calling me, saying, 'Gee, Tom, I heard the new Doritos ad.'"[8] It was a nightmare.

Waits filed suit against Tracy-Locke and Frito-Lay in November, charging that the Doritos ad gave the false impression that he was endorsing the product and claiming that his persona had been misappropriated in violation of the *Lanham Act*. Waits did not include Stephen Carter in the suit because Carter had only been paid scale for his participation. In fact, Carter became one of Waits's strongest witnesses. He felt badly about his part in the fiasco and wanted to redeem himself.

The case went to court in 1990, and at the outset the jury didn't know what to make of the plaintiff. One juror admitted when it was all over that he'd initially thought that he was there to participate in a criminal trial and Waits was the defendant. But, after a month of duty, the ladies and gentlemen of the jury grew fond of Waits and became fans of his work.[9]

The defense attorneys did their job and tried every possible means of extricating their clients from the mess they had created for themselves. Suggesting that Waits was not covered by the *Lanham Act* because he was not as famous as Midler, one Frito-Lay attorney stated, "A professional singer's voice is widely known if it is known to a large number of people throughout a relatively large geographic area. A singer is not widely known if he is only recognized by his own fans, or fans of a particular sort of music, or a segment of the population." The defense went on to insist that the extent of celebrity also determines the extent of awarded damages. The court struck down that argument on the grounds that it would leave artists who did not rank as superstars vulnerable to misappropriation. Furthermore, the court stipulated, it was a moot point because, "the great weight of evidence produced at trial indicates that Tom Waits is very widely known." The jury was instructed to deliberate on the question of whether "ordinary consumers" would be "confused." Would these consumers naturally conclude that it was Tom Waits singing the commercial and endorsing Salsa Rio Doritos?[10]

The four-week trial came to an end when the jury decided unanimously that Waits had been wronged. So convinced were the jurors of the fact that Waits had been harmed by the actions of Frito-Lay and Tracy-Locke that they awarded him a grand total of $2.475 million in compensatory damages. The defendants appealed several times, but the decision was not overturned. It took years for Waits to see a penny of the settlement, but that was okay. He had been vindicated.

Although he'd won the corn-chip battle, Waits still had legal problems of another variety to contend with. The repercussions of his relationship with former manager Herb Cohen persisted. For a long time, Cohen had been claiming that Waits still owed him money for the original Elektra recording sessions. "[Waits's] business manager called me up," recalls Bones Howe. "He said that [Cohen and Mutt, his brother and business partner] were trying to say that they paid the studio costs and they wanted to recoup those from Tom. I said, 'Wait a minute. Asylum paid the studio costs. I have the files on every record we made, so if you want the files, you can have them.' So I did help Tom with that lawsuit against Herb. And rightly so. I don't know what deal he made on the publishing or all the rest of that . . . but that kind of thing is so typical of Herb and Mutt. I couldn't let them get away with it. [But], I must say, Herb made a great contribution to Tom's career as far as his stage persona and the production of his stage work and all of that goes. His live performance. Herb really did have a lot of influence and did help Tom. But I guess there's a time when you outgrow all of that."

Later, lawyers for Waits and Cohen would lock horns over several other issues. Cohen planned to release another compilation of the Asylum tracks, but Waits was able to block that project. In the early nineties, Waits filed suit against Cohen because Cohen had allowed a Screamin' Jay Hawkins remake of "Heartattack and Vine" to be used in a British Levis jeans ad. Waits sued and Cohen countersued. While the court ruled in favor of Waits, he was awarded only a fraction of the financial compensation he'd requested. However, he could take solace in the official apology he received from Levi Strauss and Company, which took the form of a full-page ad in *Billboard* magazine.

Tom did taste defeat after one legal skirmish with Cohen. In possession of that series of rough demos Waits had recorded for Bizarre/Straight before signing with Elektra, Cohen decided to release them. The series contained a few interesting rarities, but for the most part it was made up of rough drafts of songs that Waits had later improved upon. Waits was horrified at the prospect of their release, but in the end there was nothing he could do about it. Cohen owned those demos. In 1991, *Tom Waits: The Early Years* was released, and less than a year later, a second volume appeared. Says Jerry Yester, "Those Bizarre/Straight things that Herbie Cohen released, those were like what I did in my living room, recording just to hear the songs. Tom was so pissed off when those things came out. And they shouldn't have been released. Not without his permission, anyway."

In his less pissed-off moments, Waits chalked it up to experience. He said to Mark Rowland, "I must admit when I was a kid I made a lot of mistakes in terms of my songs. A lot of people don't own their songs . . . If John Lennon had any idea that someday Michael Jackson would be deciding the future of his material, if he could I think he'd come back from the grave and kick his ass. And kick it real good, in a way that we would all enjoy. I have songs that belong to two guys named Cohen from the South Bronx. Part of what I like about the last three albums is that they're mine."[11]

During the late eighties and early nineties, Waits may have become better acquainted with his legal representatives than he'd ever hoped to be, but these could hardly be described as "Frank's Litigious Years." Other things were in motion. Tom and Kathleen moved their family to a small town in remote Northern California. (Heading north made sense to Tom because, as far as he was concerned, everything south of L.A. was just more of L.A.) A realtor had showed them a house, they'd sat on the porch, a local train had put-putted past, the engineer had doffed his cap and waved; Tom and Kathleen had enjoyed a glass of wine, a bluebird had come and perched on Tom's shoulder, a deer had grazed nearby. They were enchanted with the house, and so they bought it. How could they have known? As soon as they moved in, Tom later explained, the train stopped running and the wild creatures stopped scampering; a bypass was constructed close by, and the resulting traffic noise was equal to that at the corner of 50th and Broadway during Friday rush hour.[12] The Waits clan was forced to sell their dream house and retreat even farther into the hinterland. They settled in again, choosing a house that was fifty miles away from the nearest McDonald's, out where paved roads were a luxury. Petaluma County.

Borrowing a line from Humphrey Bogart's character in *Casablanca*, Waits explained the motivation behind this radical transplant in typically deadpan fashion: "I came for the water. I was misinformed." Asked whether he missed big-city life, he had to admit that he did crave the urban sensory overload at times, but he was making do. "Now what I like to do is get three radios, turn 'em up full blast and imagine I'm back in town. There's my thrill. Sirens really kill me; I get all choked up."[13]

Petaluma County was a great place to raise a family — plenty of room for the kids to stretch and grow, good schools, little crime. Heaven on Earth. Waits was finally able to build his own recording studio. The privacy was intoxicating. Tom Waits had become virtually unfindable. He still is, and he loves it. If anyone tries to determine his coordinates, he becomes downright grumpy, and he's likely to snap, "About an hour or so out thatta way" or, "What, are you taking a census?"

In late 1989, Waits received an unexpected career boost. British superstar Rod Stewart was putting together a box set of recordings tracing his long and illustrious career. Stewart had started out as the vocalist for the Jeff Beck Group and then for the Faces. With the 1971 release of his solo album *Every Picture Tells a Story*, Rod Stewart became a household name. The album hit number one in both Britain and the United States, and it remains an all-time rock classic. Eventually, however, Stewart's bluesy, textured offerings devolved into shallow commercial fare like "Love Touch," "Do Ya Think I'm Sexy?" and "Tonight's the Night." For his box set, Stewart wanted some new songs (he needed new singles), and he chose to do covers. One was The Isley Brothers' jumping Motown nugget "This Old Heart of Mine" (done as a duet with the youngest Isley, Ronald, who hadn't even been a member of his brothers' band when the tune hit the charts in 1966); another was Tom Waits's "Downtown Train."

David Geffen had tried to convince Stewart to record a Waits song for years, and Stewart had always balked at the suggestion. Finally, a producer played the *Rain Dogs* cut for him, and something clicked. Stewart's label, Warner Brothers, loved what Rod did with the tune and elected to release it as the box set's first single. It was a smash. In early 1990, you couldn't turn on a radio without hearing Stewart pining over Brooklyn girls who ride the train. While Stewart meticulously sanded down the song's original rough edges, his interpretation is a decent one — it doesn't approach Tom's version, but it far exceeds Patty Smyth's 1987 attempt.

A major rift developed between Stewart and Bob Seger, another extremely popular rocker of the seventies and eighties, over Waits's train song. Seger insisted that he had been planning to record "Downtown Train" as a single himself, and that he'd told Stewart about his intention in confidence. At that point, Seger charged, Stewart had never even heard of the song. This led to a media war of words: Seger called Stewart a thief; Stewart returned fire by declaring that Seger was nuts. It took some time for tempers to cool on both sides.

Seger was a longtime Tom Waits fan. He once described a chance meeting he had with Waits to *Rolling Stone*. "I'm driving through Westwood [in L.A.], and I've got my Mercedes out there. I was working on a record, this is 1987 or '88. I've got a Hawaiian shirt on; it's real hot outside. I see Tom Waits, all in black, long-sleeved shirt and cowboy boots — it's 90 degrees — and he's walking through Westwood. So, I pull up next to him and I say, 'Tom!' I've got these sunglasses on, he probably thought I was with the CIA — car phone and everything — and he says, 'Heh?' and looks real startled, so I say, 'It's Bob Seger.'

"He says, 'Ooh, hi, Bob.' He jumps in the car and we start talking. I asked him what he's doin' and he says, 'Uh . . . I'm walkin'.' I've loved his stuff down through the years, so I start asking him all these dumb questions about his songs. I said, 'In "Cold Cold Ground," Tom, you say, "The cat will sleep in the mailbox." Yesterday I went and bought my cat one of those fuzzy mailboxes. Is that what you're talking about?' He looked at me like I was from Mars. 'No, no. My cats sleep under the house.' So it goes on, this strange interlude, for about fifteen minutes. Finally, I asked if I could drop him somewhere and he says, 'Tell you what, take me back where you picked me up.' So I drove around a bunch of blocks, dropped him exactly where I picked him up and he says, 'And, uh, I'll just keep on walkin'.'"[14]

In the end, Seger and Stewart recorded three Tom Waits songs each. Aside from "Downtown Train," Stewart did a credible version of "Tom Traubert's Blues" and an unsuccessful rendition of "Hang On St. Christopher." Seger recorded heartfelt, meat-and-potatoes versions of "New Coat of Paint," "Blind Love," and "16 Shells From a Thirty-Ought-Six."

Stewart's "Downtown Train," specifically, made Tom a hell of a lot of money — quite possibly more than any of his own recordings ever had. This, coupled with the settlement of the Frito-Lay lawsuit, brought him a degree of financial ease he'd never known before. He could now focus more intently on being a father and a husband. He could putter around the house. And he could take on any acting project that struck his fancy.

In fact, Waits's acting career shifted into overdrive for a while. The puttering would have to wait. He was invited to play a parade of characters in a range of vehicles, from oddball indie flicks to big-budget prestige productions. Waits jumped right in. But, for all the fun he was having, it was still hard work. "You have to put your makeup on in the car and stay sober," he told David Sheff. "It's a lot of work to try and be natural, like trying to catch a bullet in your teeth."[15] On some level, Waits actually did consider it all a trick that he was able to execute once in a while. He didn't even consider himself an actor in the strictest sense. "I wasn't drawn to it," he said to Hoskyns. "I was asked . . . I like doing it, but there's a difference between being an actor and doing some acting."[16]

It seemed clear, though, that to many film-industry players this difference was a negligible one, at least when it came to Tom Waits. Between 1989 and 1992, Waits appeared in eight films and one theatrical production. He played a hit man in the oh-so-hip New Wave western *Cold Feet*, starring Keith Carradine, Bill Pullman, and Sally Kirkland, and he stole the show. He also had small parts in the films *Bearskin: An Urban Fairytale*; *Queens Logic*, with Joe Mantegna, Kevin Bacon, and John Malkovich (making Waits one degree in the Kevin Bacon game); the *Chinatown* sequel *The Two Jakes*, in which Waits was reunited with Jack Nicholson; *The Fisher King*, with Robin Williams and Jeff Bridges; and *At Play in the Fields of the Lord*, with Aidan Quinn, Kathy Bates, and John Lithgow, which was directed by *Ironweed*'s Hector Babenco. Waits also played a DJ who is heard but never seen in Jim Jarmusch's episodic film *Mystery Train*. Then Bill Pullman suggested to Waits that he tackle a purely comedic role. Pullman was set to appear in a L.A. stage production of Thomas Babe's new work, *Demon Wine*, a tribute to French playwright Eugene Ionesco, and he thought that Waits could contribute fresh humor to the piece. Waits won the role and found himself a member of a terrific ensemble that included, aside from Pullman, Bud Cort, Phillip Baker Hall, Carol Kane, and René Auberjonois.

"I loved working with him. I loved talking with him," says Joe Mantegna, one of Waits's co-stars in the film *Queens Logic*. "Just hanging out with him. Tom was great. He's so bright, and so talented. I remember one day we were just sitting in my trailer, just talking, and he was talking about an opera he was writing. He was going to go to Germany and do it. He's such a renaissance kind of person." Mantegna also was impressed by Waits's lack of vanity as an actor, a rare and impressive attribute in the movie world. "The poster of the movie . . . he didn't feel his role even warranted him even being in it. We were all saying, Tom, you gotta [pose for it]. He was really very self-effacing in that way. He certainly wasn't driven by his ego. He was just driven by his work and what he did. I really, really, liked him as a person, let alone as a talent. I remember that fondly, working with Tom."

As this period of abundant dramatic work drew to a close, Waits landed the most appealing role of all. The vehicle was *Bram Stoker's Dracula*, a new version of the classic horror tale, to be directed by Tom's old friend Francis Ford Coppola. It was scheduled for a 1992 release. Before Waits was recruited for the project, the leads were announced, and the list was stellar: Gary Oldman, Winona Ryder, Keanu Reeves, and Sir Anthony Hopkins. Waits had his eye on the role of R. M. Renfield, a real-estate so-licitor whose relationship with the sinister count reduces him to raving lunacy and eternal slavery to the vampire. In Waits's eyes, Renfield was a plum role, and he wanted it badly. He attempted to explain why to Mark Rowland: "I got to go into this whole lurid, torrid tale, which was a meta-morphosis for me, to go into your own dark rooms. I just thought, 'Oh God, I have to stop recording and go get a bad haircut and eat bugs. And then come back home again.'"[17]

Waits begged Coppola to let him read for the role, and in the end he snared it. From that point on, he lost himself inside Renfield's dementia, never shying away from the physical ordeals the role entailed. He told Chris Douridas of *Morning Becomes Eclectic* that while he didn't actually eat the insects, he did put them in his mouth — "like I gave them a carni-val ride . . . like a fun house. I put them in the fun house and I let them move around in my mouth and then I brought them back out again. I didn't actually murder them with my teeth. But I had a good time. I had some frightening moments when I was both frightened and exhilarated — being hosed down in an insane asylum . . . dressed like a moth. I also had to wear these hand restraints that were really painful. They were based on a design they had for piano players, actually, in Italy — to keep your hands straight. They were metal braces, and they corrected anything that your fingers may want to do that's un-pianolike . . . [The device] was all metal, and [it had] these caps that went over your fingers, and [it was] really painful to your cuticles, and it looked really scary. That was the idea."[18]

Bones Howe, who hadn't seen Waits in almost a decade, finally hooked up with his old comrade during the filming of Coppola's *Dracula*. Howe had tried to reconnect with Waits once a few years earlier, but nothing had come of his efforts. "One of the guys who had been a coproducer of *Down by Law* took a job in business affairs at Columbia. We were talking about Tom one day and I said, 'Do you ever talk to him?' He said, 'Yeah . . . every

1

6

7

8

19

20

27

28

29

30

now and then.' [So I said], 'Tell him I said hello. I'd love to see him.' I ran into this guy [again] a couple of days later and he'd talked to Waits." When Howe asked what Waits's response had been, the man reported that Waits had said he wasn't ready to talk just yet. "This was, like, '87," continues Howe. "It had been five or six years. I just went, 'Okay. When Tom is ready to talk to me, he'll talk to me.' I had no idea what was going on with Kathleen and Herb and all this other stuff."

A few years later, Howe says, he was "working at Columbia TriStar, and they were shooting [*Dracula*] on the lot. I had just given my resignation. I went down to the set and just told the publicity people, 'Look, tell Tom I want to come by and see him on the set. If that's cool with him, I'll come down. If it isn't, then that's fine . . . I won't bother him.'" The publicists urged Howe to visit the set because, "'Francis would love to see you.' So I went down and we all hung out between shots and talked about *One from the Heart* and *The Outsiders* and all the rest of that junk. And it was very friendly. It was like I hadn't seen Tom since last Thursday, you know? He's like, 'You know, I moved to Northern California.' [I said], 'Yeah, I've heard that. Don't get stuck behind a bus.'"

Five years had elapsed since Waits's last studio album. This time, Jim Jarmusch motivated his return to recording by asking him to score his latest episodic film, *Night on Earth*. One night on Earth, five cab drivers in five far-flung cities have memorable — yet, true to the Jarmusch aesthetic, low-key and offbeat — encounters with their passengers. In Los Angeles, young slacker Winona Ryder ferries talent agent Gena Rowlands. In New York, immigrant and former clown Armin Mueller-Stahl picks up a bickering couple played by Giancarlo Esposito and Rosie Perez. In Paris, militant Isaach de Bankole drives beautiful, blind Beatrice Dalle to her destination. In Rome, Waits's *Down by Law* costar Roberto Benigni shocks his passenger, a priest, with an uproarious and increasingly frank account of his life. Finally, in Helsinki, a cabbie chauffeurs a group of drunks who have just lost their jobs.

These episodes are slices of life, subtle little gems that resonate like short stories. Tom and Kathleen collaborated on all the songs, creating a mostly instrumental score that endeavors to capture the comedy and the tragedy, the American and European textures of the tales. They did an admirable job. At times their music has such presence, such a congruity with the visual and narrative component of the film, that it's almost a character in itself. By turns jaunty and melancholy — whatever is called for — the score blends sounds and styles and feelings into a wonderful, adventurous suite. It is comprised of sixteen short tracks, three of which have lyrics; horns and accordion enrich the mix, and Kurt Weill's strange influence is again felt. The film *Night on Earth* found its way onto cinema screens in 1992, and Waits released the soundtrack album in April of that year.

Yet *Night on Earth* is not the type of album that most people would be moved to listen to over and over again. The tracks work well to set up and complement the shifting moods of the film, but few, if any, Waits fans would peg it as their favorite. Lacking two vital layers — Waits's strong lyrics and distinctive singing — it feels incomplete. The time had surely come for Waits to make a "real" new album.

10

WHO ARE YOU NOW?

It wouldn't take long for Waits to come through. Hot on the heels of the *Night on Earth* soundtrack, in August 1992, came *Bone Machine*. Waits was working on *Bram Stoker's Dracula* when he recorded it, and the spectre of death hangs over the album like a pall. Much like Lou Reed's *Magic and Loss*, which had come out in January of the same year, it is an extended meditation on mortality. Even the songs that don't deal directly with death exude a sepulchral quality, with their sparse arrangements and tortured vocals. *Bone Machine* is the type of album that sneaks up on the listener. Many of the songs, while not particularly melodic, compel you to return to them. Fascinating new aspects of these pieces reveal themselves with each listening.

Some musicians place a high priority on employing studio techniques to smooth the rough edges of their work. While Waits, particularly since moving to Island Records, was not so inclined, *Bone Machine* tested the limits of this aesthetic approach more aggressively than ever. Even compared to the *Frank* trilogy, *Bone Machine* is almost all rough edges. Most of the tracks are dauntingly minimalist. The overall effect is to direct the listener's attention to the basic structures of the songs. It was a daring thing to do, and only a very restless and committed artist would attempt it. In 1993, Waits said to Rowland, "You send [the songs] out there 'cause it's true that things kind of land in your backyard like meteorites. Songs can have a real effect on you — songs have been known to save lives. Some of them are little paramedics. Or maybe some will be killers. Some will die on the windshield. And some of them will never leave home. You beat them but they never leave. Others can't wait to get out of here, and will never write. They're ungrateful little bastards. There's only one reason to write more songs. It's what Miles Davis said. Because you're tired of the old ones."[1]

Advances in recording technology would now afford Waits the luxury of choosing the ideal environment in which to give birth to his compositions. With the advent of DAT (digital audio transfer), it had become easier than ever to record music virtually anywhere — in a car, in a bar, in a bathroom, in a field. These were crucial decisions for Waits; he believed that the choice of recording environment had an enormous impact on the finished product. He began by installing his band in a studio, but the space was all wrong. The vibe just wasn't there. It was sterile. He had to find another locale. Somewhere more sensual, more in keeping with the music.

"I was so disturbed; the studio we got was totally wrong," Waits later explained to Rowland, still pained by the memory. "I was stomping around thinking, nothing will ever grow in this room. I'm more and more inclined toward texture, and you can't get texture with this whole bio-regenerator-flesh approach to recording. It gets a little too scientific for me . . . The room becomes a character. And, fortunately, we stumbled upon a storage room that sounded so good — plus it already had maps on the wall. So I said, 'That's it, we're sold.'"[2]

The storage room in question was in the studio building. It had a cement floor and a broken window; furthermore, it wasn't soundproofed — if someone talked too loud in an adjoining room, if a car passed by, or if a plane passed over, it would become part of a song. In other words, the space had everything that Tom Waits would require. Additional features were a hot-water heater, a table, and a chair. And, of course, those maps. Tom and crew only had to haul out a stack of old crates and the "studio" was ready for business. Said Waits, "We invented a new place for it to happen."[3]

The music of *Bone Machine* was miles removed from Waits's early neobeatnik sound. Upon the album's release, he said that listening to those old songs again was sort of like looking at his baby pictures.[4] They summon up feelings of fondness and familiarity, but they reflect little of the long strange journey you've been on ever since. Waits told the *Morning Becomes Eclectic* audience that what he was most partial to at this point was "songs with adventure in them. I think that's what everybody's looking for: songs with adventure, and acts of depravity and eroticism, and shipwrecks, murder." With *Bone Machine*, he was trying to "make songs that felt a little more handmade. Experiments and expeditions into a world of sound and stories. I was more interested in percussion — in these Bermuda Triangles of percussion that you find and sometimes you drop off the edge of the world."[5]

To intensify that percussive clang, Waits exploited even more found sounds than usual. His favorite new instrument, created by a buddy of his, was called a conundrum. "It's just a metal configuration, like a metal cross," he explained. "It looks a little bit like a Chinese torture device. It's a simple thing, but it gives you access to these alternative sound sources. Hit 'em with a hammer. Sounds like a jail door. Closing. Behind you. I like it. You end up with bloody knuckles when you play it. You just hit it with a hammer until you can't hit it any more. It's a great feeling to hit something like that. Really slam it as hard as you can with a hammer. It's good and therapeutic."[6]

Bone Machine actually sounded scary. The effect wasn't necessarily something that Waits had been striving for — it just seemed to happen. Certainly, the fact that he was playing Renfield while he was recording it contributed to the album's macabre aura, but that didn't fully account for Waits's new direction. Waits himself didn't offer much insight, remarking to Rowland, "It just came out of the ground like a potato."[7] The music of *Bone Machine* was more disturbing than anything Waits had ever written — and it was also some of the wildest and most intense.

The album's tracks were selected from a pool of about sixty songs and ideas that Tom and Kathleen had come up with. "You always throw out a lot of songs," Waits remarked. "Not throw them out, but you cannibalize them. That's part of the process. Frankenstein that number over there. Take the head off of him and sew it onto this guy, immediately. Keep him alive until the head has been severed. It's part of song-building. Kathleen is great to work with. She's a lapsed Catholic from Illinois. She's loaded with mythology and [has a] great sense of melody. I spin the chamber and she fires it. It's Russian roulette. Sometimes you get great things."[8]

From the opening chords of the album's opening track, "Earth Died Screaming," the listener knows that he or she is in for a rough and challenging ride. Waits borrowed the title from a fifties sci-fi movie that he'd never seen and created a song that is nothing less than a musical simulation of the apocalypse. Hellfire crackles in his vocals, which are punctuated by some very weird percussion. Les Claypool, leader of the rock band Primus, weaves in a queasy bass line (he was returning a favor — Waits had contributed vocals to Primus's single "Tommy the Cat"). The strange clicking sound that carries the tune was achieved by Waits and his band members going outside and hitting on things with sticks.

The next song, "Dirt in the Ground," doesn't revel in chaos and destruction like the preceding cut. It's more of a dirge, a reflection on mortality.

The great tenor saxophonist Teddy Edwards provided Waits with the title: Edwards used to say, "We're all gonna be dirt in the ground" to the women he was trying to lure up to his hotel room. "Why worry, Sugar? It ain't gonna matter in the long run." The notion appealed to Waits, but rather than building on the line's value as a seduction ploy he took it at face value.[9] The resulting song is a low, mournful prayer that is brought into sharp focus by Ralph Carney's plaintive horns. Next up is the rock-and-roll testimonial "Such a Scream." Despite some disturbing lyrics — concerning a blood-red plow and the "dollhouse of her skull" — Waits has insisted that "Such a Scream" is actually a love song for Kathleen. Listen to the lyrics closely and you'll see exactly what he means.[10]

"Who Are You" is a gorgeous ballad of love and loss that could easily have fit onto one of Waits's Elektra albums, though in an earlier version it would most likely have been played on piano with some strings blended in. The *Bone Machine* arrangement was built on Waits's guitar and percussion and the upright bass of former Canned Heat member Larry Taylor. When Hoskyns asked Waits to explain what this cryptic little song is all about ("They're lining up / To mad dog your tilta whirl"), Waits refused. "The stories behind most songs are less interesting than the songs themselves. So you say, 'Hey, this is about Jackie Kennedy.' And it's, 'Oh, wow.' Then you say, 'No, I was just kidding, it's about Nancy Reagan.' It's a different song now. In fact, all my songs are about Nancy Reagan."[11]

"The Ocean Doesn't Want Me" is a musical suicide note. Its instrumentation is spooky and Waits's voice is like that of a drowning man. He was inspired to write it after coming across a newspaper story accompanied by two photos — the first of a woman standing on a beach, and the second of the same woman a couple of hours later, a corpse washed up on the sand. Her living image had been captured by a passing photographer; when he came back that way again, she was dead. Gone in the blink of an eye, like the click of a shutter.[12]

Tom's daughter made her contribution to *Bone Machine*, as well. As her father remarked, "Everybody gets in. Everybody wants to get into the action." Kellesimone provided a lyric for "The Ocean Doesn't Want Me." Explained Waits, "My little girl has a word — 'strangels.' It's a cross between strange and angels. Strange angels. Or you could have braingels . . . the strange angels that live in your head would be braingels. We just went around and around with it, and it wound up in 'The Ocean Doesn't Want Me.' . . . Hey, kids write thousands of songs before they learn how to talk. They write better songs than anybody. You hope you can write something a kid would like. I got a fan letter from somebody in the Midwest. They said, 'Well, my little girl is just coming around to your songs now. They scare her a little bit. She thinks you sound like a cross between a cherry bomb and a clown.' I like that. You can't fool kids. They either like ya or they don't."[13]

"Jesus Gonna Be Here" is about a con man, the kind of tortured dreamer Waits had been etching so vividly for years. "A Little Rain" feels like something from an old Kurt Weill theatrical score. "Black Wings" bolsters Waits's mounting reputation as a great modern poet and unfolds to a tune straight out of a spaghetti western.

Like "The Ocean Doesn't Want Me," "Murder in the Red Barn" is a creepy little tale with its roots in a local news story. For a long time, Waits has been scouring the papers for ideas, skimming over accounts of politics and war and digging out reports on small human tragedies. He has told Hoskyns that he buys the local papers every day, "and they are full of car wrecks. I guess it all depends on what it is in the paper that attracts you. I'm always drawn to these terrible stories. I don't know why. Black Irish? You know . . . my wife is the same way. She comes from an Irish family and she's drawn to the shadows and the darkness. 'Murder in the Red Barn' is just one of those stories, like an old Flannery O'Connor story. My favorite line is, 'There's always some killin' / You got to do around the farm' . . . It's true."[14]

Waits cowrote "That Feel" with Keith Richards, and Richards played and sang on the track. "It's great to have somebody to write with," Waits confided to Rowland. "It's still really a mystery why songs come around and then leave. Keith is always pondering these same questions; he's extremely down-to-earth and very mystical at the same time." In fact, Richards' influence extended even further into *Bone Machine* — on "Such a Scream," Waits lays down a scorching Stones-style guitar riff. Speaking to Rowland, he laughed, "You can't help it if you're around [Keith]. You start walking like him, and you know, it's just impossible. He's got arms like a fisherman. He's physically very strong, and he can outlast you. You think you can stay up late? You can't even come close. He can stay up for a week — on coffee and stories."[15]

So *Bone Machine*, like so many of Waits's earlier projects, draws on a disparate web of sources to produce unexpected results. Tom has confessed that even he and Kathleen haven't a clue how it all came together. It was like concocting a dish that you'd been longing to taste without benefit of a recipe. Waits said to Douridas, "When do you put the cinnamon in? Is it after the nutmeg? Or do you first put the scallions in and you dice? What, do you brûlé that? Sauté that? I dunno. Sometimes. Do you lift the lid, or do you not lift the lid?"[16]

Of course, sometimes your best efforts will only produce an unappetizing mess. "Well, some [songs] never come to life," Waits continued, shifting metaphors. "Sometimes you have to be like a doctor. You have to look at them medically — 'What's wrong with this?' You have to diagnose them. Some have maladies that are impossible to deal with. Some of them you can't diagnose. Some songs, you work on them for months and they'll never make the journey. They'll be left behind, and someone has to break the news. We had a lot. We had one called 'Filipino Box Spring Hog.' It was a song about this old neighborhood ritual, and the song didn't make it on the record. It broke my heart, but it just couldn't come. It was good. Maybe it'll come out on something else."[17] It did. The song eventually made its way onto the charity album *Born to Choose* and later onto Waits's *Mule Variations*.

Yet another aspect of *Bone Machine*'s creation was compromise. Waits's mandate, beyond perfecting new modes of self-expression, was to communicate with others. To reach into the hearts and minds of his listeners. To avoid making them run for cover. "Well, you know, I always make compromises," he told Douridas. "If I really put it down the way I really want to hear it, nobody else would want to listen to it but me. I clean everything up, within reason. 'Cause . . . I like to step on it. Step on the negative. Grind it into the gutter and put that through the projector." Waits went on to say that Keith Richards called these stepped-on sounds the "hair in the gate."[18] The hair that somehow gets trapped inside a movie projector, abruptly drawing the audience's attention away from the narrative that's been unreeling before them. Suddenly, that small imperfection holds more fascination than the film itself, but then, as quickly as it has come, the hair vanishes. And for a moment the audience misses it.

Having compromised and cleaned up as much as he could bear, Waits declared *Bone Machine* finished. Everyone involved stood back for a moment and had a good look at what they had wrought. "When I was done with *Bone Machine*," Waits told Hoskyns, "we listened back and we were like, 'Oh, man, everybody's got problems on this record.' The whole arc of it . . . you don't really get a sense of it until it's completely done. In the meantime, we were just doing the finer, closer work. You don't stand back from it and see how it all works together. Then when it's all over you have to decide if it has four legs and a tail or what."[19]

A number of critics included *Bone Machine* in their top-ten-albums-of-1992 lists. The album won the Grammy for Best Alternative Album of the Year (an award that too often goes to work that is unworthy of the "alternative" designation). An array of musicians and critics sang its praises. But sales were slow, at best. Business as usual.

The following year, Robert Altman's film *Short Cuts* was released, featuring Tom Waits as an alcoholic limo driver. It was a high-profile gig. Altman, the fiercely independent director of some vivid pieces of American film culture — such as *Nashville* and *M*A*S*H*, both made in the seventies — had just come roaring out of an extended dry spell with *The Player*. This pitch-black send-up of the Hollywood motion-picture business was released in 1992, and it was Altman's first hit in years. Everyone was clamoring to work with him. Casting *Short Cuts*, a dissection of life in contemporary L.A. based on several intertwined Raymond Carver stories, Altman was able to build a powerhouse ensemble. Altman was renowned for assembling and coordinating huge casts, and he didn't hold back now. *Short Cuts* would star Tim Robbins (who'd anchored *The Player*), Andie MacDowell, Lily Tomlin, Julianne Moore, Madeleine Stowe, Matthew Modine, Jack Lemmon, Robert Downey Jr., Lili Taylor, Jennifer Jason Leigh, Christopher Penn, Frances McDormand, Bruce Davison, Buck Henry, and Peter Gallagher, as well as actor-musicians Lyle Lovett, Huey Lewis, and Tom Waits.

Waits described his part to Douridas: "I played Earl Piggot, a limo driver who drinks, and I was married to Lily Tomlin." He also spoke about how much he'd enjoyed working with Altman: "He's like a good sheriff in a bad town." At that point in the interview, Waits began to ruminate on the film actor's life: "Film is difficult sometimes, because they don't pay you to act, they pay you to wait. Somebody told me acting makes a woman more of a woman and a man less of a man. Oh God — so that's what's been bothering me! Fussing around with your hair. Getting up six in the morning and having all these people fussing all around. I like it when I can actually leave the ground. That's rare in film. It's more common in a play where you can actually experience flight. Film is so broken up. It's a mosaic. In working with good people it's always enriching and always satisfying. But some films are like you bought the last ticket on a death ship." Laughing, Waits then assumed a sinister tone — "and you'll never come home!"[20]

Short Cuts was released in 1993 and was greeted with critical raves. Altman was nominated for a 1993 Best Director Oscar, and the film garnered a number of prestigious foreign awards. The irascible Earl Piggot was seen by audiences the world over.

A few years earlier, in 1988, Waits had been asked to work on an operetta called *The Black Rider*. New York theater producer Robert Wilson, who had turned down Tom and Kathleen's request to help them get *Frank's Wild Years* off the ground, wanted to know whether Tom was interested in scoring the piece, which was based on a German legend, circa 1811, called "Gespensterbuch." This story of a man who sells his soul to the Devil to win the love of a fair maiden had, in 1821, been turned into the opera *Der Freischutz (The Marksman)* by Carl Maria Von Weber, though Von Weber had substituted a happy ending for the original tragic one. The big inducement that Wilson could hold out for Waits was that Beat icon William Burroughs would write the contemporary version; and Burroughs, presumably, wasn't afraid of tragic conclusions.

Waits and Wilson met while Wilson was staying at the Roosevelt Hotel on Hollywood Boulevard, a historic establishment just blocks away from some of Waits's old Hollywood haunts. At that point, Waits had only seen one of Wilson's plays, *Einstein at the Beach*, at the Brooklyn Academy of Music. He claimed that he'd left the theater afterward and entered a dreamworld that he could not escape for weeks.[21] There, at the Roosevelt, Wilson presented his offer to Waits. While flattered, Waits was also a little intimidated, primarily by the prospect of working closely with his hero William Burroughs.

More discussion was needed. "We all went to meet William in Lawrence [Kansas]," Waits told Hoskyns. "Greg Cohen and Robert Wilson and myself. And we talked about this whole thing. It was very exciting, really. It felt like a literary summit. Burroughs took pictures of everyone standing on the porch. Took me out into the garage and showed me his shotgun paintings. Showed me the garden. Around three o'clock he started fondling his wristwatch as we got closer to cocktail hour. He was very learned and serious. Obviously an authority on a wide variety of topics. Knew a lot about snakes, insects, firearms."[22]

Waits signed on. As the enterprise got under way, he found that the amazement he'd felt at finding himself collaborating with the likes of Burroughs wasn't waning. Burroughs "was Bull Lee in *On the Road*," Waits said. "He was the one that was more like Mark Twain with an edge. He was more suited to the whole notion of the country having some type of alter ego. He seemed to be ideally suited to the position of poet laureate. He seemed to have an overview, and one of maturity and cynicism. I've heard a lot of the stuff he did with Hal Willner. 'The Thanksgiving Prayer' and all that stuff. It just really killed me. He had a strongly developed sense of irony, and I guess that's really at the heart of the American experience. If you read the papers over the years, you have to see that there's something very ironic about everything."[23]

The Black Rider is the saga of Wilhelm, a clerk who falls in love with a beautiful maiden named Katchen. Katchen's father, Kuno, is determined that his daughter marry a hunter, so he sets up a shooting contest for her hand. Though he can't shoot, Wilhelm is desperate to win Katchen, so he makes a pact with a dark, mysterious horseman named Pegleg. Pegleg gives Wilhelm five magic bullets that will hit any target the gunman chooses, but he insists on retaining one bullet for himself. Thanks to the magic bullet, Wilhelm wins the contest, but Kuno decrees that on Wilhelm and Katchen's wedding day, there will be one final contest. Wilhelm begs Pegleg for the last bullet; Pegleg finally gives in, but when Wilhelm shoots the bullet, it flies straight into Katchen's pure heart.

For several months during the early nineties, Waits lived in Hamburg, Germany, and worked on the music for *The Black Rider*. His domestic headquarters was a ratty old hotel, and his workplace was a facility called Gerd Bessler's Music Factory. He had brought Greg Cohen along to work on the songwriting and the arrangements. The two sustained themselves with cold coffee, hard rolls, and little sleep. Day after day, they toiled with a group of local musicians they alternately called The Black Rider Orchestra or The Devil's Rhubato Band. On his occasional day off, Waits meandered around Hamburg, browsing in old shops and exploring flea markets.

The Black Rider played in Hamburg, Vienna, Paris, Barcelona, Genoa, Amsterdam, and Berlin. In 1993, it finally made it to American shores, where its home became the Brooklyn Academy of Music. Also in 1993, Waits released an album of the songs he'd written for the operetta. It couldn't really be called a new Tom Waits album — it was more of a side project.

In essence, the album *The Black Rider* documents Waits's attempt to reconstruct the German dance-hall style of Kurt Weill and Bertolt Brecht in order to retell a traditional tale. As such, it has an even more pronounced central theme and theatrical feel than Waits's experimental works of the past decade. Many of the songs evoke a haunted-carnival atmosphere — the opening track, "Lucky Day Overture," sets the mood with its carny-barker-from-Hell lyrics.

The title track sounds like something you'd hear on a swirling calliope in a German town (though Waits's German accent could have used some polishing). The album boasts several beautiful songs, like the ballad "November" and "The Briar and the Rose." Like a theme from a cowboy movie, "Just the Right Bullets" bumps the proceedings up to a gallop, but, as a whole, *The Black Rider* album is an uneven piece of work. Many of the songs worked better in the theatrical context; outside of that context the collection's coherence is diminished. Also, while cool in theory, having Burroughs sing the old standard "T'Ain't No Sin" only serves to demonstrate that Burroughs's voice is even more ravaged than Waits's own.

Overall, however, Waits's collaboration with Wilson was a successful one. On the heels of it, in 1992, Wilson again approached Waits with a project proposal. This time, Kathleen was invited to participate as well. Working with the Thalia Theater Company of Hamburg, Wilson wanted to mount a production called *Alice*, a musical that explored the relationship between the Reverend Charles Dodgson and Alice Liddell, otherwise known as Lewis Carroll and the Alice who tumbles into a well and lands in Wonderland.

Tom and Kathleen agreed to Wilson's request and wrote *Alice* for him. When the time came to orchestrate the material, Tom moved back to Hamburg on his own. He had just six weeks to complete this phase of the project. By the time the show opened, right before Christmas, he was practically crazed. The work was grueling, and he sorely missed his home and family. During the fine-tuning process many of those involved in the production could see how stressed out he'd become. By all accounts, *Alice* was a much more accessible work than *The Black Rider*, but Waits hadn't released any of the songs from it. He often, however, ventured to say that he'd like to record some of the *Alice* material — and he finally would get to release it in 2002.

Waits's musical adventures have taken many forms. One night, years back, he and Kathleen were listening to the radio when they heard a mesmerizing hymn called "Jesus' Blood Never Failed Me Yet." Waits managed to tape the song, but it was eaten by a tape deck. After spending years trying to track down a recording of the hymn, Waits gave up hope. Then, out of the blue, a friend asked him if he'd ever heard the song. The friend had a copy of his own and was happy to make one for Waits. On *Morning Becomes Eclectic*, Waits related what little he knew about that mysterious profession of faith in Jesus. "What I understand is that it was a recording made of an old man on the beach in the middle of the night, digging clams. Somebody taped him singing all by himself and then they brought the tape home and added strings to the recording and that's what this is. But it's very eerie . . . it's just a strange little song."[24]

Gavin Bryars had heard the song, too. Like Waits, the British composer found the lyrics, and the crude yet extremely affecting voice that sings them, impossible to forget. Bryars, however, explains the song's origins like this. In 1971, a friend of his named Alan Power was making a documentary about a group of London tramps. He asked Bryars to work on some of the audiotapes from the footage he'd shot — "bits of opera, sometimes folk songs, sometimes sentimental ballads." Among these bits and pieces was a man singing "Jesus' Blood Never Failed Me Yet." In the end, Powers opted not to use the song in his film and gave it, along with other unused audio segments, to Bryars.[25]

Over the years, Bryars tinkered with the piece of tape. He knew beyond a doubt that its magic was highly communicable after he left it playing on a continuous reel one day and left the studio for coffee. When he returned, he found several people weeping quietly and others in an uncharacteristically subdued frame of mind, overcome by "the emotional power of the music." From that volatile scrap of music Bryars created an orchestral concert piece, which he presented to live audiences and then recorded in 1975 for Brian Eno's Obscure Records label. When, some time later, "the possibility arose of making a CD version," Bryars "resolved to reconsider the piece for this extended medium." He fleshed out the instrumentation considerably and hit upon the idea of mixing Tom Waits's voice with that of the old man.[26]

Waits, of course, didn't need to be coaxed. He was thrilled to accept Bryars' invitation to participate in the project, a CD that would be released in 1993. And he wasn't simply drawn to it by his fascination with the tramp's particular refrain. He had always been enthralled by bums and vagabonds, and Bryars' project was a way for him to slip on the tattered hat and slide down into that underworld again. By recording "Jesus' Blood," he could reassume the familiar persona of the starving old man warming his hands over a trash-can fire in some decaying shantytown.

Clearly, it was all just playacting. And Waits was again blurring the distinction between inhabiting the slums and slumming. He had escaped skid row years ago, if "escaped" is even the word — he was never actually imprisoned by it in the first place. Waits was going home to a place that he'd never really occupied. Still, this was all done in the service of art. And it was art of the highest caliber. When Waits's voice meshes and builds with that of the tramp in Bryars' seventy-four-minute symphony, the results are poignant and mysterious beyond words.

Tom Waits was on top of the world in 1993. The critics hailed his music. Acting opportunities abounded, and he was doing interesting work in theater. No one could predict what he'd do next. As it turned out, his next move was to walk away from it all. He embarked on an extended vacation.

Waits had been working constantly for over twenty years, and he was due for a break. He had achieved financial security. The *Alice* episode had demonstrated to him that pushing too hard just makes you crazy. Finally, there was this important motivator: the birth of another son, Sullivan. Now, more than ever, Waits was determined not to be the clichéd rocker who fits in his kids between tour dates and stints in the studio. He wanted to hang out at the diner until everyone in the neighborhood knew him. He wanted to become a local character, to travel the back roads in his metallic-gold '67 Caddy Coupe DeVille. ("Drives great, but the driver's side door doesn't open, so if ya don't mind me scooching over top of you . . .") Eventually, he trashed the old boat and had to replace it, choosing a newer model, a '70 Coupe DeVille. The day the '67 Caddy died, Casey Waits had found his dad wiping the blood from his forehead with a sack of McDonald's takeout and persuaded him to go to the hospital.

Waits happily set about taking it easy. On any given day, he might go shopping — pick up old artillery shells or maps or rings made from spoon handles at the local salvage shop. He might impress the kids by bringing home the latest Primus or Beck or Rage Against the Machine CD. He might suggest to the family that they eat out, but no one would let him pick the restaurant anymore. Kathleen and the kids valued tasty and nutritious food over atmosphere, so there went Tom's beloved greasy spoons. Family life was something to contend with, Waits admitted to *Morning Becomes Eclectic* listeners. "Well, sometimes it's like log-rolling and if you see just a shot of it, a still picture of somebody log-rolling, it's one thing . . . but as a moving picture you see what's required. Yeah, we're keeping a good balance on it."[27]

When asked by Hoskyns whether he now considered himself a homebody, Waits hedged. "Gee, I don't know. That sounds like a loaded question. If I say no, I'll get into trouble with my family, and if I say yes I get in trouble with everybody else. You know, I live in a house with my wife and a lotta kids and dogs, and I have to fight for every inch of ground I get. Mostly my kids are just looking for any way I come in handy. Clothes, rides, money . . . that's all I'm good for. But I think it's the way it's supposed to be."[28]

Music had become something that Waits would indulge in when the mood struck. He provided music for several film soundtracks. He performed at charity functions, devoting time to causes that moved him. He protested the death penalty at Tim Robbins's *Dead Man Walking* concert; he contributed a cover of "Brother Can You Spare a Dime?" to the album *Brother Can You Spare a Dime Day* put out by the Harburg Foundation, which benefits the poor and the homeless; as well, his song "Filipino Box Spring Hog" appeared on the pro-choice fund-raiser album *Born to Choose*, and his cover of Cole Porter's "It's Alright with Me" graced the AIDS-research charity album *Red Hot and Blue*. Waits was happy. He had room to breathe. Inevitably, however, it wasn't enough. The old itch to be in the game began to act up. By 1998, Tom Waits was finally ready to get back to work.

One of the first things he did was leave Island Records, where he'd been a fixture for fifteen years. It was an amicable parting. Chris Blackwell, who had originally signed Waits to the label, had sold Island to Polygram years before, but he'd stayed on to run the company. When Universal Music Group snapped up Polygram, Blackwell departed to form his own new entertainment company, Islandlife/Palm Pictures. Universal went on to gut Island, merging it with rap label Def Jam and reducing the staff and talent rosters of both significantly. Waits didn't become a casualty of the corporate slash-and-burn campaign, but his contract was up for renewal with Island/Def Jam and he could see the writing on the wall. He was sure that if he stayed on he'd get lost inside a giant, impersonal superstructure, so he saved himself by declining a new contract. To fulfill his final obligation to Island/Def Jam, Waits helped to assemble a compilation of twenty-three songs from the seven albums he'd released during his Island Records tenure. The compilation would be called *Beautiful Maladies*, and it would symbolize the closing of another door for Tom Waits.

11

WHAT'S HE BUILDING IN THERE?

So why did it take Tom Waits six years to put out an album of new material? "I was stuck in traffic," is his standard reply. If you push him on the point, he'll say that he was actually stuck in traffic school all that time. If you point out that one can graduate from traffic school in a few days, he'll say that he had a really bad lawyer and the judge wanted to hold him up as an example. He'd been doing hard time at the California Department of Motor Vehicles, chopping that cotton, toting that bale, and parking parallel. He might then go on to confess that all of this was a crock and what he'd really been up to was breaking in new shoes for people too busy to do it themselves. And he'd also dug a hole in his backyard . . . Well, this is what you get for expecting a straight answer from Tom Waits.

In early 1999, Waits surprised many people by signing with Epitaph Records, an independent label formed by former Bad Religion member Brett Gurewitz. Epitaph, specializing in punk and ska, boasted groups like The Offspring, Rancid, and Pennywise. It seemed like a weird fit — one scribe suggested that Waits's next album be called *Mohawks at the Diner*.[1] Yet on one level it made perfect sense. Waits had always appreciated individuality above all else, and Epitaph steadfastly adhered to a do-it-yourself philosophy.

Waits was impressed by the fact that Epitaph was one of the few labels owned and operated by musicians. After meeting with Gurewitz and staff, he said he liked their musical diversity, he liked their eagerness — and, he joked, he liked the brand new Caddy they gave him. Waits gave Epitaph a "long-term lease" on the new album he was working on, which was called *Mule Variations*. The label would release the album, but Waits would retain all rights. Their contract was for that album alone, though both Waits and Gurewitz would be pleased to extend their agreement if all went well.[2]

Waits was positioned as the cornerstone act of Anti, Epitaph's offshoot imprint for respected artists who did not share the punk/ska sensibilities of the label's other acts. By the year 2000, Anti was also home to bluesman R. L. Burnside, punk pioneer and former Clash leader Joe Strummer, and country outlaw Merle Haggard. The Epitaph people are "easier to be around than folks from Dupont," Waits told David Fricke of *Rolling Stone*. "Not to generalize about large recording companies, but if you're not going platinum, you're not going anywhere."[3]

But before getting down to *Mule Variations*, Waits had another job to do, one that he felt strongly about. His pal Chuck E. Weiss had been a popular live performer for years but had only one album to show for it, a demo tape that was released against his wishes in 1981. It was titled *The Other Side of Town*, and it was pulled from the market soon after it appeared. In the meantime, Weiss had been writing and singing, but he never seemed to get around to recording his stuff. He claimed to have gotten sidetracked by his regular club gigs, the odd acting job, and some movie-scoring work. Furthermore, due to his fear of flying, his reputation had not extended much beyond the Los Angeles area — he'd hardly ever toured. Waits was anxious to rectify the situation. He felt that Weiss was far too talented to languish in obscurity any longer. His music had to be brought to a broader audience. Tom was at last able to drag Chuck E. into the studio and there Weiss concocted his first real album. It was called *Extremely Cool*. Waits coproduced and added vocals to the mix.

The album is a rib-tickling mixture of rock, blues, jazz, and zydeco. "I'd like [people] to see it as some kind of alternative jungle music," comments Weiss. It kicks off with the infectious "Devil with Blue Suede Shoes," followed by the love-triangle blues "Deeply Sorry," in which a man finds his girlfriend having sex with his mother. Laughing, Weiss swears that this particular song is in no way autobiographical.[4]

Other terrific cuts include the jazzy "Sonny Could Lick All Them Cats"; "Oh Marcy," a zydeco love song as tangy as gumbo; and the straight-ahead rocker "Jimmy Would." Waits produced, cowrote, and sang on the sad lament "It Rains on Me" and the structurally intriguing "Do You Know What I Idi Amin?" Waits, Weiss insists, was the brains behind "Idi Amin," which starts a cappella and gradually builds as instrumentation is added. Weiss is continually surprised at how few people seem to remember the murderous Ugandan dictator of the 1970s.[5]

When the album was finished, Waits helped Weiss to land a recording contract, and *Extremely Cool* was released in early 1999. *Mule Variations'* moment had arrived. Tom and Kathleen managed to create a pool of about sixty songs. "I want to do a whole record of [Kathleen's] dreams," said Waits. "She has amazing dreams . . . I think they should all be turned into songs."[6]

It was an exciting period, because the songs were coming on fast and thick but Waits had no sense of what the end product would be. It could be fish; it could be fowl. The thrust of the album could be painful introspection, death and decay, like *Bone Machine*, or the reflections of a contented family man. Each harbored its own mysterious potential. It was a piece of a puzzle, a picture that was slowly being revealed. At first, Waits wanted to name the album *Eyeball Kid*, after a song he'd cobbled together about a circus freak — literally, a walking, talking eyeball. After a while, that stopped feeling right, so he began sorting through other songs to find the key to the album. Eventually, Tom and Kathleen settled on the album title *Mule Variations*, because Kathleen would always tell Tom that she hadn't married a man, she'd married a mule.[7]

Life tends to intrude on those who are caught up in a fever of creation and want to put everything else temporarily on hold. The writer needs to escape both mentally and physically, but for the writer who is a parent this is often impossible. When the writing team and the parenting team are one and the same, it becomes a matter of seizing the moments whenever they present themselves. Says Waits, "I usually keep a tape recorder with me all the time. It's little. The quietest place for me is in the car, driving on the road. Because at home, if I go into a room and close the door the kids all want to know what I'm doing in there. Then when Kathleen and I are in there together writing, then they really go crazy. It's like the whole bottom just dropped out. 'What are you guys doing in there?' It's funny, but the car is a better place, really."[8]

By now, collaborating with Kathleen was second nature to Tom. They had it down cold. "One person holds the nail, the other swings the hammer," Waits commented to Hoskyns. "We collaborate on everything, really. She writes more from her dreams and I write more from the world. When you're making songs you're navigating in the dark, and you don't know what's correct. Given another five minutes you can ruin a song. So time's always a collaborator. Over the years [Kathleen's] exposed me to a lot of music. She doesn't like the limelight, but she's an incandescent presence on all songs we work on together. We've got a little mom-and-pop business. I'm the prospector. She's the cook. I bring the flamingo, she beheads it; I drop it in the water, she takes off the feathers. No one wants to eat it."[9]

The next order of business was to assemble the musicians. Waits wanted to hire a gang of the usual suspects, people who could decipher his musical shorthand, so he got on the phone. Longtime bassist (and brother-in-law) Greg Cohen committed. Guitarist Marc Ribot would lend a hand if he could spare the time away from his new band, Los Cubanos Postivos. Fortunately, Ribot was able to lay down some tracks for the album. Saxophonist Ralph Carney and blues bassist Larry Taylor, both Waits standbys, came along for the ride. Rounding out this solid crew were bluesman Charlie Musselwhite and John Hammond on harmonica and Les Claypool of Primus on bass.

Then Waits started casting around for people who could add a whole new sound dimension to his set of variations. Having become a big fan of hip-hop folk alchemist Beck, Waits invited multi-instrumentalist Smokey Hormel from Beck's band to sit in on many of the songs. Rap, Waits had come to believe, was the true folk music of the inner city, and he was deeply interested in the way sampling creates a sound collage, a pattern of diverse tones and textures. Waits himself had been striving to fabricate such collages for years through other means. Now he was ready to sample. He integrated DJ M. Mark "The III Media" Reitman's turntable work into three album tracks.

When the recording process was under way, Waits's hands were full. He was producing, bending and prodding the material, directing his team of old and new contributors, playing, and singing. He was in his element. Speaking to Hoskyns, he remarked, "You have to decide what your role is going to be. You farm out or subcontract the rest of the job. I don't always do my own electrical work at home. I usually hire an expert. So we hired professional musicians — and I don't know if I can honestly consider myself part of that group. I am the creator of forms and I sometimes get my own way. The main thing is to have people working with you that will succumb to the power of suggestion. The whole thing is kind of a hypnotic experience, and when you say you want musicians to play like their hair is on fire, you want someone who understands what that means. Sometimes that requires a very particular person that you have a shorthand with over time."[10]

Mule Variations was recorded at Prairie Sun Studios, a converted chicken ranch way out in the sticks. "If you set up right outside with the dogs and chickens," Waits told the *Times* of London, "it's amazing how your surroundings will collaborate with you and be woven into the songs."[11] Shades of *Bone Machine*.

With *Mule Variations*, Waits wedded the two eras of his sound. Songs like "Filipino Box Spring Hog" and "Big in Japan," wild sonic experiments, recall *Bone Machine*; smoother, piano-based cuts, like "House Where Nobody Lives" and "Hold On," regenerate his Elektra period sensibilities. Strangely, it all comes together quite naturally.

"Big in Japan" starts things off with a thundering intonation. It shocks the listener with its violent musicality. Waits had actually made this intro years before in a Mexican hotel room by switching on his tape recorder and yelling and banging on a chest of drawers until it was reduced to kindling. He was trying to find the music in the chaos, attempting to make a simple savage act sound like the stylings of a hopped-up band.[12] The experiment was successful, and for the price of a cheap piece of furniture Waits had a little symphony of destruction. Every once in a while he'd pop the tape onto his cassette player and laugh. He had no plans to use it until it occurred to him that "Big in Japan" would benefit from an intro that could jolt the listener into sitting up and taking notice.

The song is about Japan as a haven for entertainers. Celebrities who can no longer draw a crowd anywhere else often find that their popularity lives on in Japan; and A-list stars who are too proud to hawk cars, whiskey, television sets, or cigarettes at home can shill with impunity there. Visiting Japan is like visiting Mars, says Waits. He, himself, isn't big in Japan — except in a Godzilla-steps-on-Tokyo kind of way.[13]

Songs like "Big in Japan" and *Bone Machine*'s "Such a Scream" are far more rock-oriented than anything Waits did when he was young. "I always start at the wrong end of everything," he told Hoskyns. "Throw out the instructions, and then wonder how you put this thing together. Maybe I'm raging against the dying light. What do they say? Youth is wasted on the young? You're more in touch maybe with those feelings the further you get from them. Time is not a line or a road where you get further away from things. It's all exponential. Everything that you experienced when you are eighteen is still with you."[14]

With the Mississippi John Hurt–meets–Bruce Springsteen story song "Hold On," Waits proves his point. His ability to manufacture more accessible music has never left him. "Hold On" is a sensitive ballad about escaping bad relationships in a town that hobbles the spirit. Over a bed of acoustic guitars, Waits spreads his detailed analysis of small-town existence and the ties within it that bind. Just like a good short story, the song dramatizes the problems of its characters, pulling us in, making us care.

"Get Behind the Mule" is like an old-time blues lament. Waits had heard the story of legendary bluesman Robert Johnson — that he'd sold his soul to the Devil at a Mississippi crossroads for the ability to deliver sublime blues. The music came pouring out of him, and within the space of a couple of years he had recorded some timeless tunes, including "Crossroad Blues," "Love in Vain," and "Sweet Home Chicago." But then, like many of those who deal with the Devil, Johnson died young. When he had first run away from home in pursuit of his dream, Johnson's father had said, "Trouble with Robert is he wouldn't get behind the mule in the morning and plow."[15]

The gorgeous, melancholy love song "House Where Nobody Lives" builds on a strong lyrical idea, comparing an abandoned house to a person who lacks the capacity for love. Waits told David Fricke that the notion had been triggered by an old house he'd seen in the vicinity of his own. "It had busted windows, weeds, junk mail on the porch. It seems like everywhere I've ever lived, there was always a house like that. And what happens at Christmas? Everyone else puts their lights up. Then it looks even more like the bad tooth on the smile of the street. This place in particular, everybody felt so bad, they all put some Christmas lights on the house, even though nobody lived there."[16]

Another of Waits's Ken Nordine–inspired spoken-jazz numbers, "What's He Building?" is told from the perspective of a man keeping an eye on his neighbor because he's persuaded that the man is up to no good. He's not exactly sure how, but the guy has no friends, receives a lot of mail, and reads funny magazines. And what about those strange sounds coming from his house? It's not just an echo. It's not the T.V. Something evil is afoot . . . "We seem to be compelled to perceive our neighbors through the keyhole," says Waits. "There's always someone in the neighborhood, the Boo Radley, the village idiot. You see that he drives this yellow station wagon without a windshield, and he has chickens in the backyard, and doesn't get home 'til 3:00 A.M., and he says he's from Florida but the license says Indiana . . . so, you know, 'I don't trust him.' It's really a disturbed creative process."[17]

"Chocolate Jesus" is an ironic look at the selling of religious figures. Tom's father-in-law, the type who's always on the lookout for a new way to make a buck, provided the inspiration. He'd once brought his powers of persuasion to bear on Tom and Kathleen in order to get them to invest in something called Testamints — little lozenges for religious people who have trouble finding time to worship in this hectic modern world. The mints had a cross on one side and a Bible quotation on the other. Tom and Kathleen thought this was hilarious and started playing around with the idea. They came up with a new product concept — the chocolate Jesus. "He died for our sins, and He's a yummy treat, too."[18]

A radical mood shift is achieved with "Georgia Lee," a somber requiem for a little girl named Georgia Lee Moses who was murdered not far from Waits's home. While friends and neighbors turned to each other for comfort and support at her funeral, Waits sensed that everyone was wondering why Georgia Lee had gone unaided while she was still alive. Where were the police? The social workers? Could anyone have saved her? Why wasn't God there to protect her? With "Georgia Lee," Waits helped to ensure that this little girl did not wind up as an anonymous statistic.[19]

When *Mule Variations* was ready to be sent out into the marketplace, there was a danger that it would sink without a trace. After all, it had been six years since Waits's last album, and that's an eternity in the music business. Things had happened. Since the release of *The Black Rider* in November 1993, multiplatinum artist Bruce Springsteen had seen his spare, subdued *Ghost of Tom Joad* sell a fraction of the pace his offerings normally sold at. Prince had released the equivalent of ten full-length CDs. Rap and R&B had pretty much replaced rock and roll in the hearts of a hefty portion of the music-buying public. The top-of-the-pops position had been wrested away from Nirvana and Pearl Jam by Britney Spears and The Backstreet Boys.

In the larger arena, the world seemed a confusing and scary place as the century drew to a close. Speculation was rampant that when the clock chimed midnight on December 31, 1999, systems would crash worldwide, bringing civilization as we know it to an end. A sex scandal had nearly toppled Bill Clinton, one of the most popular American presidents of our time. School violence had reached terrifying new levels. America Online, an upstart Internet company that had been in business only for the time it had taken Waits to record three albums, had become powerful enough to purchase Time Warner, the largest media conglomerate in the world. The sense that almost anything could happen permeated the atmosphere.

The music world was in turmoil. Record companies were swallowing each other up. Polygram bought A&M, Geffen, Motown, Island, Def Jam, and many of the other more successful small labels. Universal bought Polygram, slashing and shuffling its cache of small labels. The industry was also up in arms about Napster, the computer program through which music fans were downloading musical selections from the Internet for free, seriously impacting on record sales. Many established acts — among them superstars like Springsteen, Paul McCartney, The Rolling Stones, Neil Young, Rod Stewart, and Madonna — found that their sales figures were dwindling alarmingly. Tom Waits could never begin to match the commercial clout of artists such as these. By the time *Mule Variations* came out would even a sliver of the pie be left for him?

"It's like looking for your waitress," Waits said to Fricke. "People get like that with artists. We are a product-oriented society. We want it now, and we want an abundance of it in reserve. But there are limits to what you can do. One is not a tree that constantly blooms in the spring; the fruit falls and you put it in a basket . . . There's something to be said for longevity. For some people, being in pop music is like running for office. They court the press in a very conscientious fashion. They kiss babies. No matter how black their vision is, their approach is the same. I'm more in charge of my own destiny. The songs are coming all the time. Just because you don't go fishing today doesn't mean there aren't any fish out there. So you don't fish for a couple of weeks, a couple of years? The fish will get along fine without you."[20]

As it turns out, there was nothing to worry about. *Mule Variations* became the highest-charting album of Waits's career, debuting (and peaking) on the *Billboard* album charts at number thirty. Less surprisingly, it was also critically acclaimed. *Mojo* named it best album of the year, and Waits was nominated for two Grammys, winning the award for Best Contemporary Folk Album. Not only had Tom Waits been remembered during that long silent stretch between albums, but also the music world had caught up with him a bit. Industry insiders and fans alike were according him a new respect. His influence had loomed over the previous decade, and not just in the area of music. It can be no coincidence that the ultimate hipster doofus of nineties' pop culture, Kramer of the wildly popular T.V. sitcom *Seinfeld*, mimicked the trademark wardrobe and hairstyle. A growing number of musicians considered cutting edge in their own right were citing Waits as a key influence — among them Les Claypool of Primus, Mark Linkous of Sparklehorse, and Beck.

Those feelings of appreciation were mutual. "I like Beck very much," Waits remarked to Hoskyns. "Saw him in concert a couple of times, and it really moved me. He's got real strong roots. It's funny. I heard him talking about Sonny Terry and Brownie McGhee, and I used to open shows for them in the old days. It was nice to hear a kid as young as he is talking about them, because I loved those guys. There's a really rich cultural heritage there, and it's nice to see that it's living on in someone as well rounded and as good a spokesman as Beck seems to be. He's got some street credibility too, because from what I hear he was a busker and really went out there and stood on a corner and drew a crowd. I love that. Those are some real important chops to have. And when he goes up onstage and throws that guitar around like a hula hoop, it's pretty remarkable what he can do to an audience."[21]

As well, Waits told many of his interviewers that Sparklehorse's 1996 debut album, *Vivadixiesubmarinetransmissionplot* (the title was a tribute to *Swordfishtrombones*, itself a tribute to Captain Beefheart), was one of his favorites. Singer/songwriter Mark Linkous, essentially a one-man band, had been crippled by an accidental drug overdose — he lay unconscious for fourteen hours with his legs pinned beneath him. Regaining his strength, he'd resumed working on his music, putting together the breathtaking *Good Morning Spider*. When he heard that his hero Tom Waits was also a big fan of Sparklehorse's work, Linkous invited him to contribute to one of the album's tracks. Unfortunately, the timing wasn't right, but Waits has agreed to lend a hand with Sparklehorse's next disc.[22] Waits also continued to work with his pal Les Claypool; he sang and played mellotron on, as well as produced, "Coattails of a Dead Man," a song from Primus's 1999 album *AntiPop*.

Waits feels for young musicians struggling to break out of the rigid molds that exist in today's music world. These days, when radio is formatted within an inch of its life and record companies have lost whatever taste they had for creative gambling, it is frustratingly difficult for such artists to make themselves heard. "It's gotta be hard for someone starting out now," Waits said to Fricke. "All the business you have to go through, making the videos, all this competition. I thought it was bad when I started out."[23]

Waits thought it would be a good idea to boost his new album's chances for survival by doing some live shows — not a grueling tour like those he would undertake in days gone by, but a five-month-long string of performances in a few strategic locations. "A tour usually implies fifty cities," he said to Hoskyns. "I'll play some major cities. As to whether I'm gonna be wearing a leotard or not, nothing is planned. All these things have yet to be decided."[24]

The first such show actually predated the release of *Mule Variations* by a month and a half. The venue was the annual South by Southwest Music and Media Conference in Austin, Texas — the biggest showcase of new talent in the music business. Waits's show was the event of the conference. It was one of the few live performances he'd given in over a decade and the first time he'd played Austin in over fifteen years. Tickets for it were like gold. Local fans, record execs, and journalists fought one another for them. Several people were caught trying to sneak in. Everyone knew it was going to be an amazing show.

Taking the stage, Waits won over the crowd immediately, happily preaching to the converted. He played a strong and varied set, previewing the new album with "House Where Nobody Lives" and "Filipino Box Spring Hog." He threw in several tunes from his Island years and, to the delight of those assembled, dusted off the classic Elektra cuts "Tom Traubert's Blues" and "(Looking For) The Heart of Saturday Night." The band was smoking, and Waits was visibly enjoying his rapport with the crowd.

It's sad that such an event had to end on a sour note. Waits was obviously shaken when a woman started heckling him from the crowd, calling him a sellout for allowing so many music-biz types to snatch up tickets, effectively shutting out his "real," nonprofessional fans. While it's highly unlikely that Waits had decreed how the tickets would be divvied up, the woman's words seemed to sting him nonetheless.

It might have been because the heckler wasn't completely off base. The days of intimate gigs played in smoky little bars to audiences of twenty or so were long over for Waits. He could no longer lead the life of the troubadour who passes through town and has a drink with the patrons after the show. It was the classic irony of the entertainment business reasserting itself: the more successful you are at connecting with your audience, the more that audience swells, the more isolated you become from it.

Waits had no choice but to shrug off the taunts of "sellout" and continue his minitour of world hot spots, including Los Angeles, New York, Denver, Boston, Toronto, Florence, Berlin, and Stockholm.

The *Get Behind the Mule* trek was far more low-key than 1987's theatrical tour de force, the *Frank's Wild Years* tour. Waits had called *Mule Variations* "surrural," and he wanted the tour to be, too.[25] He wore a rumpled old sports coat and hat. Ably supported by his band, he tore through his back catalog, his face pushed into the microphone, deconstructing and reimagining his tunes. Waits did pull a few of his old concert tricks out of the bag, however — that familiar knock-kneed strut, the police bullhorn, the glitter dust that wafted across the stage. He also stomped on a platform sprinkled with a fine powder, and swirls of dust would rise — like the dust that rises in the wake of a cruiser on a dry dirt road. During "Eyeball Kid," Waits wore a hat constructed of mirrors, creating a weird human-disco-ball effect. The movements of the band members were syncopated with the lights as he conducted their solos. During "What's He Building?" Waits, lit only by a flashlight, performed as an electric fan blew dust wildly into the rafters. The tour's set lists were much more open than usual, and Waits did more of his early Elektra songs than he'd done on any tour since signing with Island.

Like so many other artists, Waits turned to the Internet to deliver his music to his fans in a whole new way. Though adamantly computer illiterate — "I don't surf," he has insisted — he was a presence on the Web as *Mule Variations* was coming out. He previewed the album by releasing "Big in Japan" on the official Tom Waits Web site nearly three weeks before its release date. Five other *Mule Variations* cuts were released to Sonicnet in the week leading up to the album's release. The Austin show was broadcast online in its entirety the day before. And, finally, on the day the album came out, Waits had his first online chat. Tom Waits had entered the new millennium.

Waits's other profession was calling him back, as well. He signed to play a role in yet another ensemble piece with some of the best film actors around. *Mystery Men*, a parody of superheroes, was released in 1999 and starred Ben Stiller, Janeane Garofalo, William H. Macy, Hank Azaria, Greg Kinnear, Geoffrey Rush, and Paul Reubens. It tells the story of a group of superhero wannabes whose pathetic little powers include shoveling, throwing silverware, and extreme anger. They must all pool these limited resources to rescue Captain Amazing, the metropolis's true crime stopper, who's been kidnapped by his nemesis. It's either that or hand the city over to the forces of evil.

Waits plays one Dr. A. Heller, a mad scientist with unusual taste in women. Heller likes them old, but Waits didn't find that strange. "Perverted?" he said to Hoskyns. "I don't know. There's a scene with a woman in her nineties at a rest home where we watch television and I make advances, but I wouldn't necessarily call that perverted. Dr. Heller likes older women, and I guess it's so radically different from the Hollywood cycle of older men with younger women. What's really perverted is these old-timers going and picking up these young gals. I respect maturity and longevity."[26]

Heller specializes in creating weapons — of the nonlethal variety. Guns hold no appeal for him, but diabolical devices that disable a person do, like a tornado in a can or a clothes-shrinker. As Heller, explained Waits, he got to "make something called a blame-thrower. You aim it at people and they start blaming each other; 'It's your fault!' 'No, it's your fault!' It's a nutty movie."[27]

187

To adorn Heller's lair, Waits gathered up many of the contraptions and instruments he had around the house and brought them to the set. And director Kinka Usher was pleased at the way that Waits contributed to the film's largely improvised dialogue; it was his idea, for example, to offer the clothes-shrinker with its own clamshell holster and a full warranty. Usher also gave this explanation for why Waits often talked with his hands in the film: he'd jotted many of his scripted lines on his fingers so he wouldn't forget them.[28]

Another project that Waits took on was a television special created by buddy John Lurie, his *Down by Law* costar. *Fishing with John* was a postmodern version of that old daytime-T.V. staple, the fishing show. Lurie mustered his hip friends and they all headed off to an exotic Caribbean island to fish, banter with one another, and soak up a little local color. At one point, Waits and Lurie are stranded in the middle of nowhere when their car breaks down (strangely, the invisible camera crew that is capturing it all on film never lends them a hand). Then, when they go deep-sea fishing on a tugboat accompanied by a local guide, Tom suffers a serious bout of seasickness. As the show continues, we see Waits enjoying a high-stakes poker game, negotiating who gets the big bed, and arguing that driftwood art is a travesty.

The show's humor is at times sophomoric — Waits catches his first red snapper and stuffs it down his shorts — but the scenery is breathtaking, the local people play nicely off their strange visitors, and Waits and Lurie's discussions flow naturally. As the special ends, we see the carless Waits and Lurie trudging across the island while Waits grouses that he should have his head examined for agreeing to come on the trip.

So what was next on the agenda for Tom Waits? Hot on the heels of releasing *Mule Variations*, he provided songs for two movie soundtracks. He agreed to appear in a movie called *The Boom Boom Room*, which was to be shot in Philadelphia in 2000 but ended up never getting off the ground. Early in 2000, Waits, for the first time in his long career, produced a full album for another artist. He sat behind the knobs for blues artist and old friend John Hammond. Throughout the years, Waits also participated in projects with various musicians he respected, guesting on albums by the Tin Hat Trio and c-side (California Sonic Instrument Designers Ensemble) with Petit Mal; as well, he contributed two songs to a Ute Lemper album.

In the summer of 2000, Waits embarked on a brief tour of Europe, playing in Poland for the first time, as part of the TPSA Film and Music Festival at Warsaw's Sala Kongresowa. That short tour also included three nights at the Grand Rex Theater in Paris. Robert Wilson again approached Tom and Kathleen with another proposal for a musical collaboration, and in February 2000 the couple traveled to Copenhagen. There they constructed a new version of Georg Büchner's tragic 1837 play *Woyzeck*. Based on a true story, *Woyzeck* is the story of a soldier who is tormented by military personnel, mysterious doctors, and circus performers. Slowly descending into madness, he murders his unfaithful common-law wife in a jealous rage. Considered a socialist document, the play exposes the social and economic pressures that have triggered these terrible events. Tom and Kathleen's version of the play premiered on November 14, 2000, at Denmark's Betty Nansen Theater, as part of the Culture Bridge 2000 celebration.

It appeared that Tom Waits had had it, at least for the time being, with the quiet life. He's puttered enough. Once again, he hurled himself into a dizzying variety of projects.

12

THE LONG WAY HOME

With Waits's musical renaissance going full steam ahead, one of his old labels started looking backwards. Rhino Records, the record company which pretty much single-handedly sparked the whole compact disk reissue craze, had been bought up by Warner/Elektra/Asylum Records. WEA saw Rhino as the ready-made home for releasing their vast musical catalogue (and saddled the imprint with the much more corporate moniker Warner Strategic Marketing). Execs at Rhino/WSM started planning an anthology covering Waits's Elektra/Asylum tenure: the first official U.S. collection of this period since *The Anthology of Tom Waits*, which had come out in the very early days of the compact disk and was never released on CD. In the time since, only the imported *Asylum Years* and the inferior demo collections *The Early Years (Volumes 1 & 2)* had been released. It seemed a long time past due for a collection of Waits's early years.

They planned a two-disk compilation (tentatively entitled *Low-Rent Romeo: a Tom Waits Anthology*) which would include songs from all the albums for the label, as well as a few non-album rarities like the single B-side "Blue Skies" and "Mr. Henry" (which was only on the long out-of-print compilation *Bounced Checks*). They briefly considered including some *One From The Heart* songs, but that idea was dropped when the label had trouble cross-licensing the songs from Sony. The idea of plumbing the vaults for some interesting unreleased tracks appealed to them as well, although they agreed with Bones Howe when he insisted that they could only be used with Waits's express permission. Rhino contacted Waits and Brennan early on in the process, and for a while they were on-board with the idea. Then they decided that the compilation should only be a single disk and include no rarities. The label had their hearts set on a two-disk set, so the project went into limbo for over a year.

Finally, they decided to see if they could put together a good proposal and try to sell the collection to Waits and Brennan. When Waits found out that they were again thinking about a two-disk set he went ballistic, calling nearly everyone on the Warner Music food chain from the project's producer to the head of Warner Brothers Records to complain. While they had the legal right to release it that way, the label had no interest in having a pissed-off star on their hands, so they agreed with Waits and Brennan to make it a single disk. They also conceded to the singer's request to only include previously released album tracks and asked the couple once again to be involved in the making of the set, which would eventually be called *Used Songs (1973–1980)*.

Bones Howe, who as the producer of many of the songs that would be included had also been approached at the early phases of the project, was not too surprised by Waits's hesitance. "I think that Tom was dragging his feet on it," Howe said. "Tom has never been big about the past. . . . Part of it was that there were four tracks that sit in the can to this day that were done during the various LPs that I did with him. . . . Tom's attitude about the past was [to] leave the past alone. Don't screw with it."

When the decision was made, the label's A&R guys made some song suggestions. Howe also pointed out some favorite tracks. "The list went to Tom, and he thinned it out until it was what is actually on the CD now," Howe recalls. Waits chose the songs he wanted to be included and also was responsible for much of the sequencing, which was not the typical chronological approach. Instead, Waits sequenced the album much like he did with his new material, in a way that the songs led into each other like chapters of a good book. Then, he returned his ideas to the label. "Tom said that these were the songs that [he] will approve," Howe recalls. "When I say Tom now, I always put in parentheses 'and Kathleen.' I think it is Tom and Kathleen [who make these decisions together]."

So for the first time since parting company that day at Marconi's so many years ago, Bones Howe and Tom Waits were working together on a project again. Well, sort of, but not as closely as Howe would have liked. "When it came to doing this record, I dealt with Tom through his assistant, who was very nice to me. She treated me with the appropriate respect. [However] I would have rather have had a fight with Waits on the phone than be treated with appropriate respect, you know what I'm saying?" Howe laughs. "I'd rather have had him growl at me, like we did over the sequence of various albums and stuff. To just be talking with him on the phone, even if I couldn't see him personally, instead of being [dealt with] politely."

Once the song sequencing was determined, Rhino sent Howe a recording of the proposed album. "They were kind enough to say you were the producer on these tracks and the engineer. Would you please listen to these and say what you think about the levels and that sort of thing? I can't remember which track — I think it was the second track on the album [which was 'Eggs and Sausage'] — I thought was a little bass light. I called Tom's assistant and said before I talk to the people at Rhino, let me just tell Tom to see if he agrees with me. One track sticks out because I think it needs a little more bottom. She called me back the next day and said, 'I talked to Tom, and he listened to it and he thinks you're right.'" That type of thing was basically Howe's role on the project; as he referred to it, he was "just on the sidelines coaching."

Howe is very proud of the finished product. "My opinion of the record is that it's a wonderful selection of material from the time that Tom and I worked together. Certainly, 'Ol' 55' [the only song from the *Closing Time* album produced by Jerry Yester] is an appropriate addition to that, because that's the tune that he's really known for. It belonged on there. I'm very pleased with the record. I think it's a lovely record. I've given it to a lot of the people that knew Tom during that period, guys that used to come around the studio like Michael Collins, the documentary filmmaker. People like that who just really adore this record. Of all the tracks we made together, it's certainly a wonderful representation. I like it a lot."

Not all collections of music from the past ended up quite so happily for Waits. A more distressing look backwards came when a European record label called Burning Airplane claimed that they had secured the rights to release an album from a live show that Waits had performed in the mid-seventies. While the company's claims of contractual legitimacy seemed rather tenuous at best, they were able to officially release *The Dime Store Novels (Volume 1) — Live at Ebbett's Field* in Europe, where some of the copyright laws were less stringent. The concert the label used for the album was an often-bootlegged bicentennial performance at the Denver club where Waits had originally befriended Chuck E. Weiss. Though it disturbed Waits to have an "official" boot reaching store shelves, his protests could not halt the CD. Waits may have been unable to stop the release of that first disk at the time, but four years later a promised *Volume 2* has still never shown up.

From the more recent past, Waits had wanted to record the music from *Alice* since it was originally staged in 1992. However, problems with his old record label Island slowed down the process, undoubtedly stemming back to the fact a similar project for *The Black Rider* had led to one of Waits's more impenetrable and slowest-selling albums. So, even though the music from *Alice* was a lot more digestible, it was unavailable to Waits fans, except through low-quality bootlegs of the songs. The project got pushed back farther when Waits moved over to Anti/Epitaph. He wanted to immediately release his latest, freshest work with *Mule Variations.* Waits was pleased with the experience of working with the label and thought it may finally be the moment to officially record songs from the musical. "Well, you know, time is always a collaborator with music," he explained to *Time Out.* "Invariably, you record things when they're new, but it's not necessarily the law."[1]

However, it made no sense to record these older songs when he had music from his more recent show, *Woyzeck*, which was also not yet available to fans. In a bold marketing move, Waits decided to record and release the soundtracks for the two plays at the same time. He did change the name of *Woyzeck* to the more fan-friendly album title *Blood Money.* It is rare for any artist to drop two records at the same time, and when it does happen, it is usually done by superstar acts like Bruce Springsteen (who released *Human Touch* and *Lucky Town* simultaneously in 1992) or Guns N' Roses (*Use Your Illusion I* and *Use Your Illusion II* in 1991). Industry pundits questioned whether there were enough buyers out there to justify Waits's simultaneous releases, even though he had a large cult following. "If it turns out to be a good idea, I'll take credit for it. If not, I'll blame it on someone else," Waits joked to *USA Today.* "When you haven't had a record out for seven years, people get upset. When you put two out at the same time, they get upset. It's either 'Why've you been away so long?' or 'Why are you here all the time?'"[2]

Waits decided to make sure that the albums were respectful of their theatrical pasts, while at the same time stood alone as Tom Waits disks. He also continued his fascination with quirky instruments and disdain for the expected. In fact, only four of the songs on the two albums had that staple of modern composition, the electric guitar. Those four were "Everything You Can Think" from *Alice*, and "God's Away On Business," "Knife Chase," and "Starving in the Belly of the Whale" from *Blood Money.* Only a few other songs, all on *Blood Money*, used acoustic guitars. "The electric guitar thing is so overused," Waits explained to *Time Out.* "They show up on everything, it almost seems like it's the guiding force of popular music. Without it I wonder what people's music would sound like. It was like tying one hand behind your back just for the hell of it. See how you do. See if you can electrify some of these other instruments, or get them to be just as expressive.

There's a reason guitar is in everything — it's portable, it's powerful, it's potent, and it comes in so many different forms, and it's simple to play. I still love it, but we tried to omit it on these records to see what will happen."[3]

Of the two albums, *Alice* is the more immediately accessible — if any album with the quirky, thorny likes of "Kommienezuspadt," "Table Top Joe," and "We're All Mad Here" could be labeled accessible. *Alice* has a gentleness, a poetic sense of woe, and a throbbing, beautiful suffering that is almost mournful. For the most part, the album eschews the more carnival-like musical atmosphere that Waits has been experimenting with since *Swordfishtrombones* for a more classical feel. *Alice* is a mix of Brechtian balladry, Dixieland jazz, and chamber music. "*Alice* is kind of like taking a pill," Waits said in an interview for the electronic press kit that was on Anti's website for the albums. "It's a little dreamier. It's a little more . . . I don't know . . . druggy I'd say, more kind of an opiate. And dreamy. More of a song cycle."[4]

The song cycle starts in with the delicate, jazzy title track. "Alice" is a sax-laden ballad that would feel at home on one of Waits's Elektra albums. However, despite the refined musical backing, the lyrics catalogue a feeling of obsession. The words work in the framework of the musical about writer Lewis Carroll's strange relationship with young Alice. It also resonates outside the structure of the story, showing how people can become fixated on another person, even when they know that it is not what is best for them. "I'm imagining a whole Victorian atmosphere and someone like [Carroll], who had this obsession and compulsion," Waits told *USA Today*. "He was mystified by this peculiar, sparkling little girl. I'm trying to explore the nature of obsession, not just in his frame of mind but also as it applies to any love affair."[5]

There are other unbearably fragile songs like "Flower's Grave," "Lost in the Harbor," and "No One Knows I'm Gone," which bleed like an open wound. Ghosts of lost opportunities and squelched desires disappear into the quickly receding fog of life. Which is not to say that *Alice* is just a long group of lamentful ballads. "Kommienezuspadt" has Waits spouting guttural foreign-sounding words (and some occasional English ones) over a racing horn-laced calliope tune. "Actually there are a few words in there that have real meaning but the rest of it is just pure gibberish," Waits admitted. "But, a lot of people when they hear it they say, 'Gee, I didn't know you spoke Romanian' or 'I didn't know you spoke the odd dialect of Finland.' I have been known to tell them that I *do* speak those languages, but truthfully I don't."[6]

195

Alice continues Waits's musical fascination with the deformed. "Table Top Joe" is an old-fashioned ragtime workout about a man who is born with just a head, no body. Instead of letting his deformity destroy him, Joe uses it to his advantage, putting together an act and becoming a vaudeville star. Not all of Waits's freaks are so lucky, though. "Poor Edward" tells the tragic story of a man who was literally two-faced; he had the full face of a woman on the back of his head. She is Edward's doppelganger, constantly belittling him and tempting him with evil thoughts. Eventually the face drives Edward to madness and suicide. These two songs are the opposite sides of a fever dream.

This dichotomy of joy and pain comes naturally to Waits as a songwriter. "I'm an old softie," Waits said. "Most songwriters are probably writing one or two songs over and over again in one way or another. Kathleen said that with me, it's either Grand Weepers or Grim Reapers. Yeah, I run hot and cold. I like melody, and I like dissonance. I guess maybe it's an alcoholic personality. I get mad, and I cry."[7]

Blood Money tends to be a darker, more acidic, yet less emotionally draining, listen. It also delves more into the tonal experimentation of Waits's later music. This probably stems from the bleak storyline of the source material, the musical *Woyzeck*. "It's a story that continues to surface in Europe," Waits told *USA Today*. "[Producer Robert] Wilson told me about this lowly soldier who submitted to medical experiments and went slowly mad from taking medications and herbs. He finds out his wife is unfaithful. He slits her throat and throws his knife in the lake, goes in after it and drowns, and then his child is raised by the village idiot. I said, 'OK, I'm in. You had me at "slit her throat."'"[8]

Musically as well as lyrically, *Blood Money* is more jagged, more screaming, more percussive. It has a playful black sense of humor behind the apocalyptic yowls of anger. "Misery is the River of the World" contradicts an enraged howl at the moon on the human conditions with a carnival oom-pah band backing. A subtle samba beat percolates underneath the resigned bitterness of "Everything Goes to Hell." More stomping, clanging instrumentation reminiscent of *Bone Machine* appears on "God's Away On Business" as Waits spits out every word with poisonous bile only experienced by the betrayed. A similar sense of mental instability crops up in the raging "Starving in the Belly of the Whale." The instrumental "Knife Chase" weds a martial backbeat to a spy-film throb.

"There's certain sounds that I am attracted to," Waits said. "I always like things that sound like they're trying to reach you from far away, so I feel like I need to lean in and give them some help. I like clank and I like boom and I like steam. I thought that would be a good title for a record: 'Clank, Boom and Steam.' Clank, boom, pssssst! There's something kind of locomotive about it, coal-driven."[9] It turns out that Waits would save that title for his next album, the song "Clang Boom Steam" would become one of the last tunes on the 2004 album *Real Gone.*

Strangely, in the middle of all this dark experimentation, there are a couple of Waits's more touchingly romantic songs. Over a soft old-fashioned bed of music, "Coney Island Baby" features a lead played on a chamberlain. Waits reserves his simplest lyrics of straightforward devotion for this song, calling his love a princess, a rose, a pearl. Much like the earlier "Johnsburg, Illinois" and "Jersey Girl," this song celebrates the little, subtle moments in a relationship. The song closes out with a piano quote from "Innocent When You Dream." The next song, "All the World is Green," is a similarly lovely ballad about trying to remember the moments when romance is pure and possibilities are endless. There is also a sense of desperate romantic resignation on the charming tunes "Another Man's Vine" and "The Part You Throw Away."

For a few weeks before the disks were released, Anti's website previewed the two albums, allowing people to listen to the music online. *Blood Money* and *Alice* debuted on the *Billboard* album charts at #32 and #33 respectively. This made the albums Waits's second and third best-charting albums ever, with only *Mule Variations* charting higher. As usual, the chart positions were not as important to Waits as was the fact that he was able to finally complete the long journey to get this music out into the world. "I just try to walk my own path," he told the *New York Times.* "You have to believe in yourself and you have to ride out the seasons. Everybody wants it to be summer all the time, in relationships and with their career. And when the weather starts to turn, they think they better get out. So it takes a certain amount of persistence."[10]

While it was summertime for his music, the movie career was going through a cold spell. *The Boom Boom Room* movie project never got off the ground, and another film he acted in called *Cadillac Tramps* was never released. But Waits continued to work on movie projects that interested him, contributing original tunes to the films rather than acting in them. He and Kathleen composed the music to the Academy Award–winning Best Animated Short Film *Bunny* by Chris Wedge. Wedge had been working in film animation going back to the 1982 Disney computer thriller *Tron,* and had been chief animator for MTV's cockroach film *Joe's Apartment* and the fourth *Alien* movie, *Alien Resurrection. Bunny* was an odd, slightly whimsical computer-animated ten-minute film about a bunny making a cake. While she is stirring the batter a moth flies in the room. She kills the moth, but doesn't realize that it has fallen into the cake batter. After she cooks the cake, she eats it and promptly dies. This brief description doesn't explain the quirky allure, astonishing computer graphics, and thoughtful poetry of the film. The success of *Bunny* led to the opportunity for Wedge to direct the feature-length movies *Ice Age* and *Robots.* In fact, *Bunny* is included on the DVD for *Ice Age.*

Waits also contributed the end-title tune "The World Keeps Turning" to Ed Harris's critically acclaimed *Pollock*, the story of the life of revolutionary painter Jackson Pollock. "I asked Tom Waits, who I met some years back, if he'd write me a song for the end of the film," Harris said in the director's commentary of the DVD.[11] Waits also did two new songs, "The Long Way Home" and "Jayne's Blue Wish," for Arliss Howard's movie *Big Bad Love.*

In May of 2001, Waits got together with fellow artists Randy Newman and Ann and Nancy Wilson of Heart to file a $40 million lawsuit against the Internet file-sharing site MP3.com for copyright infringement. The singers all found their songs stored and available without permission on the company's site as part of its My.MP3 service, including tracks from Waits's album *Mule Variations* and Newman's old singles "Short People" and "I Love L.A." Their attorney, Bruce Van Dalsem of the law firm Gradstein, Luskin & Van Dalsem, explained, "This is a case of artists banding together to protect their most valuable assets — their songs. More successful songwriters of this caliber need to stand up against copyright infringement in order to protect their own rights and discourage the theft of music written by lesser-known artists who cannot afford to protect their smaller catalogs of work." The My.MP3 program had been shut down earlier by a lawsuit by major record labels including Sony, Universal, BMG, Warners, and EMI. MP3.com had reached a licensing agreement with the labels and had re-launched in December of 2000. The suits differed by the fact that the labels had sued the company for unauthorized use of their master recordings, while the artists focused on the use of the compositions.[12]

While Waits was still recording the two albums, the world was interrupted by tragedy. On September 11, 2001, the whole earth stood still with the terrorist attacks on the World Trade Center in New York and the Pentagon in Washington, DC. As someone who had spent so much time (both good and bad) in Manhattan, the disaster touched Waits deeply, causing him to examine his life and his calling. "Artists are trying to figure out what they do that has value," he told *USA Today*. "A lot of things have to happen before you turn on your record player. You want to be safe and warm and held. At times I think, 'What am I doing? Making jewelry for the ears?' The world's on fire and we're on a bus without a driver. We're all very much awake now. It's important for us to remain awake and not go back to sleepwalking in our pajamas, playing golf, and contemplating our navels. The rest of the world is tapping us on the shoulder with the oldest conflict of time: the haves and have-nots. It's time for great men to step forward with wisdom and depth and compassion, and I don't know who they are. We all feel impotent politically. I don't know the answer. You have to start with self, family, and community."[13]

As has been a pattern throughout his career, a lot of respected artists continued to try to put their own individual stamp on Waits's songs. On her 2001 cover album *Strange Little Girls,* acclaimed singer/songwriter Tori Amos recorded a series of songs that were very specifically from a male songwriter's viewpoint and gave them a feminine twist. This led to some extremely radical rethinking of songs like Neil Young's "Heart of Gold," Depeche Mode's "Enjoy the Silence," Slayer's "Raining Blood," Boomtown Rats' "I Don't Like Mondays," and Eminem's "'97 Bonnie & Clyde." The one song on the album that Amos was relatively faithful to the source material was a sparse, beautiful take of "Time" from *Raindogs.* "I thought about taking [it] to the organ, but I stripped it back," Amos explained to *ICE* magazine. "It's from the point of view of Death, so I felt you need to feel like you are sitting on the piano stool. No masks, no effects, it's right here, dry, with a little compression on the vocals."[14]

Waits contributed a tune to the first major record in over ten years for classic soul singer Solomon Burke. Burke had had many hits for Atlantic Records in the sixties such as "Cry To Me," "Everybody Needs Somebody To Love," and "Just Out of Reach (Of My Two Open Arms)." However, Burke was never the type to play the record label games. He didn't like the songs he was being asked to record and that he was getting paid the bare minimum for his shows and recordings. In fact, it was so bad that Burke would make the record companies pay him to cook for the band, and he would sell anything he felt he could get money for. Eventually, he stood up for his rights and left Atlantic in the late sixties. After that he floated from one label to another, but he never replicated his early success. As an artist he was left behind, forgotten by the labels and soon by listeners in general.

In the years since, Burke has plied many trades, including undertaker, hot dog manufacturer, and currently an ordained minister in Los Angeles. He also had to spend a lot of time raising his family — he has twenty-one children and sixty-three grandchildren. Burke never stopped singing, though, he just stopped recording. He toured often through the eighties and nineties, and even did a little acting in movies like the 1986 Mickey Rourke–Robert DeNiro thriller *Angel Heart.* In 2002, when Andy Kaulkin, one of the heads of Epitaph Records, told Burke he was interested in making a new album, Burke considered it "divine intervention." When he signed up with Fat Possum Records (another imprint of Epitaph) to do a comeback album at age sixty-three, many of the biggest names in music wanted to play a part in the project. Amazingly, Bob Dylan, Elvis Costello, Brian Wilson, Van Morrison, Nick Lowe, Dan Penn, and Waits all gave Burke songs to record. Critically acclaimed singer/songwriter Joe Henry signed on to produce. Burke came in to sing the songs without having heard any of them. Still, the album *Don't Give Up on Me* was recorded in four days. It became a surprise success, even netting Burke a Grammy nomination for Best Contemporary Blues album.

The song Waits offered up was a tune he had written with his wife called "Diamond in Your Mind." While Burke liked the song very much, there was some of Waits's tough street language that Burke felt uncomfortable saying as a minister. Burke suggested that perhaps the words could be touched up a bit to make them more suitable for him. He was met with stunned silence. "When we started to change some of Tom's lyrics, Andy came into the studio and said quietly, 'Dr. Burke, no disrespect, but you just don't change Tom Waits's lyrics,'" Burke remembers. "They got Tom on the phone, and I don't know what Andy said, but afterwards he came in and said, 'You won't believe this, but Tom said it's okay!'"[15]

Waits's music continued making its insidious way into other mainstream media, as well. HBO's critically acclaimed series *The Wire* used the Blind Boys of Alabama's celebratory cover of "Way Down in the Hole" as the theme for its first season of the show. It defiantly set the stage for the streetwise tales of drugs, violence, and death on the streets of Baltimore. Waits was impressed enough with the series that he allowed his own original recording of the song to play over the credits in the show's second season. The third season of the series was opened by yet another recording of the same song — this one done by the legendary New Orleans funk outfit The Neville Brothers, specifically for the show.

Waits's music also played a big part on the television mystery series

Crossing Jordan. The show stars Jill Hennessy as an offbeat Medical Examiner who fights her personal demons as she solves the murders of the cadavers that make it into her office. Jordan's father owns a bar, and since the M.E. (and the actress who plays her) is a frustrated singer, Jordan will occasionally take the stage at the bar. Significantly, one of the few times that she was allowed the chance, she performed a lilting version of "Innocent When You Dream" from *Frank's Wild Years.* "They submitted a few songs to me to look at," Hennessy explained about the selection process for the songs on the show. "The ones that just hit me the most were Tom Waits and the Bob Dylan, because, that's what I was raised with. Living in New York for so long, I'm a huge fan of Tom Waits. So that's how it comes about. We all try to work together and come up with something that moves us the most."

These performances also had a lot to do with the fact that the show was putting together a soundtrack CD. Hennessy's versions of "Innocent When You Dream" and Dylan's "It's All Over Now, Baby Blue" were included, as well as a lovely cover of Waits's "Hang Down Your Head" by respected folk singer/songwriter Lucinda Williams. "It was just great to work with people like T-Bone Burnett and Craig Street, who worked with Norah Jones," Hennessy continued. "The end product was phenomenal. Alison Krauss was on it, Lucinda Williams, Cassandra Wilson. . . . It was just a brilliantly done album. We were really well reviewed, which was the biggest thrill for me."

In April of 2003, Waits was asked to present actor Dustin Hoffman a Lifetime Achievement Award at the 46th annual San Francisco International Film Festival. Waits and Hoffman had been friends since the late seventies, when they met through Bette Midler. Hoffman was in the middle of getting a divorce and staying at a cheap hotel. Midler brought Waits to visit, and as Waits explained to the audience, "Dustin was sitting at a piano playing, and there was a lot of alcohol involved." Hoffman recalled the situation of their meeting to the crowd as well: "Tom sang all the songs from his album *Closing Time* because my marriage was ending, and you know how you think your first marriage will last forever. And you know, Tom, there wasn't just alcohol involved."[16] Hoffman asked Waits to sing "Tom Traubert's Blues" and the standard "Moonglow," and Waits obliged. Later in the evening, Waits proudly pointed out that those days were past him; he hadn't drunk any alcohol in ten years.

Another Lifetime Achievement Award that night was given to Robert Altman, Waits's director in the film *Short Cuts.* Actress Lily Tomlin (who played Waits's wife in that film and was part of the ensemble for Altman's classic film *Nashville*) presented the award to Altman, complete with a performance of her old *Laugh-In* character Ernestine the telephone operator. Waits also played his skid-row ballad "On the Nickel" at the special request of Altman.[17] "I am not someone who can cry," the venerable director explained from the podium. "I mean, I don't think I'm physically able to cry. The only time I recall ever crying at all is when I was listening to Tom Waits sing."[18] Altman continued to respect Waits's work as an actor, as well, and in 2004 rumors started circulating that the veteran director was making a movie version of Garrison Keillor's respected radio and book series *The Prairie Home Companion*, with Waits pegged to play a starring role. Though at the time of this writing, Waits's management insists that no official overture had been made towards having him in the film, the rumor will not die. Also supposedly chosen for parts in the film, projected for a 2006 release, were Keillor, Meryl Streep (who also worked with Waits in *Ironwood*), teen star Lindsay Lohan, Maya Rudolph, and Waits's *Short Cuts* co-stars Lily Tomlin and Lyle Lovett. As the movie has come closer and closer to completion, rumors of Waits's participation in the film never seemed to come to fruition.

A great honor was bestowed on Waits when he was invited to perform at the Lincoln Center in New York in a special benefit concert called Healing the Divide, which was "dedicated to a theme of peace and reconciliation."[19] Opening the show with a speech was the Dalai Lama, who spoke first because he started his spiritual practices at 3:30 in the morning and couldn't stay up for the entire show. "So His Holiness goes to bed at 7:30?" Waits joked with the crowd in his closing set. "That's not the holiness I used to know." Waits performed with the Kronos String Quartet and longtime bassist Greg Cohen. During the set he did stunning versions of songs like "Way Down in the Hole," "What's He Building?," and the song he wrote for Solomon Burke, "Diamond in Your Mind."[20]

A much more low-key performance came exactly one month later, when Waits joined old friend and touring partner Bonnie Raitt for the "Little Kids Rock" program at Spring Valley Elementary School in San Francisco. The program supports music education in schools. Raitt talked Waits into performing a duet of the song "Sweet and Shiny Eyes," which they had recorded together on her 1975 album *Home Plate*. They were joined by former Metallica bassist Jason Newsted and Norton Buffalo on harmonica. Waits informed the children that his first piano had been left out in the rain so that many of the keys were not functioning. "I was fine with that, though," Waits told the kids. "I just played the ones that were working. I used to make up little songs when I was angry or sad. I'm still doing that."[21]

In a move to help celebrate new artists, Waits was added to an eclectic group of music industry judges to decide the winner of the third annual Shortlist Music Prize. Based on the Mercury Music Prize in England, the Shortlist Prize is formed to find the most daring and original new album of the year, spanning every genre and style. The star-studded list of judges for the 2003 prize included Waits, Dave Matthews, Tori Amos, Chris Martin of Coldplay, Erykah Badu, Flea of the Red Hot Chili Peppers, the Chemical Brothers, ?uestlove of the Roots, Josh Homme of Queens of the Stone Age, Musiq, Mos Def, Perry Ferrell, and the Neptunes, as well as music-oriented filmmakers Cameron Crowe and Spike Jonze. The judges had to pick from a pool of nominees that included eclectic musical talents such as the Yeah Yeah Yeahs, Cody Chestnutt, Sigur Ros, Floetry, the Streets, Bright Eyes, Cat Power, Interpol, and the Black Keys. The award was given to singer/songwriter Damien Rice, for his acclaimed debut solo album *O*.[22]

History repeated itself in 2004 when Waits successfully sued a Spanish advertising agency in a case that mirrored his earlier suit with Frito-Lay. The company, Tandem Campany Guasch, had approached Waits to use "Innocent When You Dream" from *Frank's Wild Years*, in a commercial for Audi. As is his custom when approached for advertising, Waits turned down the offer flat. However, the company, perhaps not familiar with the earlier cases, but more likely hoping that Spanish laws would be less stringent, decided to create the commercial anyway. The song they used had the same structure as "Innocent When You Dream" and also featured a singer who nearly sounded identical to Waits. The ad ran in 2000, and soon Waits's people heard about it through postings on Internet sites. Again, Waits had to come out and explain that he was not the jingle vocalist, and he was not going against his fervent belief that celebrities should not endorse products. The original suit also named Volkswagen-Audi España as a co-defendant, but the Spanish courts cleared the car company of any wrongdoing.[23]

In 2003, Waits was approached to add a song to a tribute to the seminal punk group the Ramones. Two of the band's members, lead singer Joey Ramone and bassist Dee Dee Ramone, had died in the past couple of years. A group of high profile fans of the band got together to create the disk *We're a Happy Family — A Tribute to the Ramones*. Included on the album were such artists as U2, Red Hot Chili Peppers, Eddie Vedder,

Metallica, Kiss, The Pretenders, Marilyn Manson, Rob Zombie, Garbage, and Green Day. Perhaps in appreciation of the scrappy recording of "I Don't Wanna Grow Up" that the legendary band did on their final album, Waits decided to do a feisty cover of "The Return of Jackie & Judy." On the track, friend Les Claypool of Primus played bass, Epitaph head (and former Bad Religion member) Brett Gurewitz played guitar, and Waits's son Casey sat in on the drums. This led to yet another one of Waits's off-beat Grammy nominations; in 2004 he was nominated for Best Male Rock Vocal Performance for the track. Surviving Ramone member Johnny Ramone said, "It took the Ramones thirty years to be eventually nominated for a Grammy. Thanks to Tom Waits for finally getting us there."[24] Johnny Ramone would also die soon after, a victim of cancer.

In a sort of return tribute, Waits's ex-girlfriend Rickie Lee Jones took to sometimes performing Waits's early song "(Looking For) The Heart of Saturday Night" on her tour for her latest album, the politically charged *The Evening of My Best Day*. Jones has been famous for her reluctance to discuss their relationship, but in her own way she paid tribute to those days and her respect for his music.

Another artist that piqued Waits's interest was a singer named Norah Jones. Jones, who is the daughter of famous Indian musician Ravi Shankar, had released a jazzy album in 2002 that had, against all odds, become one of the biggest hits of the year. Waits was impressed by her debut album *Come Away with Me*, which ended up winning five Grammys in 2003, including Artist of the Year and Record of the Year. Waits's friend Keith Richards called her the best new singer he'd heard in twenty-five years in an interview in *Q* magazine. Waits thought that Jones may be able to do an interesting version of his song "The Long Way Home," which Waits had recorded himself for the 2002 soundtrack album for the film *Big Bad Love*. Jones was also an admirer of Waits's music. "I met Tom and Kathleen at a concert he was doing. Tom asked me if I had listened to the demos he sent me," Jones said. "I didn't even know he had sent me anything, but I assured him I would track them down." She loved the song, a country-tinged lament that would show off her Texas roots. However, she admitted the idea of recording a Tom Waits song was a little intimidating. "We've covered a couple of his tunes in concert, but it's hard to do because I like his versions so much. I'm a huge fan. We pretty much recorded it like he did."[25]

Waits continues working with friends and artists he respects. He appeared on Mexican roots-rock band Los Lobos's 2004 album *The Ride*, returning the favor of Los Lobos member Steve Berlin for appearing on his albums. Waits sang on the song "Kitate," cut together with additional vocals by singer Martha Gonzales of the band Quetzal. "We sent Tom a rough demo and he said, 'I love this track and want to collaborate, but I want to do it my way,'" Berlin told *ICE*. "He demanded that no one else be there, and he recorded it on this archaic, multi-track cassette. . . . So we had to find one of those machines — of which there aren't many left. . . . The funny thing Tom said was, 'You know, I've always wanted to sing in Spanish. My dad spoke Spanish.' So we were like, 'Great! Awesome!' We got it back and it was just Tom chanting, 'Quitate' ['Stop it']. That was the extent of his Spanish."[26]

Also in early 2004, Francis Ford Coppola re-released *One from the Heart* as a two-disk DVD, and reissued Waits's soundtrack album. The whole idea came to being a couple of years before, when Coppola decided that he wanted to completely re-edit the film for DVD release. Coppola had the full right to do whatever he wanted with the film, because in the years of paying off the debts that came from closing his studio, American Zoetrope, (a closing caused greatly by the box-office failure of the film) he had regained the complete ownership of the film's rights. When recutting the film, Coppola and his editors realized that they needed the original music because the song snippets they had access to were specifically timed for the older cut. The problem was that the tapes had been lost somewhere along the line during the studio closing.

At this point, Coppola had lost touch with Bones Howe. He wanted to reach him because some of the DVD bonus items would include film footage about the making of the soundtrack, and he wanted to make sure that Howe was amenable to being included in the documentaries, particularly one called "Tom Waits and the Music of *One from the Heart*." Luckily, a mutual acquaintance who lived near Howe in central California heard that Francis was looking to contact Bones. "Somebody mentioned to him that they couldn't find me," Howe laughs. "He said, 'Oh, he lives in Montecito, I see him every day.'" So Coppola gave the man a release for Howe to sign to use the film footage of Howe, Waits, Coppola, Bob Alcivar, and Crystal Gayle, that included their work in the studio and their first big meeting at Coppola's house in Napa.

A few months later, Howe got a call from Kim Aubry, who was working with Coppola to produce the DVD. "He said, 'We've been through the vaults here, do you know where the music is?'" Howe recalls. "I said funny you should ask me that, because in between when you called me I went back and looked. . . . What happened was when Zoetrope went under and fell into bankruptcy, the studio [Wally Heider Recording] called me and said, 'We have all these tapes from *One from the Heart* and Zoetrope is gone. What should we do with them?' They said we have to get rid of these tapes or destroy them, because we need the space in the library. I had a tape store-room at Heider, so I said just move them into my storage vault." They sat there until Howe left Los Angeles in the nineties, and then he moved all of his tapes to a storage facility called Iron Mountain.

Howe told Aubry that he had all of the demos, including some things that probably never saw the light of day. "He said, 'Oh, God that would be wonderful. Because some of the stuff that we want is like there's an intro missing from one of the songs and we've made the thing longer and if we had the intro, we could put the intro in.'" Howe said he was glad to send the original master tapes to them, only asking in return that when they go through the demos they would burn all the songs on DVD for him. They burned everything for Howe who said, "It's a wonderful collection of stuff. Of course there is a lot of stuff there that isn't of any value, but it does have some nostalgic value."

The new version of the soundtrack included two unreleased tracks from the original sessions, "Candy Apple Red" and "Once Upon a Town/ Empty Pockets." "That's where those two songs came from," Howe continued, "and it was a great idea to do that, because it made it a brand new album." The DVD gives bonus work-in-progress versions of the songs "The Wages of Love," "Picking Up After You," "I Beg Your Pardon," "Candy Apple Red," and "Take Me Home." But perhaps the most eye-opening of these is a really raw live-in-studio version of "This One's from the Heart," under its original title, "Cold Chisel." This includes studio chatter between Waits and Bones Howe and shows the song coming to life as they massage it into shape. Coppola's son Roman also created a new music video for "This One's from the Heart," using scenes from the film. "That album is still one of the best examples of [Waits's] work," Howe says.

Howe also helped a bit in setting up the music in the new cut and tracking down the musicians who worked on the songs to make sure they received proper compensation and credit. "Francis is much happier with [the new cut of the movie]," Howe says. "Again, it sort of got the same attention the movie got when it came out. People who love Francis's work loved it. People who hated the movie still hate it. But, the one thing that becomes obvious when people look at it now is how much influence that movie had on video filmmakers and music-clip filmmakers, MTV clip-makers and all. How far ahead of the times it was at the time we made it."

In summer 2004, another older film that Waits had worked on was released to theaters. Waits's good friend, film director Jim Jarmusch released *Coffee and Cigarettes*, a long-planned melding together of a series of eleven related short films in which, as the title suggests, different personalities sit down together in funky diners and chat over java and smokes. Waits's segment had actually been filmed back in 1993 (back when he was still smoking; he finally gave up this last vice just a few years ago). In the short, Waits chats with punk-rock forefather Iggy Pop of the Stooges. "Iggy Pop and I play two characters in the short film. It was actually rather funny," says Waits. "It's just a little bit that Jarmusch does called *Coffee and Cigarettes*. Using different people that you cast in it, you talk about coffee and you talk about cigarettes, and then it's over. Iggy and I did one, and it was really great."[27] He was right, Waits and Pop were truly entertaining playing themselves (well, highly stylized versions of themselves) as they meet over coffee and size each other up, engaging in a subtle game of career one-up-manship. Two segments starring Cate Blanchett and Alfred Malina with Steve Coogan were also terrific little slice-of-life vignettes — but the other shorts seemed rather slight, unfocused, and kind of boring. Other people who took part in the project are actors Steve Buscemi, Roberto Begnini, Joie Lee, and Bill Murray and musicians Jack White and Meg White (The White Stripes), RZA and GZA (Wu-Tang Clan), and comedian Steven Wright.

In the meantime, the world was waiting patiently for Waits's next full-length studio album. An article in *Billboard* magazine in the summer of 2003 promised Waits's next album was to be released in March of 2004. But when that anticipated month arrived, there was still no word of a release date.[28] That word came soon after; Waits was hard at work on the new album in his old *Down By Law* stomping grounds of New Orleans and the Mississippi Delta and the new album, to be called *Real Gone*, should be released in October 2004. Again, the information wasn't exactly on track — the idea of him returning to the bayous was a bit fanciful. Waits insisted to Barney Hoskyns, "People just assumed it was the Mississippi Delta. But see, there's a Sacramento [California] delta, and that's where we were."[29] People took the release date with a bit of a grain of salt since earlier deadlines had been missed, but on October 5, 2004, the album was finally available for the patient fans. Not that the missed deadlines meant that Waits had been lazing around instead of working. "I'm up early every morning," he insisted on KFOG radio. "I take the kids to school and all that."[30]

Waits previewed the album, like he had several times before, by releasing one of the songs on a charity album. However, this was the only way that it was business as usual for Waits. As a singer, he had always been stubbornly silent about his politics, undoubtedly thinking that the political views of a singer/songwriter should only be of interest to himself. All of this had changed in the America of George W. Bush. Like so many others, he saw so many of the basic rights promised in the Constitution being trampled. So, while he did not seem to go out of his way to bring up politics, he would not back down in interviews when asked to discuss the 2004 Presidential Elections and what he thought of candidates George W. Bush and John Kerry. And most everyone was asking. "Well I'd say this is probably one of the most important elections that we've had in a long time," Waits said on *The Dave Fanning Show*. "Not that they aren't all important, but I join the voices of a lot of Americans and hope that he's voted out of office. . . . I can't say that Kerry is a logical and the most effective alternative, I think maybe we're kinda one party with two heads. . . . I like what Bill Hicks said. I think when you are elected president in the United States they [should] take you into a small room. And they run a film clip of the Kennedy assassination from an angle no one has ever seen before. And then they turn to you and say: *'Are there any questions?'*"[31]

He took it even further in an interview with Barney Hoskyns for the British magazine *Rock's Back Pages,* in which he stated, "This is an enormous global cartel. We're going 90 miles an hour down a dead-end street. Bush has probably set us back about 75 years."[32] It was really quite astonishing, in interviews leading up to the release of *Real Gone* (and the elections) Waits discussed George W. Bush almost as much as he discussed his own music. In the *Toronto Star* he bemoaned the "you're-either-with-us-or-against-us" idea that had sprouted in the Bush administration, the suggestion that if you were against Bush or against the Iraq War that you were anti-American. Waits charged that Bush wanted to go to war with Iraq from day one, comparing him to a doctor who smashed your foot and then tried to cast it.[33] When a British newsman suggested that polls seemed to indicate that Bush would probably win, Waits reacted with horror, begging him not to say that.[34]

More importantly, he put his money where his mouth was. One of the cornerstones of the upcoming *Real Gone* was the song "Day After Tomorrow," a touching protest of the Iraq war told from the point of view of a soldier writing home. Weeks before the new album was released, Waits contributed the tune to a charity album called *Future Soundtrack for America.* The collection also included songs by R.E.M., Blink-182, David Byrne, Bright Eyes, Death Cab for Cutie, The Flaming Lips, Fountains of

Wayne, Jimmy Eats World, They Might Be Giants, and the Yeah Yeah Yeahs. All proceeds for the album went to MoveOn.org, a political group that was dedicated to the ouster of George W. Bush. Waits was also long-rumored to play a part in the Vote For Change Tour, a group of concerts played throughout the U.S. in the months leading up to the election, with all of the benefits going towards John Kerry's election. Artists who did participate in the tour included Bruce Springsteen, R.E.M., John Fogerty, Pearl Jam, Bonnie Raitt, The Dixie Chicks, James Taylor, Neil Young, Bright Eyes, The Dave Matthews Band, John Mellencamp, and Death Cab for Cutie. The whispers that Waits would participate in the tour never came to be, though.

As had become his habit over the last few albums, Waits allowed the new work to be premiered on the Internet. All of the songs for *Real Gone* were released to the music-download site iTunes.com on September 24, almost two weeks before the album would be available in stores. This may have contributed to the fact that the album debuted at #28 on the *Billboard* albums chart on October 13, making it his highest charting record ever, beating *Mule Variations* debut and peak at #30.

Waits had called up many of his favorite collaborators to work on the album. Missing in action on *Alice* and *Blood Money*, guitarist Marc Ribot was shanghaied back into the studio. Other familiar faces included Larry Taylor and Les Claypool (who undoubtedly had more time on his hands with his band Primus on "indefinite hiatus" since 2001). The two handled all the duty on bass (Taylor played some guitar, too) replacing the conspicuously absent Greg Cohen, who was now AWOL from a third straight Waits disk after being a lynchpin of his group since *Heartattack and Vine* in 1980. At the time of the *Real Gone* recordings, Cohen was working with jazz innovator Ornette Coleman's latest quartet.

On drums was Claypool's former bandmate in Primus Brian "Brain" Mantia, who had left the band right before the breakup to join the current line-up of celebrated metal band Guns N' Roses, helping lead singer Axl Rose record the legendarily slow-to-birth album *Chinese Democracy*. At this writing, that album is still essentially an urban legend; the perfectionist (and more than somewhat unstable) Rose has been threatening to release the album on-and-off since breaking up the classic lineup of his band in the mid-nineties, with no end in sight. Harry Cody, formerly of the band Shotgun Messiah, also contributed some guitar and banjo work to *Real Gone*.

After getting his feet wet with the Ramones cover, Waits's son Casey, now nineteen years old, wanted to take the plunge and play percussion and work the turntables on the old man's album. (This further proved Kathleen Brennan's long-ago point that the boy should not be named Senator, although it does bring up the question of whether he should have been called Drummer.) Musically, Casey Xavier Waits has vastly different influences from his father — as is the way with parents and children everywhere. Casey would rather listen to Ol' Dirty Bastard of the Wu-Tang Clan or Rage Against the Machine than Mose Allison or Harry Partch. Still, it was Casey's first chance to work on an album, and he went into the musical mix with a determination that his father referred to as "somewhere between euphoria and embarrassment."[35] However, as Waits pointed out, Casey had gotten what he most needed from the opportunity — the experience of working on a record — and more importantly, he got a paycheck for it.

His son's presence also seemed to influence the musical direction of the album. Though Waits had been experimenting with it for a few years, *Real Gone* has much more of an urban, street vibe than any of his previous works. Waits experimented with vocal tricks of being "a human beatbox" and Casey worked the "wheels of steel" on a couple of tracks. Not to suggest that Tom Waits has recorded a rap album — that would be nearly impossible and totally impractical to pull off with any panache. However, much like his earlier experiments with Tin-Pan Alley jazz, funk, rock, bebop, and the blues, Waits used another musical style to spice up and inform his work, not necessarily to drive it. "Hip-hop is filled with the noise and the rebellion and the anger and the energy of today," Waits told the *San Diego Union Tribune*. "Most people, because it's young people's music — unless you have kids — don't stay in touch with what's going on right now. There's no reason to, you just listen to your old records, just like your mom and dad did. With kids you say, 'Shut that thing off!' Then you think, 'Maybe I better listen to it.'"[36]

While he was listening to hip-hop, he was avoiding other sounds and types of music that had been his regulars. As had become something of a habit in his later albums, Waits decided to test himself by banishing one of his basic musical building blocks from the recording of *Real Gone*. In previous albums, the instruments that got the shaft were the saxophone (*Swordfishtrombones*) and the electric guitar (*Alice* and *Blood Money*). For the new CD, Waits thought it would be interesting to do an entire album without using one of the earliest staples of his sound and his first instrument, the piano. Not that he banished the keyboards from the studio; in fact he says that just the opposite was true. "My theory is that if you don't bring it, you'll definitely need it," he told the *San Francisco Chronicle*. "So I tell them to bring everything. Then I don't use it. I brought a piano and never even sat down on it. It just didn't seem to fit."[37] He was more forceful in his explanation to the BBC, saying all piano players eventually hit the point when they just want to drop the thing off a high roof.[38]

Waits always searches for different places to record his music. Most of the work on the album was recorded in an abandoned schoolhouse. However, Waits acknowledged that a lot of the vocals were laid down in a much more private setting — his bathroom. He explained that the sound he was searching for just wasn't coming at the studio. He had to find an alternate spot to get the acoustics perfect, and somehow it ended up being in the loo. Still, he acknowledged he wasn't sure what exactly it was about the cramped space which made it so conducive to the sounds that he was stalking. "I don't know. It was just kind of a mystical place."[39]

Waits starts the album at the "Top of the Hill." He shows his hand from the beginning: this is going to be a new variation on his sound. The song has Waits rapping over a jittery bass and guitar line with a jumble of sounds skittering around in the background; Casey's turntable work, strangely flat percussion by Brain, and Waits's own distracted vocal booms accenting the whole thing. Waits's label suggested the song was reminiscent of seventies jug band Mungo Jerry (best known for the classic single "In the Summertime"). Musically, it is vaguely evocative of some tracks from *Bone Machine*, and yet at the same time it's like nothing he's done before. This ain't your father's Tom Waits.

The odd Waits take on R&B continues with "Hoist That Rag." On this song, Ribot's sproingy guitar licks and old school scatting percussion by Casey Waits and Brain make the song something of an oddity — a Tom Waits song which is so effortlessly funky that it could undoubtedly be covered by George Clinton of Parliament-Funkadelic fame. The third song on the album is in many ways the centerpiece of the collection. "Sins of the Father" is a lament on the state of the world that runs for an astonishingly long (at least for Waits) ten-and-a-half minutes. In some ways, it seems like a more traditional Waits lament, all pained vocals and deep simmering regret with just a vague hint of reggae. Yet the lyrics reflect the newly political Waits worldview, taking a cynical look at how governments can become fat and lazy and not recognize that they are putting their own survival ahead of their citizens and how the younger generations must pay for what has come before them. When asked by Jonathan Valania of *Magnet* if it was specifically about Bush, Waits replied, "I'm talking about my father, I'm talking about your father, I'm talking about his father. The sins of the father will be visited upon the son. Everybody knows that."[40]

The song also included what was undoubtedly a tip of the hat to one of Waits's esteemed peers. Canadian Leonard Cohen is another cult artist well known and respected for his songwriting talent. In fact, Cohen started his career as a novelist and poet — penning several books including *Beautiful Losers, Parasites of Heaven*, and *Book of Mercy.* In the sixties, Cohen became fascinated with folk music — writing such standards of the form as "Suzanne," "Hallelujah," and "Bird on a Wire." As his career extended over the years, Cohen's artistic scope continued to expand, creating such acclaimed albums as *New Skin For the Old Ceremony* (1973), *Death of a Ladies' Man* (1977), *I'm Your Man* (1988), and *The Future* (1992).

The "Sins of the Father" line "Everybody knows that the game was rigged" seems to be a tribute to Cohen's apocalyptic love song "Everybody Knows" from *I'm Your Man.* That song features the extremely similar line, "Everybody knows the fight was fixed: the poor stay poor, the rich get rich." Months after *Real Gone* was released, the *Observer* asked Waits to list his twenty favorite albums, and *I'm Your Man* was there, ranked ninth. "Important songs, meditative, authoritative," Waits wrote about Cohen's album, "and Leonard is a poet, an extra large one."[41]

The deceptively simply titled "Shake It" features the album's most guttural vocal over a siren of a guitar line by Larry Taylor. It is one of the more experimental tunes on the album, a dissonant, clanging swirl of sound and motion — and a song that is more impressive as an exercise than it is an enjoyable listen. Critic Michael Toland suggests that Waits was channeling "Howlin' Wolf as interpreted by an impressionist painter,"[42] which explains the song's odd mixture of allure and disorientation as well as anything. Put more simply, it is one of the experiments that Waits has always slipped onto recent albums to push the envelope of musicality and artistic scope (see also: "Filipino Box Spring Hog" from *Mule Variations,* "Kommienezuspadt" from *Alice,* or "Such a Scream" from *Bone Machine*).

Musically more interesting is the gothic mystery of "Don't Go Into the Barn." It is a melding of several styles in one track. In the midst of a disturbing tale of rural death and mayhem, there is an offbeat interlude reminiscent of enduring basic training in the military. As he has often done before, Waits's rant has an evangelical fervor of a man just barely avoiding damnation — a man who feels the hell hounds nipping at his heels. The lyrics are vaguely insane and the whole thing has the feel of a darkly surreal opiate-fever dream.

If he is screeching for salvation in that song, in "How's It Gonna End?" Waits uses his sometimes underappreciated soft-spoken vocal style — he damn near croons in this quietly mournful dissection of a man's almost eternal bad luck streak. The song has a subtle polka melody — the mixture of Harry Cody's banjo, Waits's guitar, and Larry Taylor's bass sounds amazingly like an accordion. The subtle instrumentation and unadorned vocals show off Waits's evocative lyrics and imagery in a way reminiscent of his early work. "How's It Gonna End?" got additional exposure being widely released as a free download on the Internet through services like Amazon.com and AOL.

"Instructional dance songs are a rarity these days. When I was a kid, it seemed that every single that came out was an instructional dance song," he told the *Toronto Star*, name checking such long ago dance crazes as "The Locomotion," "The Jerk," "The Peppermint Twist," "The Grind," and "The Mess Around."[43] Therefore, Waits stepped into the void and came out with the "Metropolitan Glide." Of course, "Metropolitan Glide" is a Waits dance song — which means that you will never hear it at a club and it ends with Waits wheezing over the beats like he has tuberculosis. However there are some concessions to rhythm and blues; a rubbery bass line and the *faux*–James Brown screams of "Are you ready?" in the background. That screech is very similar to a dance floor sample from John Kongas' seventies single "He's Gonna Step on You Again," which was long a hip-hop staple. It had been used on Rob Base and DJ E-Z Rock's eighties rap hit "It Takes Two," Happy Mondays' cover of the Kongas's song (renamed "Step On '91"), and at least two Janet Jackson songs, amongst many, many others. Oddly enough, this little dance number earned Waits yet another one of his strange Grammy nominations, for Best Solo Rock Vocal Performance, in 2005.

Not too surprising on an album so steeped in mortality and suffering, the most beautiful and traditionally structured song is an ode to a corpse. The mournful murder ballad "Dead and Lovely" asks the question "What's more romantic than dying in the moonlight?" It tells the quietly affecting story of a girl who trusts the wrong man and pays for it with her life. Like "How's It Gonna End?" before it, the song has the sepia glow of an old photograph. The song feels like it is from another time, particularly the jazzy noir guitar lines and the subtle percussion which sounds an awful lot like quiet snaps of the fingers.

"Circus" channels the word jazz that Waits has taken to heart, most successfully in "What's He Building?" and "Frank's Wild Years." The music is just barely there, a music-box melody with nearly inaudible snares. The vocals have a tinny disembodied sound, like they were recorded over an intercom. "It was a song first, that I did with some hip-hop I looped from the radio," Waits told *The Globe and Mail*. "But it felt too cheerful, too bouncy. I wanted it more pathetic and tawdry. So I spoke it, and got my son to play drums on it, and it worked out better."[44]

There is more lovely desperation in "Trampled Rose." The album preview on the website for his label Anti described it evocatively as "West Africa joined with Appalachia and a furtive tarantella."[45] That unlikely description actually captures the vibe of the song quite well, with Waits's tortured and drawn-out vocals dripping with desperate longing. This middle section of the album contains more examples of Waits's great skill as an old-timed balladeer. The next song "Green Grass" paints a vivid portrait with some of the most evocative lyrics on the album. Then he returns to the raw throbbing avant-blues of "Baby Gonna Leave Me," the industrial thud of "Clang Boom Steam" and then the calliope-salvation of "Make It Rain."

Then comes the hushed acoustic song which he previewed the album with on the charity CD, "Day After Tomorrow," Waits's quiet and heartfelt protest of the Iraq War. However, it was more than just Iraq that inspired him, he admitted to the Australian radio show *The Deep End*. "It's a letter home. From a soldier . . . I've got kids that are draft age. And it's a troubling time we are all living through. You know, it was written to try and be a song about the Civil War or Vietnam War. Just war, you know . . . a war song."[46] The narrative may not have been specifically about the Iraq War as he claimed; however the timing was not just a coincidence. Waits was very much concerned with Iraq. "All you really can do is put a human face on the war. These are my feelings. I just tried to imagine a soldier writing home from anywhere. This is your war. You have lost, both sides have lost," Waits said on a radio interview with the BBC. "We're killing off our children. They're sending our children to war. They're sending *their* children to war. It's a mess, man. Anybody knows that."[47]

The album closes with another human beatbox experiment — an untitled a capella track without actual lyrics except for the word *chickaboom* repeated constantly over an indecipherable backing vocal. "I was making sounds that weren't words but once I listened back I could actually determine certain syllables," Waits told *Mojo*. "It was like going back in time with the language where the sound came first and slowly shaped itself around items and experiences. I'm one of those people that if I don't have my knees skinned and a cut on my hands, I don't really feel like I've had much of a days work. That's where the [album] title came from — the blues thing, like I'm really gone."[48]

The album came out as promised, and when the day of reckoning came, for the first time since *Nighthawks at the Diner*, a Waits album was released to decidedly lukewarm reviews. Not bad ones, not good ones, just blah ones. "On *Real Gone*, Tom Waits walks a fraying tightrope," Thom Jurek said in the *All Music Guide* and this seemed to be the general consensus.[49] People tended to point out that Waits was a genius, but then give the proviso that it was not his strongest work. *Seattle Weekly* was impressed by Waits's ability to "coax alien sounds out of acoustic instruments."[50] *Splendid* magazine suggested that his flirtation with hip-hop was "almost as if he's daring people to call him a washed up old fogey, going further with this musical stunt than most of his diehard fans can stomach, probably just to make them uncomfortable."[51]

This refusal to do what is expected from him, of course, is totally in keeping with Waits's musical leanings and should be of little surprise. Perhaps the most accurate description of *Real Gone*'s place in the Waits canon is Dean Truitt's of *One Way*, "With the passage of time, *Real Gone* may not go down as the jewel in Tom Waits' artistic crown." And that was a good review.[52] Waits took it all in stride, drolly telling the *Los Angeles Times*, "Kids love the record, little kids. They like songs about death."[53]

Bones Howe thinks that the vast differences of opinions on the latest work may be attributed to a very simple fact. As Waits's music has gotten more and more experimental, it has become harder for the casual listener to embrace. "I think that as time goes on, he gets tougher and tougher to just pick up on if you don't have any history with him," Howe admits. "It becomes more and more dissonant, more and more noisy. I think noisy is the best adjective. It's noisy music now. I used to call it his junkyard music, but it's noisy music now. There are some [terrific] songs on each album, like the *Mule* album; [but] there are too many songs on there. That's where he could have used a producer, to say, 'Hey, Tom . . .' We used to leave stuff out of the other records. He didn't leave anything out of that record. It would have been much better if a couple of those songs had been dropped."

However, Bones recognizes that it is not in Waits's nature to pander with his music. It goes back to the days when they were working together. Howe always felt that the door could be opened even wider if Waits would play the music biz game a little more. He respected Waits's integrity, but "thought it was a shame that Tom never got any pop attention." Howe acknowledges, "He didn't want any pop attention. He wanted success his way, and as it turned out, he got his success his way. [But] I always thought that one record that got him on A.M. radio would really do what it did for Laura Nyro. But, Tom was always against that."

However, "success his way" has continued to expand. Waits has been able to make a living doing what he wants for over thirty years. While he still has never had a smash hit, his influence and reputation are as strong as ever. He finally got a million-selling album *(Mule Variations)*, but even that is not the real test of Tom Waits's career. It is said of the first Velvet Underground LP that when it was released, it sold maybe a hundred copies, but at least eighty of those buyers went on to form a band. Waits, to this day, has that kind of power — the ability to influence listeners about the range of music and its possibilities. Not everyone is going to get it, but those who do will likely become converts. Maybe Waits describes his restless muse best: "Part of my compulsion is I'm unable to repeat myself in certain things. Other people are nervous when they have to digress or deviate from the scripts, and I'm compelled to change things all the time."[54]

Sometimes Waits will return the favor, as well. When he finds a band he really likes, he will try to lend a hand. One big fan of Waits was singer/songwriter E (born Mark Oliver Everett) of the band the Eels. He'd heard through the grapevine that Waits was also a fan of his work, "but my low self-esteem refused to accept that," E told *ICE*. When Waits suggested a Shortlist Prize nomination for the Eels' album *Shootenanny!*, E was "forced to believe the rumors." Waits later called him and they chatted, and E asked if they could work together. Waits agreed, added some guttural vocals to the Eels song "Going Fetal" on the album *Blinking Lights and Other Revelations*. "It's always nice when one of your heroes turns out to be a really great guy," E said.[55]

Singer Rob Thomas of the hugely popular rock band Matchbox Twenty, who has worked with legendary performers like Carlos Santana and Willie Nelson, is another artist who counts Waits as an inspiration. In fact, Thomas says that one of the songs on his solo album *Something to Be* was an attempt to emulate Waits's sound. "Paul [Matchbox Twenty drummer Doucette] and I are huge Tom Waits fans," Thomas says enthusiastically. "One of the things about 'Now Comes the Night' that I loved was that when I listen to old Tom Waits albums, I love that you can hear his foot on the foot pedal. That was one of the reasons that I wanted to record that song live, because I wanted to have that feeling. I play it for my friends and I'm like, 'Listen, listen, not to the music, listen to that *bomp bomp, bomp*

bomp. That's my foot on the pedal, man!' It comes from that, when I listen to 'Tom Traubert's Blues' or something like that, you know? I think he's an American treasure."

Singer Adam Cohen, who leads a band called Low Millions, also finds himself getting lost in the world of Waits music. "I love it," he says unequivocally. "I'm inspired by it. [I'm] in awe of it. It's so insular in its genius that I often forget it, because I'm incapable of mimicking it or incorporating it into my world. It's so unique." Cohen must know something about quality songwriting, because beyond his own good work, he's learned just a bit about great lyrics from his father, Leonard Cohen, who recorded Tom Waits's ninth favorite album.

Of course, it can go the other way around as well; Waits can get just as awestruck as the next guy. Singer Jakob Dylan, leader of the rock group the Wallflowers and son of Waits's inspiration — folk and rock music god Bob Dylan — learned this first-hand when he was backstage at the encounter between Waits and his father. Jakob was rather shocked to find that meeting his father had rendered Waits nearly speechless. "I'd be like, 'Come on, you're Tom Waits, the coolest guy in the world . . . say something,'" Jakob Dylan said. "I know my dad is very charismatic and that can freak people out but he's also a great guy if you deal with him right. So Tom Waits is going, 'Mnnub, mnubbb,' and I'm like, 'Don't fall apart on me, man, you're my hero.'"[56]

However, this makes a certain amount of sense. Not necessarily in putting Waits in his place in the musical hierarchy, it's just a reminder that long before he became an alt-rock figurehead, he was just a fan himself. He's just a kid who pinned Dylan lyrics to his walls who is rather shocked that he has had the wonderful opportunity — and the talent — to make a career of his first true love. This fascination with, and passion for, art has touched his work for thirty years. It has inspired him to seek out his own muse and poke and prod the music that moved him. This depth and range of influences was pointed out, yet again, when Amazon.com invited him to pick his ten favorite albums and he came up with this eccentric list: *Let the Buyer Beware* by Lenny Bruce, *In the Wee Small Hours* by Frank Sinatra, *The Abyssian Baptist Gospel Church Choir*, *Y Los Cubanos Postizos* by his guitarist Mark Ribot, *Purple Onion* by the Les Claypool Frog Brigade, a side project by his friend and Primus leader, *The Delivery Man* by Elvis Costello, *Ompa Til du Dør* by Kaizer's Orchestra, *Flying Saucer Tour* by Bill Hicks, *Masked Man* by Charlie Patton, and *The Specialty Sessions* by Little Richard.[57] A few months later, he came up with a different list of twenty for *The Observer* which had many of the same albums, but was also even deeper and quirkier.

Waits assimilates all of these sounds and more in his imagination and in the studio to try and reach others. Besides, as is his way, Waits likes to downplay all the talk about his music being so special or revolutionary, telling *The San Francisco Chronicle* simply, "I'm not original. I'm doing bad impersonations of other people. I like to sound like Ray Charles. Who wouldn't? So, you're hearing my poor, failed attempt at a Ray Charles imitation."[58]

Of course, the imitation spreads well beyond the music. In the end, Waits has pumped up his music and myth for several reasons. Yes, the romantic stories and the off-the-wall interviews probably helped him to get noticed and made him unique. But they were also a tool of survival. "The fact is that everybody who starts doing this to a certain extent develops some kind of persona or image to survive," Waits told Mick Brown of *Word*. "Otherwise it's very dangerous to go out there. It's much safer to approach this with some kind of persona, because if it's not a ventriloquist act, if it's just you, then it's really scary. . . . The whole thing's an act. Nobody would ever show you who they are — nobody would ever dare to do that, and if they do, they change their minds after a while because it gets to a point where you don't know what's true any more. The dice is throwing the man, instead of the man throwing the dice."[59]

So, whether it is the man, the music, or the self-made myth, Tom Waits soldiers on, periodically poking his head up from his hole to check the weather, release an album, or play a live show. He sometimes indulges his acting hobby, most recently taking a surreal supporting role in the big-budget adventure *Domino,* starring Keira Knightley, Christopher Walken, and Mickey Rourke.[60] He can watch bemusedly as his musical *The Black Rider* is finally performed around the world by several different companies. And he can putter around on his long-rumored rarities box set *Orphans,* which Anti does acknowledge is on the way . . . someday. Waits has earned the right to take his career and his life at his own pace, so even if he'll lay low for a few years between albums, he's always there because the music is there. In fact, in this age of the Internet, it is available to more people in more ways than ever before. This can be a boon and a curse. It opens up his potential audience significantly. However, the Internet has also opened up the same old wound that Waits has tried to heal for years.

The legal wrangling with former manager Herb Cohen just keeps on keeping on. In June of 2005, a suit was filed against Warner Music claiming that Waits was getting underpaid for digital downloads of his Elektra/ Asylum albums. A story on ABCNews.com explained: "According to the suit, under the terms of the two contracts, Waits was entitled to royalties of either 25% or 50% from revenues derived from third-party licenses. Third Story maintains that digital music downloads constitute a form of third-party license, and that Waits is entitled to payment at that level."[61] Despite the altruistic description being handed to the news organizations, the suit was placed by Cohen's company Third Story Music, not by Waits. Add to this the fact that Cohen still gets the royalties for this music. Given their history, it seems unlikely that Cohen was just looking out for his old protégé in filing this suit. However, Bones Howe has been assured by his lawyers that this case will, indeed, be beneficial to all of them.

In late 2005 word came out that many years earlier Waits had done a commercial, despite his vocal disdain of the idea. While he did not sing or allow his music to be used, he did act as a voiceover performer in a 1981 ad for dog food. He decided to take the job around the time he was severing his ties with Herb Cohen. With Waits's contract status what it was, his financial state was becoming highly precarious. He read the following copy in the commercial for Purina's Butcher's Blend Dog Food:

> As dog travels through the unbeaten and often tempting world of man, there's one thing, above all, that tempts him most — the taste of meat! And that is why Purina makes Butcher's Blend. Butcher's Blend is the first dry dog food with three tempting meaty tastes. Beef, liver 'n' bacon. All in one bag. So c'mon, deliver your dog from the world of temptation. The world of Butcher's Blend. The first dry dog food with three meaty tastes.[62]

The commercial was well respected in the advertising industry; it won major industry awards in 1982 at the Clio Awards and the Cannes Lions International Advertising Festival.

While Waits had never exactly made a secret of this, it still came as a bit of a shock to fans. Not just that he had done a commercial after so many years of decrying them but that such a well-known one had flown under the radar for all these years. Waits had even made an offhand acknowledgement of it to writer Jonathan Valania of *Magnet* in 1999, "They always want me to do ads for underwear and cigarettes, but I never do them. I did one and I'll never do it again."[63] Waits's name is plainly mentioned in the credits listed for the Clio Award. Still, the ad was pretty much forgotten until the copywriter for the ad tried to sell the original masters of Waits's voiceover, along with the signed Screen Actors Guild contract, on eBay. The sale was quickly withdrawn from the site, undoubtedly due to legal pressure, with the auction notice reading curtly, "The seller ended this listing early because the item is no longer available for sale."[64]

Since *Real Gone* has made it into the stores, no word of a follow-up of new material has surfaced. But that is no cause for alarm. In fact, it has become par for the course. Waits is a notorious perfectionist, and he's undoubtedly right now in a Northern California studio getting the kinks out (or putting the kinks into?) a new set of tunes. Or maybe he's trying to channel the inspiration he found at the Salvador Dali exhibit in the Philadelphia Museum of Art with his family.[65] He is choosing from amongst a voluminous catalogue of musical snippets and songs that he has birthed, hammering and ratcheting them into shape. Trying desperately to capture the sounds he hears in his mind. When it is as close as possible to the perfect aural junkyard that he imagines, he will share it with the rest of the world. Of this, you can be sure. You can also be pretty darned sure that it will be tonally interesting and lyrically stimulating.

No one knows what he'll come up with next, but at least one thing is certain. Whatever it is will be stimulating and thought-provoking. Waits is an artist who can still surprise and challenge himself and his audience thirty years into his career. How many others can make a similar claim?

To a degree, Waits's longevity can be attributed to the fact that he has never been a flavor of the month. And you can't plunge from the heights if you've never scaled them. Waits is no superstar; he's a craftsman and an artist. He fabricates good, functional, sturdy, eclectic art and then dares his audience to try it out. Some people can't get beyond his raspy vocals, and that is a pity. They are missing something vital, something elemental, something that is at once both sexual and pure, violent and benign, profane and strangely spiritual. Tom Waits is a man with a highly original artistic vision that he has never allowed to become corrupted. Bones Howe recalls Waits saying to him, "The reason I got into music is so that I wouldn't have to conform. And if I have to conform with my music, then I shouldn't be in music anymore."

Howe concludes, "I just think that [Tom Waits] has a lot of scope. He has a very wide vista to look from. I think that he's an immense talent. He's always looking. He's always experimenting. He's always trying to move from where he is. He doesn't sit still. He doesn't stay in one place. He wants to keep moving."

As 1999 drew to a close, *Rolling Stone* asked a host of celebrities from different niches of the entertainment industry to articulate their thoughts about the new millennium. Waits was asked what he would say to the students of the class of 2000. "Run away and join the circus," he told them. "Get a tattoo, hop a train. Plant a garden and save the seeds. Get married, have kids, wear a hat. Get good with a bullwhip. Don't lie, don't cheat, don't steal. Everyone must put beans on the table. Be devoted to the unification of the diverse aspects of yourself. Remember, most of what is essential is invisible to the eye. The quality of time you spend with someone far outweighs the quantity. And, there's a lot you can do with a wah-wah pedal and a bullet mike."[66]

DISCOGRAPHY

ALBUMS

Closing Time
Elektra 5061 (1973)

1. Ol' 55
2. I Hope That I Don't Fall in Love with You
3. Virginia Avenue
4. Old Shoes (And Picture Postcards)
5. Midnight Lullaby
6. Martha
7. Rosie
8. Lonely
9. Ice Cream Man
10. Little Trip to Heaven (On the Wings of Your Love)
11. Grapefruit Moon
12. Closing Time

All songs written by Tom Waits.
Produced by Jerry Yester for Third Story Productions.

The Heart of Saturday Night
Asylum 1015 (1974)

1. New Coat of Paint
2. San Diego Serenade
3. Semi Suite
4. Shiver Me Timbers
5. Diamonds on My Windshield
6. (Looking For) The Heart of Saturday Night
7. Fumblin' with the Blues
8. Please Call Me, Baby
9. Depot, Depot
10. Drunk on the Moon
11. The Ghosts of Saturday Night (After Hours at Napoleone's Pizza House)

All songs written by Tom Waits.
Production and sound by Bones Howe for Mr. Bones Productions.

Nighthawks at the Diner
Asylum 2008 (1975)

1. Opening Intro
2. Emotional Weather Report
3. Intro
4. On a Foggy Night
5. Intro
6. Eggs and Sausage (In a Cadillac with Susan Michelson)
7. Intro
8. Better Off Without a Wife
9. Nighthawk Postcards (From Easy Street)
10. Intro
11. Warm Beer and Cold Women
12. Intro
13. Putnam County
14. Spare Parts I (A Nocturnal Emission) *(Tom Waits and Chuck E. Weiss)*
15. Nobody Intro
16. Big Joe and Phantom 309 *(Tommy Faile)*
17. Spare Parts II and Closing

All songs written by Tom Waits except where noted.
Production and sound by Bones Howe for Mr. Bones Productions.

Small Change
Asylum 1078 (1976)

1. Tom Traubert's Blues (Four Sheets to the Wind in Copenhagen)
2. Step Right Up
3. Jitterbug Boy (Sharing a Curbstone with Chuck E. Weiss, Robert Marchese, Paul Body and the Mug and Artie)
4. I Wish I Was in New Orleans (In the Ninth Ward)
5. The Piano Has Been Drinking (Not Me) (An Evening with Pete King)
6. Invitation to the Blues
7. Pasties and a G-String (At the Two O'Clock Club)
8. Bad Liver and a Broken Heart (In Lowell)
9. The One That Got Away
10. Small Change (Got Rained on with His Own .38)
11. I Can't Wait to Get off Work (And See My Baby on Montgomery Avenue)

All songs written by Tom Waits.
Production and sound by Bones Howe for Mr. Bones Productions.

Foreign Affairs
Elektra 1117 (1977)

1. Cinny's Waltz
2. Muriel
3. I Never Talk to Strangers *(duet with Bette Midler)*

4. Medley: Jack and Neal/California, Here I Come *(Tom Waits/Joseph Meyer, Al Jolson, and Buddy G. De Sylva)*
5. A Sight for Sore Eyes
6. Potter's Field *(Tom Waits and Bob Alcivar)*
7. Burma Shave
8. Barber Shop
9. Foreign Affair

All songs written by Tom Waits except where noted.
Production and sound by Bones Howe. A Mr. Bones Production.

Blue Valentine

Elektra 162 (1978)

1. Somewhere (from *West Side Story*) *(Leonard Bernstein and Stephen Sondheim)*
2. Red Shoes by the Drugstore
3. Christmas Card from a Hooker in Minneapolis
4. Romeo Is Bleeding
5. $29.00
6. Wrong Side of the Road
7. Whistlin' Past the Graveyard
8. Kentucky Avenue
9. A Sweet Little Bullet from a Pretty Blue Gun
10. Blue Valentines

All songs written by Tom Waits except where noted.
Production and sound by Bones Howe. A Mr. Bones Production.

Heartattack and Vine

Elektra 295 (1980)

1. Heartattack and Vine
2. In Shades
3. Saving All My Love for You
4. Downtown
5. Jersey Girl
6. 'Til the Money Runs Out
7. On the Nickel
8. Mr. Siegal
9. Ruby's Arms

All songs written by Tom Waits.
Production and sound by Bones Howe. A B.H. Production.

Bounced Checks

Asylum 7200 (1981)

1. Heartattack and Vine
2. Jersey Girl *(alternate take)*
3. Eggs and Sausage (In a Cadillac with Susan Michelson)
4. I Never Talk to Strangers *(duet with Bette Midler)*

5. The Piano Has Been Drinking (Not Me) *(live version)*
6. Whistlin' Past the Graveyard *(alternate take)*
7. Mr. Henry
8. Diamonds on My Windshield
9. Burma Shave
10. Tom Traubert's Blues (Four Sheets to the Wind in Copenhagen)

All songs written by Tom Waits.
Production and sound by Bones Howe.

One from the Heart (Original Soundtrack)
Columbia CK37703 (1982)

1. Opening Montage
a) Tom's Piano Intro
b) Once Upon a Town *(duet with Crystal Gayle)*
c) The Wages of Love *(duet with Crystal Gayle)*
2. Is There Any Way Out of This Dream? *(vocal by Crystal Gayle)*
3. Picking Up After You *(duet with Crystal Gayle)*
4. Old Boyfriends *(vocal by Crystal Gayle)*
5. Broken Bicycles
6. I Beg Your Pardon
7. Little Boy Blue
8. Instrumental Montage
a) The Tango
b) Circus Girl
9. You Can't Unring a Bell
10. This One's from the Heart *(duet with Crystal Gayle)*
11. Take Me Home *(vocal by Crystal Gayle)*
12. Presents
13. Candy Apple Red*
14. Once Upon a Town/Empty Pockets*

* CD bonus tracks on 2004 reissue.

All songs written by Tom Waits.
Production and sound by Bones Howe.

Swordfishtrombones
Island 422-842 469-2 (1983)

1. Underground
2. Shore Leave
3. Dave the Butcher *(instrumental)*
4. Johnsburg, Illinois
5. 16 Shells From a Thirty-Ought-Six
6. Town with No Cheer
7. In the Neighborhood
8. Just Another Sucker on the Vine *(instrumental)*
9. Frank's Wild Years

10. Swordfishtrombone
11. Down, Down, Down
12. Soldier's Things
13. Gin Soaked Boy
14. Trouble's Braids
15. Rainbirds *(instrumental)*

All songs written by Tom Waits.
Produced by Tom Waits.

Rain Dogs
Island 7 90299-2 (1985)

1. Singapore
2. Clap Hands
3. Cemetery Polka
4. Jockey Full of Bourbon
5. Tango 'Til They're Sore
6. Big Black Mariah
7. Diamonds and Gold
8. Hang Down Your Head *(Kathleen Brennan and Tom Waits)*
9. Time
10. Rain Dogs
11. Midtown *(instrumental)*
12. 9th & Hennepin
13. Gun Street Girl
14. Union Square
15. Blind Love
16. Walking Spanish
17. Downtown Train
18. Bride of Rain Dog *(instrumental)*
19. Anywhere I Lay My Head

All songs written by Tom Waits except where noted.
Produced by Tom Waits.

Anthology of Tom Waits
Asylum 9 60416-4-E (1985)

1. Ol' 55
2. Diamonds on My Windshield
3. (Looking For) The Heart of Saturday Night
4. I Hope That I Don't Fall in Love with You
5. Martha
6. Tom Traubert's Blues (Waltzing Matilda)
7. The Piano Has Been Drinking (Not Me)
8. I Never Talk to Strangers *(duet with Bette Midler)*
9. Somewhere (from *West Side Story*) *(Stephen Sondheim and Leonard Bernstein)*
10. Burma Shave

11. Jersey Girl
12. San Diego Serenade
13. A Sight For Sore Eyes

All songs written by Tom Waits except where noted.
Production and sound by Bones Howe for Mr. Bones Productions, Inc.
Produced by Jerry Yester for Third Story Productions

Asylum Years
Asylum/WEA International 960 494-2 (1986)

1. Diamonds on My Windshield
2. (Looking For) The Heart of Saturday Night
3. Martha
4. The Ghosts of Saturday Night (After Hours at Napoleone's Pizza House)
5. Grapefruit Moon
6. Small Change
7. Burma Shave
8. I Never Talk to Strangers *(duet with Bette Midler)*
9. Tom Traubert's Blues (Waltzing Matilda)
10. Blue Valentines
11. Potter's Field *(Tom Waits and Bob Alcivar)*
12. Kentucky Avenue
13. Somewhere (from *West Side Story*) *(Stephen Sondheim and Leonard Bernstein)*
14. Ruby's Arms

All songs written by Tom Waits except where noted.
Production and sound by Bones Howe for Mr. Bones Productions, Inc.
Produced by Jerry Yester for Third Story Productions.

Frank's Wild Years: Un Operanchi Romantico In Two Acts
Island 422-842 357-2 (1987)

Act I
1. Hang On St. Christopher
2. Straight to the Top (Rhumba) *(Tom Waits and Greg Cohen)*
3. Blow Wind Blow
4. Temptation
5. Innocent When You Dream (Barroom)
6. I'll Be Gone *(Tom Waits and Kathleen Brennan)*
7. Yesterday Is Here *(Tom Waits and Kathleen Brennan)*
8. Please Wake Me Up *(Tom Waits and Kathleen Brennan)*
9. Frank's Theme

Act II
10. More Than Rain
11. Way Down in the Hole
12. Straight to the Top (Vegas) *(Tom Waits and Greg Cohen)*
13. I'll Take New York
14. Telephone Call from Istanbul

15. Cold Cold Ground
16. Train Song
17. Innocent When You Dream (78)

All songs written by Tom Waits except where noted.
Produced by Tom Waits.

Big Time
Island 7 90987-2 (1988)

1. 16 Shells From a Thirty-Ought-Six
2. Red Shoes
3. Underground*
4. Cold Cold Ground
5. Straight to the Top*
6. Yesterday Is Here
7. Way Down in the Hole*
8. Falling Down
9. Strange Weather
10. Big Black Mariah
11. Rain Dogs
12. Train Song
13. Johnsburg, Illinois*
14. Ruby's Arms*
15. Telephone Call from Istanbul
16. Clap Hands*
17. Gun Street Girl
18. Time

* CD bonus tracks

All songs written by Tom Waits.
Produced by Tom Waits and Kathleen Brennan.
Recorded live in Los Angeles, San Francisco, Dublin, Stockholm, and Berlin

The Early Years (Volume One)
Bizarre/Manifesto PT3 40601 (1991)

1. Goin' Down Slow
2. Poncho's Lament
3. I'm Your Late Night Evening Prostitute
4. Had Me a Girl
5. Ice Cream Man
6. Rockin' Chair
7. Virginia Ave.
8. Midnight Lullabye
9. When You Ain't Got Nobody
10. Little Trip to Heaven
11. Frank's Song
12. Looks Like I'm Up Shit Creek Again

13. So Long I'll See Ya

All songs written by Tom Waits.
Produced by Robert Duffey.
Recorded July to December 1971, Los Angeles.

The Early Years (Volume Two)
Bizarre/Rhino R2 71089 (1992)

1. I Hope That I Don't Fall in Love with You
2. Ol' 55
3. Mockin' Bird
4. In Between Love
5. Blue Skies
6. Nobody
7. I Want You
8. Shiver Me Timbers
9. Grapefruit Moon
10. Diamonds on My Windshield
11. Please Call Me, Baby
12. So It Goes
13. Old Shoes

All songs written by Tom Waits.
Mastered by Robert Duffey and Ken Perry.
Recorded July to December 1971, Los Angeles.

Night On Earth (Original Soundtrack Recording)
Island 314-510 725-2 (1992)

1. Back in the Good Old World (Gypsy) *(vocal)*
2. Los Angeles Mood (Chromium Descensions)
3. Los Angeles Theme (Another Private Dick)
4. New York Theme (Hey, You Can Have That Heartattack Outside Buddy)
5. New York Mood (A New Haircut and a Busted Lip)
6. Baby, I'm Not a Baby Anymore (Beatrice Theme)
7. Good Old World (Waltz)
8. Carnival (Brunella Del Montalcino)
9. On the Other Side of the World *(vocal)*
10. Good Old World (Gypsy Instrumental)
11. Paris Mood (Un de Fromage)
12. Dragging a Dead Priest
13. Helsinki Mood
14. Carnival Bob's Confession
15. Good Old World (Waltz) *(vocal)*
16. On the Other Side of the World *(instrumental)*

All songs written by Tom Waits and Kathleen Brennan.
Produced by Tom Waits.
Songs arranged by Tom Waits and Francis Thumm.

Bone Machine

Island 314-512 580-2 (1992)

1. Earth Died Screaming *(Tom Waits)*
2. Dirt in the Ground
3. Such a Scream *(Tom Waits)*
4. All Stripped Down *(Tom Waits)*
5. Who Are You
6. The Ocean Doesn't Want Me *(Tom Waits)*
7. Jesus Gonna Be Here *(Tom Waits)*
8. A Little Rain
9. In the Colosseum
10. Goin' Out West
11. Murder in the Red Barn
12. Black Wings
13. Whistle Down the Wind *(Tom Waits)*
14. I Don't Wanna Grow Up
15. Let Me Get Up On It *(Tom Waits)*
16. That Feel *(Keith Richards and Tom Waits)*

All songs written by Tom Waits and Kathleen Brennan except where noted.
Produced by Tom Waits.
Associate Producer: Kathleen Brennan.

The Black Rider

Island 314-518 559-2 (1993)

1. Lucky Day Overture
2. The Black Rider
3. November
4. Just the Right Bullets
5. Black Box Theme
6. T'Ain't No Sin *(vocal by William Burroughs) (Walter Donaldson and Edgar Leslie)*
7. Flash Pan Hunter (Intro)
8. That's the Way *(Tom Waits and William Burroughs)*
9. The Briar and the Rose
10. Russian Dance
11. Gospel Train (Orch)
12. I'll Shoot the Moon
13. Flash Pan Hunter *(Tom Waits and William Burroughs)*
14. Crossroads *(Tom Waits and William Burroughs)*
15. Gospel Train
16. Interlude *(Greg Cohen)*
17. Oily Night
18. Lucky Day
19. The Last Rose of Summer
20. Carnival

All songs written by Tom Waits except where noted.
Produced by Tom Waits.

Beautiful Maladies — The Island Years
Island 314-524 519-2 (1998)

1. Hang on St. Christopher
2. Temptation
3. Clap Hands
4. The Black Rider
5. Underground
6. Jockey Full of Bourbon
7. Earth Died Screaming
8. Innocent When You Dream (78)
9. Straight to the Top *(Tom Waits and Greg Cohen)*
10. Frank's Wild Years
11. Singapore
12. Shore Leave
13. Johnsburg, Illinois
14. Way Down in the Hole
15. Strange Weather *(Live)*
16. Cold Cold Ground *(Live)*
17. November
18. Downtown Train
19. 16 Shells From a Thirty-Ought-Six
20. Jesus Gonna Be Here
21. Good Old World (Waltz) *(Tom Waits and Kathleen Brennan)*
22. I Don't Wanna Grow Up *(Tom Waits and Kathleen Brennan)*
23. Time

All songs written by Tom Waits except where noted.
Produced by Tom Waits.

Mule Variations
Anti/Epitaph 86547-2 (1999)

1. Big in Japan
2. Lowside of the Road
3. Hold On
4. Get Behind the Mule
5. House Where Nobody Lives *(Tom Waits)*
6. Cold Water
7. Pony *(Tom Waits)*
8. What's He Building? *(Tom Waits)*
9. Black Market Baby
10. Eyeball Kid
11. Picture in a Frame
12. Chocolate Jesus
13. Georgia Lee
14. Filipino Box Spring Hog *(Tom Waits)*

15. Take It with Me
16. Come Up to the House

All songs written by Tom Waits and Kathleen Brennan except where noted.
Produced by Tom Waits and Kathleen Brennan.

Used Songs 1973-1980
Elektra/Rhino R2 78351 (2001)

1. Heartattack and Vine
2. Eggs and Sausage (In a Cadillac with Susan Michelson)
3. A Sight For Sore Eyes
4. Whistlin' Past the Graveyard
5. Burma Shave
6. Step Right Up
7. Ol' 55
8. I Never Talk to Strangers *(duet with Bette Midler)*
9. Mr. Siegal
10. Jersey Girl
11. Christmas Card from a Hooker in Minneapolis
12. Blue Valentines
13. (Looking For) The Heart of Saturday Night
14. Muriel
15. Wrong Side of the Road
16. Tom Traubert's Blues (Four Sheets to the Wind in Copenhagen)

All songs written by Tom Waits.
Original Recordings Produced by Bones Howe and Jerry Yester.

The Dime Store Novels (Volume 1) — Live at Ebbets' Field
Burning Airlines/Pilot 82 (2001)

1. I Hope That I Don't Fall in Love with You
2. San Diego Serenade
3. Good Night Loving Trail *(Bruce "Utah" Phillips)*
4. Diamonds on My Windshield
5. Ice Cream Man
6. Please Call Me, Baby
7. Better Off Without a Wife
8. The Ghosts of Saturday Night
9. Big Joe and Phantom 309 *(Tommy Faile)*
10. Semi Suite
11. Ol' 55
12. On a Foggy Night
13. Martha

All songs written by Tom Waits except where noted.

Alice

Anti/Epitaph 86632-2 (2002)

1. Alice
2. Everything You Can Think
3. Flower's Grave
4. No One Knows I'm Gone
5. Kommienezuspadt
6. Poor Edward
7. Table Top Joe
8. Lost in the Harbor
9. We're All Mad Here
10. Watch Her Disappear
11. Reeperbahn
12. I'm Still Here
13. Fish & Bird
14. Barcarolle
15. Fawn

All songs written by Tom Waits and Kathleen Brennan.
Produced by Tom Waits and Kathleen Brennan.

Blood Money

Anti/Epitaph 86629-2 (2002)

1. Misery is the River of the World
2. Everything Goes to Hell
3. Coney Island Baby
4. All the World is Green
5. God's Away On Business
6. Another Man's Vine
7. Knife Chase
8. Lullaby
9. Starving in the Belly of the Whale
10. The Part You Throw Away
11. Woe
12. Calliope
13. A Good Man is Hard to Find

All songs written by Tom Waits and Kathleen Brennan.
Produced by Tom Waits and Kathleen Brennan.

Real Gone

Anti/Epitaph 86678-2 (2004)

1. Top of the Hill
2. Hoist That Rag
3. Sins of the Father
4. Shake It

5. Don't Go Into the Barn
6. How's It Gonna End?
7. Metropolitan Glide
8. Dead and Lovely
9. Circus
10. Trampled Rose
11. Green Grass
12. Baby Gonna Leave Me
13. Clang Boom Steam
14. Make It Rain
15. Day After Tomorrow
16. Untitled (Chickaboom)

All songs written by Tom Waits and Kathleen Brennan.
Produced by Tom Waits and Kathleen Brennan.

SINGLES

"Downtown Train" b/w "Tango 'Til They're Sore" (Island IS253) (7" single) (1985)

"Downtown Train" b/w "Tango 'Til They're Sore" and "Jockey Full of Bourbon" (Island IS235) (12" single) (1985)

"Goin' Out West" b/w "A Little Rain" (Island) (7" single) (1992)

"Hang on St. Christopher" *(extended mix)* b/w "Hang on St. Christopher" *(instrumental)* (Island 096750) (12" single) (1987)

"Hold On" b/w "Big in Japan" and "Buzz Fledderjon" (Anti/Epitaph Europe 1020-2) (CD single) (1999)

"I Don't Wanna Grow Up" (Island promo PRCD 6748-2) (CD single) (1992)

"In the Neighborhood" b/w "Frank's Wild Years" (Island IS141) (7" single) (1983)

"In the Neighborhood" and "Singapore" b/w "Tango 'Til They're Sore" *(Live)* and "16 Shells From a Thirty-Ought-Six" *(Live)* (Island IS12260) (12" single) (1986)

"Jersey Girl" b/w "Heartattack and Vine" (Asylum E 47077) (7" single) (1980)

"(Looking For) The Heart of Saturday Night" b/w "(Looking For) The Heart of Saturday Night" *(alternate take)* (Asylum E 45262) (7" single) (1975)

"New Coat of Paint" b/w "Blue Skies" (Asylum E 45233) (7" single) (1974)

"Ol' 55" (Asylum 11014) (7" single) (1973)

"San Diego Serenade" (Asylum E 45213) (7" single) (1974)

"16 Shells From a Thirty-Ought-Six" b/w "Big Black Mariah" (Island I07761) (7" single) (1987)

"16 Shells From a Thirty-Ought-Six" b/w "Big Black Mariah" and "Ruby's Arms" (Island IS370) (12" single) (1987)

"Somewhere (from *West Side Story)*" b/w "Red Shoes by the Drugstore" (Asylum E 45539) (7" single) (1978)

"Somewhere (from *West Side Story)*" b/w "Somewhere (from *West Side Story)*" (Elektra) (7" single) (1978)

"Step Right Up" (single edit) b/w "The Piano Has Been Drinking (Not Me)" (Asylum E 45371) (7" single) (1976)

"Who Are You?" b/w "A Little Rain" (Island 74321 1226612) (CD single) (1992)

MUSIC VIDEOS

Another Man's Vine (2002)
Blow Wind Blow (1987)
Cold Cold Ground *(live)* (1988)
Downtown Train (1985)
God's Away On Business (2002)
Hold On (1999)
I Don't Want To Grow Up (1992)
In the Neighborhood (1983)
It's Alright With Me (1990)
16 Shells From a Thirty-Ought-Six (1988)
The One That Got Away (1976)
Temptation (1987)
This One's from the Heart (2004)
What's He Building? (1999)

GUEST APPEARANCES ON VARIOUS ARTIST COLLECTIONS OR SOUNDTRACK ALBUMS

"Annie's Back in Town"
Paradise Alley: Original Soundtrack Album (MCA 5100) (1978)

"Anywhere I Lay My Head"
Dead and Gone #1: Trauermärsche Funeral Marches (Trikont 0234) (1997)

"Babbachichuija"
Orbitones: Spoon Harps and Belloephones (Ellipsis Arts 3610) (1998)

"Baby Gonna Leave Me"
Uncut 2004 (Volume 1): 15 Tracks from the Year's Best New Albums (Uncut) (2004)

"Bend Down the Branches"
For the Kids (Nettwerk 30288) (2002)

"Big in Japan"
Balling the Jack: Birth of the NU-Blues (Ocho 12) (2002)

"Big in Japan"
Punk-O-Rama 4: Straight Outta the Pit (Epitaph 86563) (1999)

"Black Wings"
Condo Painting: Original Motion Picture Soundtrack (Gallery Six 16) (2000)

"Book of Moses"
More Oar: A Tribute to the Skip Spence Album (Birdman 23) (1999)

"Brother, Can You Spare A Dime?"
Brother, Can You Spare A Dime Day (The Harburg Foundation DIME 93) (1993)

"Buzz Fledderjohn"
Connections 2: In Benefit of KCRB-FM (Jackalope 02) (2004)

"Buzz Fledderjohn"
Groundwork: Act To Reduce Hunger (Groundwork/Starbucks) (2001)

"Date For Church" *(with the Replacements)*
Just Say Mao: Volume III of Just Say Yes (Sire 9 25947-2) (1989)

"Day After Tomorrow"
Future Soundtrack for America (Bark 37) (2004)

"Diamonds On My Windshield"
The Beat Generation Box Set (Rhino R2 70281) (1992)

"Downtown Train"
Smoke: Original Motion Picture Soundtrack (Miramax/Hollywood MH-62024-2) (1995)

"Earth Died Screaming"
Twelve Monkeys: Original Soundtrack (UNI/MCA MCAD-11392) (1995)

"Emotional Weather Report"
Onxert — Live from the Archives Volume 4 (Onxert 4) (1998)

"The Fall of Troy"
Dead Man Walking: Music From and Inspired by the Motion Picture (Columbia CK 67522) (1995)

"The Fall of Troy" *(Live)*
Rare On Air Volume Four: Still More Selections from KCRB-FM On Air Performances (Mammoth 354 980 193-2) (1998)

"Filipino Box Spring Hog"
Beyond Mississippi: The Blues That Left Town (Manteca 209) (2002)

"Filipino Box Spring Hog"
Born To Choose (Rykodisc RCD10256) (1993)

"Georgia Lee"
Seka: Sister Volume 2 (Twah 115) (2001)

"Get Behind the Mule"
Blues: The Essential Album (Essentials 230) (2004)

"God's Away on Business"
Enron: The Smartest Guys in the Room — Original Soundtrack Album (Commotion 7) (2005)

"A Good Man Is Hard To Find"
Songs Inspired By Literature: Chapter 2 (Sibl Project 1063) (2003)

"Good Old World"
International Film Channel: In Your Ear (Warner/Hybrid 20010) (1999)

"Hang on St. Christopher"
The Island Tape (Island/Select SEL IS11)

"Heigh Ho (The Dwarfs' Marching Song)"
Stay Awake: Various Interpretations of Music from Vintage Disney Films (A&M CD 3918 DX 003644) (1988)

"Highway Café"
Pearls In the Snow: The Songs of Kinky Friedman (Damian/BMG 12217) (1999)

"Hold On" *(Live in studio)*
On the Mountain: Volume 6 (KMTT) (2000)

"I'm Still Here"
Rough Trade Shops: Counter Culture (Mute England 218) (2003)

"Innocent When You Dream (Barroom)"
The Island Story 1962-1987 (Island 7 90684-2) (1987)

"Innocent When You Dream (Barroom)"
Smoke: Original Motion Picture Soundtrack (Miramax/Hollywood MH-62024-2) (1995)

"It Rains on Me"
Free the West Memphis 3 (Koch International 8150) (2000)

"It's All Right with Me"
Red, Hot and Blue (Chrysalis F2 21799) (1990)

"It's Over"
Liberty Heights: Original Soundtrack (Warner Sunset/Atlantic 83270-2) (2000)

"Jack and Neal/California, Here I Come" *(Medley)*
The Beat Generation Box Set (Rhino R2 70281) (1992)

"Jayne's Blue Wish"
Big Bad Love: Original Soundtrack Album (Elektra/Asylum 79637) (2002)

"Jockey Full of Bourbon"
Things To Do In Denver When You're Dead: Original Soundtrack (A&M 0424) (1995)

"Jockey Full of Bourbon"
Coded (Columbia 24072) (2000)

"King Kong"
Late Great Daniel Johnston: Discovered Covered (Gammon 2112) (2004)

"Little Drop of Poison"
The End of Violence: Original Soundtrack (UNI/Outpost OPRD-30008) (1997)

"Little Drop of Poison" *(new recording)*
Shrek 2: Motion Picture Soundtrack (Geffen 9862698) (2004)

"The Long Way Home"
Big Bad Love: Original Soundtrack Album (Elektra/Asylum 79637) (2002)

"(Looking For) The Heart of Saturday Night"
Folk Scene Collection Volume Two (Red House 137) (1999)

"(Meet Me In) Paradise Alley"
Paradise Alley: Original Soundtrack Album (MCA 5100) (1978)

"More than Rain"
Gun Shy: Original Soundtrack Album (UNI/Hollywood 162267) (2000)

"Ol' 55"
Classics In Digital – Storytellers: Singers and Songwriters (Warner Brothers 2-27615) (1987)

"Ol' 55"
From the Asylum (Asylum Promo) (1973)

"Ol' 55"
Masterpieces (WEA 32252) (1993)

"On the Other Side of the World"
Mondays in the Sun: Original Soundtrack (Milan 36014) (2002)

"Please Call Me, Baby"
Keeping the Faith: Original Soundtrack (Hollywood 162275) (2000)

"The Pontiac"
Smack My Crack (Giorno Poetry Systems GPS 038 1987) (1987)

"Putting On the Dog"
Liberty Heights: Original Soundtrack (Warner Sunset/Atlantic 83270-2) (2000)

"Rat's Theme"
Streetwise: Original Motion Picture Soundtrack (1984)

"The Return of Jackie & Judy"
We're A Happy Family — A Tribute to the Ramones (DV8/Columbia 86352) (2003)

"River of Men"
Fishing with John: T.V. Soundtrack (Strange and Beautiful 14) (1998)

"Sea of Love"
Sea of Love: Original Motion Picture Soundtrack (Mercury 842 170-2) (1989)

"Silent Night"
SOS United (EMI IC 098 7 92988-1) (1989)

"Step Right Up"
Year of the Ear Sampler — Volume 1 (Elektra EA277) (1977)

"Take Care Of All Of My Children"
Streetwise: Original Motion Picture Soundtrack (1984)

"Tommy the Cat" *(with Primus)*
Bill & Ted's Bogus Journey: Original Soundtrack (Interscope 91725-2) (1991)

"Tom Traubert's Blues (Four Sheets to the Wind in Copenhagen)"
Basquiat: Original Soundtrack (Island 314-524 260-2) (1996)

"Walk Away"
Dead Man Walking: Music From and Inspired by the Motion Picture (Columbia CK 67522) (1995)

"What Keeps Mankind Alive?"
Lost In the Stars: The Music of Kurt Weill (A&M SP 9-5104) (1985)

"The World Keeps Turning"
Pollock: Original Soundtrack (Unitone 5301) (2001)

"World of Adventure"
Fishing With John: T.V. Soundtrack (Strange and Beautiful 14) (1998)

GUEST APPEARANCES ON THE ALBUMS OF OTHER MUSICIANS

Blind Boys of Alabama
"Go Tell It on the Mountain"
On the album *Go Tell It on the Mountain* (Real World 90600) (2003)

Gavin Bryars
"Jesus' Blood Never Failed Me Yet" (Tramp and Tom Waits with full orchestra) (vocals) and *"Jesus' Blood Never Failed Me Yet" (Tom Waits with high strings) (vocals)*
On the EP *Jesus' Blood Never Failed Me Yet* (Point Music 438-823-2) (1993)

Richie Cole
"Waiting for Waits" *(vocals)*
On the album *Hollywood Madness* (Muse MCD-5207) (1992)

C-Side and Petit Mal
All songs
On the album *Moanin' Parade: The Gatmo Sessions Vol. I* (Jackalope) (2000)

Dave Douglas
"Mahfouz" *(vocals)*
On the album *Witness* (RCA 63763) (2001)

Teddy Edwards
"Little Man" and "I'm Not Your Fool Anymore" *(vocals)*
On the album *Mississippi Lad* (Antilles 314-511 411-2) (1991)

The Eels
"Going Fetal" *(vocals)*
On the album *Blinking Lights and Other Revelations* (Vangrant 406) (2005)

Ramblin' Jack Elliott
"Louise" *(vocals)*
On the album *Friends of Mine* (Hightone/Rhino R2 8089) (1998)

John Hammond
All songs *(guitar, piano, vocals and production)*
On the album *Wicked Grin* (Pointblank/Virgin 7243 9 50764 2 8) (2001)

Dan Hicks and His Hot Licks
"I'll Tell You Why That Is" *(vocals)*
On the album *Beatin' the Heat* (Surfdog SD-67113-2) (2000)

Jack Kerouac
"On The Road" *(guitar, percussion, vocals)*
On the album *Reads On the Road* (Rykodisc 10474) (1999)

Los Lobos
"Kitate" *(vocals)*
On the album *The Ride* (Hollywood 162443) (2004)

Bette Midler
"I Never Talk to Strangers" *(vocals)*
On the album *Broken Blossom* (Atlantic SD 19151) (1977)

Martin Mull
"Martin Goes and Does Where It's At" *(vocal as bartender)*
On the album *I'm Everybody I've Ever Loved* (ABC AB997) (1977)

Ken Nordine
"The Movie" and "Thousand Bing Bangs" *(spoken word vocals)*
On the album *Devout Catalyst* (Grateful Dead Records GDCD40152) (1991)

Roy Orbison
All songs *(guitar and organ)*
On the album *Roy Orbison & Friends: A Black & White Night* (Virgin 91292-2)
(1989); reissued (Orbison ROBW2000-2) (1997)

Primus
"Coattails of a Dead Man" *(vocals, mellotron, and producer)*
On the album *AntiPop* (Uni/Interscope 490414) (1999)

Primus
"Tommy the Cat" *(vocals)*
On the album *Sailing the Seas of Cheese* (Uni/Interscope 91659-2) (1991)

Bonnie Raitt
"Sweet and Shiny Eyes" *(vocals)*
On the album *Home Plate* (Warner Brothers 2864-2) (1975)

The Replacements
"Date for Church" *(vocals)*
B-side to 7" single "I'll Be You" (Sire 7-22992-B) (1989)
On the various artists album "Just Say Mao: Volume III of Just Say Yes" (Sire 9
25947-2) (1989)
Also on the album *All For Nothing, Nothing For All* (Reprise 9 46807-2) (1997)

The Rolling Stones
"Sleep Tonight" *(vocals)*
On the album *Dirty Work* (Rolling Stones 40250) (1986)

Sparklehorse
"Dog Door" *(vocals)*
On the album *It's A Wonderful Life* (EMI 525616) (2001)

Thelonious Monster
"Adios Lounge" *(vocals)*
On the album *Beautiful Mess* (Capitol 80227) (1992)

Tin Hat Trio
"Helium Reprise" *(vocals)*
On the album *Helium* (Angel 7243 5 56935 2 5) (2000)

Chuck E. Weiss
"It Rains On Me" and "Do You Know What I Idi Amin" *(vocals, guitar, producer)*
On the album *Extremely Cool* (Slow River/Rykodisc SRRCD 41)

TOM WAITS'S SONGS RECORDED BY OTHER ARTISTS

"Better Off Without A Wife"
Pete Shelley
On the various artists album *Step Right Up: The Songs of Tom Waits* (Manifesto
PT3 41101-2) (1995)

"Better Off Without A Wife"
Johan Verminnen (recorded in Dutch as "Beter Zonder Wijf")
On the album *Stilte Als Refrein* (Biram Records) (1973)

"Big in Japan"
Wolfgang Ambros (recorded in German as "Gross in Kagran")
On the album *Ambros Singt Waits* (BMG Ariola München) (2000)

"Big Black Mariah"
The Carnival Saloon
On the album *The Carnival Saloon Live* (2001)

"Big Black Mariah"
John Hammond
On the album *Wicked Grin* (Pointblank/Virgin 7243 9 50764 2 8) (2001)

"The Black Rider"
Frank Black and the Catholics
On the album *Black Letter Day* (spinArt 113) (2002)

"Black Wings"
Astrid Seriese
On the album *Into Temptation* (Briga) (1996)

"Blind Love"
Bob Seger and The Silver Bullet Band
On the album *The Fire Inside* (Capitol CDP 7 91134 2) (1991)

"Blind Love"
Fjorton Sånger (recorded in Swedish)
On the album *Bad Liver and Hans Brustna Hjärtan* (Nonstop Records NSM 33-15) (1989)

"Blow Wind Blow"
Astrid Seriese
On the album *Secret World* (Briga) (1994)

"Blue Skies"
Floyd Dixon
On the various artists album *New Coat Of Paint: The Songs of Tom Waits* (Manifesto MFO 42101-2) (2000)

"Blue Valentines"
Long John Baldry Trio
On the album *Live* (Stony Plain 1268) (2000)

"Blue Valentines"
The Carnival Saloon
On the album *The Carnival Saloon Live* (2001)

"Blue Valentines"
Jumbones
On the various artists album *Big Change* (self-released by Yahoo Groups Tom Waits List) (2001)

"Blue Valentines"
Sarah Jane Morris
On the album *Blue Valentine* (Irma/Jazzhouse) (1995)

"Blue Valentines"
Fjorton Sånger (recorded in Swedish)
On the album *Bad Liver and Hans Brustna Hjärtan* (Nonstop Records NSM 33-15) (1989)

"Blue Valentines"
Speeding or Shyness
On the album *Speeding or Shyness* (Wheelbarrow) (2004)

"The Briar and the Rose"
The Carnival Saloon
On the album *The Carnival Saloon Live* (2001)

"The Briar and the Rose"
Holly Cole
On the album *Temptation* (Metro Blue CDP 7243 8 31653 2 2) (1995)

"The Briar and the Rose"
The Cottars
On the album *Made In Cape Breton* (Rego Irish 2) (2001)

"The Briar and the Rose"
Jackie Curry and Ted Waites
On the various artists album *Hey Tom, Look What We Did To Your Songs* (self-released by Yahoo Groups Tom Waits List) (2001)

"The Briar and the Rose"
Niamh Parsons
On the album *Loosen Up* (Green Linnet 1167) (1997)

"The Briar and the Rose"
Dale Russ and Finn MacGinty
On the album *North Amerikay* (Aniar) (1999)

"The Briar and the Rose"
Tory Voodoo
On the album *Third Weeks A'lightnin* (Binky 1025) (1996)

"Broken Bicycles"
Botanica
On the various artists album *New Coat Of Paint: The Songs of Tom Waits* (Manifesto MFO 42101-2) (2000)

"Broken Bicycles"
Christine Collier
On the album *Blue Aconite* (Fledg'ling 3010) (1997)
Also on the album *Songbird* (Fledg'ling 3024) (1999)
Live version on the album *Home* (Stereoscout) (2003)

"Broken Bicycles"
Mary Foster Conklin
On the album *You'd Be Paradise* (Mock Turtle Music 00220) (2001)

"Broken Bicycles"
Mitchell Howard
On the album *Everybody Has A Dream* (Cling Peaches 00220) (2000)

"Broken Bicycles"
Bette Midler
On the video *Art or Bust* (Vestron) (1985)

"Broken Bicycles"
Willis Moore
On the album *So Far* (Orchard 5119) (2000)

"Broken Bicycles"
Maura O'Connell
On the album *A Real Life Story* (Warner Brothers 9 26342) (1990)

"Broken Bicycles"
Mathilde Santing
On the album *Out of This Dream* (Warner Brothers WEA WX96C) (1987)
Also on the album *So Far, So Good: The Best of* (Megadisc) (1992)
Also on the album *Ballads* (Megadisc SZ2 1872) (1994)

"Broken Bicycles"
Anne Sofie Von Otter and Elvis Costello (recorded in a medley with Paul McCartney's "Junk")
On the album *For the Stars* (Deutsche Grammophon 289 469 530-2) (2001)

"Buzz Fledderjohn"
John Hammond
On the album *Wicked Grin* (Pointblank/Virgin 7243 9 50764 2 8) (2001)

"Cemetery Polka"
Primus
Never officially released

"Cemetery Polka"
Fjorton Sånger (recorded in Swedish)
On the album *Bad Liver and Hans Brustna Hjärtan* (Nonstop Records NSM 33-15) (1989)

"Cemetery Polka"
Gary Tausch
On the various artists album *Hey Tom, Look What We Did To Your Songs* (self-released by Yahoo Groups Tom Waits List) (2001)

"Chocolate Jesus"
Cani Randagi
On the various artists album *Hey Tom, Look What We Did To Your Songs* (self-released by Yahoo Groups Tom Waits List) (2001)

"Chocolate Jesus"
Emily Richards
On the album *Valhalla* (Rillriver 43950) (2003)

"Christmas Card from a Hooker in Minneapolis"
Wolfgang Ambros (recorded in German as "Weihnachtsgrüsse Von Aner Hur Aus Floridsdorf")
On the album *Ambros Singt Waits* (BMG Ariola München) (2000)

"Christmas Card from a Hooker in Minneapolis"
Ataris
On the various artists album *The Year They Recalled Santa Claus* (KROQ 111710) (2002)

"Christmas Card from a Hooker in Minneapolis"
Neko Case
On the various artists album *New Coat Of Paint: The Songs of Tom Waits* (Manifesto MFO 42101-2) (2000)

"Christmas Card from a Hooker in Minneapolis"
Kacey Jones
On the album *Every Man I Love Is Either Married, Gay or Dead* (IGO) (2000)

"Christmas Card from a Hooker in Minneapolis"
Magnapop
On the various artists album *Step Right Up: The Songs of Tom Waits* (Manifesto PT3 41101-2) (1995)

"Christmas Card from a Hooker in Minneapolis"
Fjorton Sånger (recorded in Swedish)
On the album *Bad Liver and Hans Brustna Hjärtan* (Nonstop Records NSM 33-15) (1989)

"Cinny's Waltz"
Holly Cole
On the album *Temptation* (Metro Blue CDP 7243 8 31653 2 2) (1995)

"Clap Hands"
Claudia Bettinaglio
On the album *Saving All My Love* (Taxim HE 024) (2001)

"Clap Hands"
John Hammond
On the album *Wicked Grin* (Pointblank/Virgin 7243 9 50764 2 8) (2001)

"Clap Hands"
Peter Mulvey
On the album *Deep Blue* (Eastern Front 112) (1997)

"Clap Hands"
Bo Ramsey and the Backsliders
On the album *Live* (Trailer 04) (1995)

"Clap Hands"
Fjorton Sånger (recorded in Swedish)
On the album *Bad Liver and Hans Brustna Hjärtan* (Nonstop Records NSM 33-15) (1989)

"Clap Hands"
Sign of 4
On the album *Dancing with St. Peter* (Track/Navarre 1027) (2003)

"Cold Cold Ground"
Claudia Bettinaglio
On the album *Saving All My Love* (Taxim HE 024) (2001)

"Cold Cold Ground"
John Gogo
On the album *Leave A Light On* (JG-3) (1997)

"Cold Cold Ground"
Grievous Angels
On the album *Miles on the Rail* (Bloodshot BS 038) (1998)

"Cold Water"
Claudia Bettinaglio
On the album *Saving All My Love* (Taxim HE 024) (2001)

"Diamond in Your Mind"
Solomon Burke (never recorded by Waits)
On the album *Don't Give Up on Me* (Fat Possum/Epitaph 80358) (2002)

"Diamonds and Gold"
Firewater
On the album *Songs We Should Have Written* (Jetset 67) (2004)

"Diamonds on My Windshield"
Steve Glotzer
On the album *Life Imitates Art* (Six String 7163) (2000)

"Dirt in the Ground"
Claudia Bettinaglio
On the album *Saving All My Love* (Taxim HE 024) (2001)

"Dirt in the Ground"
Christine Collister
On the album *Dark Gift of Time* (Koch 8022) (1998)

"Dirt in the Ground"
Astrid Seriese
On the album *Secret World* (Briga) (1994)

"Down, Down, Down"
The Carnival Saloon
On the album *The Carnival Saloon Live* (2001)

"Down, Down, Down"
Hell Blues Choir
On the album *Greetings from Hell: The Tom Waits Songbook* (Tylden and Co. GTACD 8212) (2003)

"Down There by the Train"
Johnny Cash (never recorded by Waits)
On the album *American Recordings* (American Recordings 9 45520-2) (1994)
Alternate version on the box set *Unearthed* (American Recordings 000167902) (2004)

"Downtown"
The Carnival Saloon
On the album *The Carnival Saloon Live* (2001)

"Downtown"
Alex Chilton
On the various artists album *Step Right Up: The Songs of Tom Waits* (Manifesto PT3 41101-2) (1995)

"Downtown"
Ana Popovich
On the album *Hush* (Ruf 1063) (2002)

"Downtown"
Sunnyside Turner
On the various artists album *Big Change* (self-released by Yahoo Groups Tom Waits List) (2001)

"Downtown Train"
Mary Chapin Carpenter
On the album *Hometown Girl* (Columbia CK40758) (1987)

"Downtown Train"
Everything But The Girl
On the album *Acoustic* (Atlantic 7 82395-2) (1992)
Also on the album *82-92 Essence & Rare* (Cherry 7587) (1998)

"Downtown Train"
Frenay and Lenin
On the album *Live at Pastabilities* (Vector 1918) (1998)

"Downtown Train"
Hell Blues Choir
On the album *Greetings from Hell: The Tom Waits Songbook* (Tylden and Co. GTACD 8212) (2003)

"Downtown Train"
Zoe McCullough
On the album *Never Give Up Never Give In* (Zoe 004) (2000)

"Downtown Train"
Tom Russell Band
On the album *Road to Bayamon* (Philo/Rounder PH-1116) (1988)

"Downtown Train"
Patty Smyth
Released as a single (Columbia 07112) (1987)
Also on the album *Never Enough* (Columbia FC 40182) (1987)
Also on the album *Greatest Hits Featuring Scandal* (Columbia/Legacy CK 65616) (1998)

"Downtown Train"
Spring String Quartet
On the album *Train Songs* (CC n'C 2022) (2002)

"Downtown Train"
Starsound Orchestra
On the album *Plays the Hits Made Famous by Rod Stewart* (Delta 21738) (2001)

"Downtown Train"
Rod Stewart
Released as a single (Warner Brothers 22685) (1989)
Also on the box set *Storyteller: The Complete Anthology 1964–1990* (Warner Brothers 9 25987-2) (1989)
Also on the album *Downtown Train: Selections from Storyteller* (Warner Brothers 9 26158-2) (1990)
Also on the album *If We Fall In Love Tonight* (Warner Brothers 9 46452-2) (1996)
Also on the album *Very Best of Rod Stewart* (Warner Brothers 9 78328-2) (2001)
Live version on the video *It Had To Be You: The Great American Songbook* (J Records 20056) (2003)
Also on the various artists album *Billboard #1s: The 80s* (Rhino 78084) (2004)

"Do You Know What I Idi Amin?"
Chuck E. Weiss (co-written by Weiss and Waits; never recorded by Waits)
On the album *Extremely Cool* (Slow River/Rykodisc SRRCD 41) (1999)

"Drunk on the Moon"
Hillbilly Winos
On the album *Live from the Living Room* (Living Door) (2002)

"Earth Died Screaming"
Tuyo
On the album *Tuyo* (Nisapa 2003) (1999)

"Falling Down"
Holly Cole
On the album *Temptation* (Metro Blue CDP 7243 8 31653 2 2) (1995)

"Falling Down"
Fjorton Sånger (recorded in Swedish)
On the album *Bad Liver and Hans Brustna Hjärtan* (Nonstop Records NSM 33-15) (1989)

"Fannin Street"
John Hammond (never recorded by Waits)
On the album *Wicked Grin* (Pointblank/Virgin 7243 9 50764 2 8) (2001)

"Filipino Box Spring Hog"
Pieter Hartmans
On the various artists album *Hey Tom, Look What We Did To Your Songs* (self-released by Yahoo Groups Tom Waits List) (2001)

"Flowers Grave"
Hell Blues Choir
On the album *Greetings from Hell: the Tom Waits Songbook* (Tylden and Co. GTACD 8212) (2003)

"Foreign Affair"
Richie Cole
On the album *Profile* (Heads Up HUCD-3022) (1993)

"Foreign Affair"
The Manhattan Transfer
On the album *The Extensions* (Atlantic SD 19258) (1979)
Also on the album *The Manhattan Transfer Anthology: Down In Birdland* (Rhino R2-71053) (1992)
Live version on album *Man-Tora! Live In Tokyo* (Rhino R2-72406) (1996)

"Frank's Theme"
Holly Cole
On the album *Temptation* (Metro Blue CDP 7243 8 31653 2 2) (1995)

"Frank's Wild Years"
Paddy McMenamin
On the various artists album *Big Change* (self-released by Yahoo Groups Tom Waits List) (2001)

"Fumblin' with the Blues"
Claudia Bettinaglio
On the album *Saving All My Love* (Taxim HE 024) (2001)

"Fumblin' with the Blues"
Betsy Kaske
On the album *Last Night in Town* (Mountain Railroad 57288) (1980)

"Fumblin' with the Blues"
Gordon Payne (Medley with Payne's "Red Light")
On the album *Gordon Payne* (A&M 4725) (1978)

"Georgia Lee"
Tim Grimm
On the album *Names* (Wind River 4032) (2004)

"Georgia Lee"
Kathryn Roberts and Sean Lakeman
On the album *1* (I Scream EQCD002) (2001)

"Georgia Lee"
Solas
On the album *The Edge of Silence* (Shanachie 78046) (2002)

"Get Behind the Mule"
John Hammond
On the album *Wicked Grin* (Pointblank/Virgin 7243 9 50764 2 8) (2001)
Also on the various artists album *The Last Castle: Original Soundtrack Album* (Uptown/Universal 016193) (2001)
Live version on the various artists album *Live at the Rogue: Field of Blues* (Rockin' Rogue 1) (2003)

"Gin Soaked Boy"
John Hammmond
On the album *Ready for Love* (Back Porch 80599) (2003)

"Gin Soaked Boy"
Southside Johnny and the Jukes
On the album *Messin' with the Blues* (Leroy) (2000)

"God's Away On Business"
Hell Blues Choir
On the album *Greetings from Hell: The Tom Waits Songbook* (Tylden Co. GTACD 8212) (2003)

"Going Out West"
The Blacks
On the album *Just Like Home* (Bloodshot 63) (2000)

"Going Out West"
Dr. Feelgood
On the album *Twenty-Five Years* (Grand 20) (1999)

"Going Out West"
Forty Watt Bulb
On the album *Shovel's Length Short* (Aquarium 9320) (2004)

"Going Out West"
Gomez
On the album *Out West* (ATO 21538) (2005)

"Going Out West"
Jeff Lang
On the album *Disturbed Folk Volume 2* (Black Market Music JL CD 9901) (1999)

"Going Out West"
Wig
On the album *Detroit Rust City* (Small Stone 1) (1996)

"A Good Man Is Hard To Find"
Camille O'Sullivan
On the album *A Little Yearning* (Cat-O-Stripes) (2002)

"Good Old World"
Holly Cole
On the album *Temptation* (Metro Blue CDP 7243 8 31653 2 2) (1995)

"Grapefruit Moon"
Joy Eden Harrison
On the album *Angel Town* (Bizarre Straight/Manifesto 40501) (1995)

"Grapefruit Moon"
Soulskin
On the album *Soulskin* (Askew 3732) (2003)

"Gun Street Girl"
Canned Heat
On the album *Burnin' Live* (Aim 1033) (1994)

"Gun Street Girl"
Luke Doucet
On the album *Outlaws: Live and Unreleased* (Six Shooter 015) (2004)

"Had Me a Girl"
Anthony Frazer
On the various artists album *Hey Tom, Look What We Did To Your Songs* (self-released by Yahoo Groups Tom Waits List) (2001)

"Hang Down Your Head"
Human Drama
On the album *Pin Ups* (Triple X CD-51142-2) (1993)

"Hang Down Your Head"
Jack Ingram and the Beat Up Ford Band
On the album *Live at Adair's* (Warner Brothers 46117) (1995)

"Hang Down Your Head"
Petty Booka
On the album *Let's Talk Dirty in Hawaiian* (Weed 7911) (2003)
Also on the various artists album *Benten Lable Sampler: The Greatest Girl Bands in Asia* (Benteb) (2001)

"Hang Down Your Head"
Lucinda Williams
On the various artists album *Crossing Jordan: Original Soundtrack* (DMZ 87089) (2003)

"Hang on St. Christopher"
The Bulletboys
On the album *Freakshow* (Warner Brothers 9 26168-2) (1991)

"Hang on St. Christopher"
Rod Stewart
On the album *A Spanner in the Works* (Warner Brothers 9 45867-2) (1995)

"Heartattack and Vine"
Claudia Bettinaglio
On the album *Saving All My Love* (Taxim HE 024) (2001)

"Heartattack and Vine"
John Hammond
On the album *Wicked Grin* (Pointblank/Virgin 7243 9 50764 2 8) (2001)

"Heartattack and Vine"
Lydia Lunch featuring Nels Cline
On the various artists album *New Coat of Paint: the Songs of Tom Waits* (Manifesto MFO 42101-2) (2000)

"Heartattack and Vine"
Kathi McDonald
On the album *Kathi McDonald* (Kathi McDonald 00428) (2004)

"Heartattack and Vine"
Popa Chubby
On the album *Hit the High Hard One* (Laughing Bear/Prime 030) (1997)

"Heartattack and Vine"
Screamin' Jay Hawkins
On the album *Black Music for White People* (Demon FIEND CD 211) (1991)
Also on the album *Portrait of a Man: A History of Screamin' Jay Hawkins* (Edsel EDCD414) (1997)

"Hold On"
Mae Moore and Lester Quitzau
On the album *Oh My!* (Poetical License 3) (2004)

"Hold On"
Elliott Murphy
On the album *Soul Surfing* (Last Call 307451) (2002)

"Hold On"
Thomas Sjovard
On the various artists album *Big Change* (self-released by Yahoo Groups Tom Waits List) (2001)

"House Where Nobody Lives"
King Ernest
On the album *Blues Got Soul* (Epitaph 80334) (2000)
Also on the various artists album *Not the Same Old Blues Crap: Vol. 2* (Fat Possum 80342) (2001)

"I Beg Your Pardon"
Kyle Eastwood
On the album *From There to Here* (Sony 68013) (1998)

"Ice Cream Man"
Claudia Bettinaglio
On the album *Saving All My Love* (Taxim HE 024) (2001)

"Ice Cream Man"
Screamin' Jay Hawkins
On the album *Black Music for White People* (Demon FIEND CD 211) (1991)
Also on the album *Best of the Bizarre Sessions: 1990-1994* (Manifesto 42201)
(2000)

"I Don't Wanna Grow Up"
Holly Cole
On the album *Temptation* (Metro Blue CDP 7243 8 31653 2 2) (1995)

"I Don't Wanna Grow Up"
Hell Blues Choir
On the album *Greetings from Hell: The Tom Waits Songbook* (Tylden and Co.
GTACD 8212) (2003)

"I Don't Wanna Grow Up"
Pavers
On the album *Wrecking Ball* (CI 030) (2002)

"I Don't Wanna Grow Up"
The Ramones
On the album *¡Adios Amigos!* (Radioactive 11273) (1995)
Also on the album *Hey Ho Let's Go! The Ramones Anthology* (Rhino R2 75817)
(1999)
Live version on the album *Greatest Hits Live* (MCA 11459) (1996)

"I Don't Wanna Grow Up"
Marky Ramone Group
On the album *Ramones Forever: An International Tribute* (Radical RCL 70037)
(2002)

"I Hope That I Don't Fall in Love with You"
Wolfgang Ambros (recorded in German as "Verliab Di Ned")
On the album *Ambros Singt Waits* (BMG Ariola München) (2000)

"I Hope That I Don't Fall in Love with You"
Laurel Brauns
On the album *Swimming* (Red Tail) (2001)

"I Hope That I Don't Fall in Love with You"
Marc Cohn
On the various artists album *The Prince and Me: Original Soundtrack Album*
(Hollywood 162445) (2004)

"I Hope That I Don't Fall in Love with You"
Rodney Hayden
On the album *The Real Thing* (Rosetta 2004) (2002)

"I Hope That I Don't Fall in Love with You"
Priscilla Herdman
On the album *Forgotten Dreams* (Flying Fish 230) (1993)

"I Hope That I Don't Fall in Love with You"
Hootie and the Blowfish
Performed on the T.V. series *MTV Unplugged* (1996)
Also on the album *Scattered, Smothered and Covered* (Atlantic 63308) (2000)

"I Hope That I Don't Fall in Love with You"
Brian Kennedy
On the album *A Better Man* (BMG International 40913) (1996)

"I Hope That I Don't Fall in Love with You"
Vonda Shepard
Performed on the T.V. series *Ally McBeal*, "Out in the Cold" (2000)

"I Hope That I Don't Fall in Love with You"
10,000 Maniacs
On the U.K. CD single "These Are Days" (Elektra 156CD 7559-66372-2) (1992)
Also on the various artists album *Step Right Up: The Songs of Tom Waits* (Manifesto PT3 41101-2) (1995)
Also on the album *Campfire Songs: The Popular, Obscure and Unknown Recordings* (Rhino/Elektra 73900) (2004)

"I Hope That I Don't Fall in Love with You"
Juliet Turner
On the album *Burn the Black Suit* (Hear This Music 2) (2000)

"I'll Never Let Go Of Your Hand"
Kicki and Ozcar (recorded in German as "Slapper Aldrig Mitt Tag Om Din Hand")
On the various artists album *Big Change* (self-released by Yahoo Groups Tom Waits List) (2001)

"I'll Shoot the Moon"
Pinky McClure
On the album *From Memorial Crossing* (Global Fusion 30) (2000)

"In Between Love"
Curtis Stigers
On the album *I Think It's Going to Rain Today* (Concord 2275) (2005)

"Innocent When You Dream"
Elvis Costello
On the album *Kojak Variety (Expanded Version)* (Rhino 76487) (2004)

"Innocent When You Dream"
Nancy Harrow
On the album *Street of Dreams* (Gazelle 2005) (1995)

"Innocent When You Dream"
Jill Hennessy
On the various artists album *Crossing Jordan: Original Soundtrack* (DMZ 87089) (2003)

"Innocent When You Dream"
Lana Lane
On the album *Ballad Collection Vol. 2* (Avalon Japan 10214) (2001)

"Innocent When You Dream"
Liberty Horses
On the CD Maxi Single "Shine" (Capitol 15926) (1992)

"Innocent When You Dream"
Lisa Moscatiello
On the album *Innocent When You Dream* (Happy Cactus 1) (1997)

"Innocent When You Dream"
Camille O'Sullivan with Jack L
On the album *A Little Yearning* (Cat-O-Stripes CD1) (2002)

"Innocent When You Dream"
2227
On the 7" vinyl single "No Brains, No Tumors" (Strip Core/Forum) (1995)

"In the Coliseum"
Pearl Jam
On the album *Live 20/6/2000 – Verona, Italy* (Sony 85061) (2000)

"In the Neighborhood"
Wolfgang Ambros (recorded in German as "Durt Bin I Daham")
On the album *Ambros Singt Waits* (BMG Ariola München) (2000)

"In the Neighborhood"
The Dutchdogs
On the various artists album *Hey Tom, Look What We Did To Your Songs* (self-released by Yahoo Groups Tom Waits List) (2001)

"In the Neighborhood"
Hell Blues Choir
On the album *Greetings from Hell: The Tom Waits Songbook* (Tylden and Co. GTACD 8212) (2003)

"In the Neighborhood"
Manfred Maurenbrecher and Richard Wester (recorded in German as "In der Nachbarschaft")
On the album *Das Duo Live* (Monopol CD 35683) (1990)

"In the Neighborhood"
Fjorton Sånger (recorded in Swedish)
On the album *Bad Liver and Hans Brustna Hjärtan* (Nonstop Records NSM 33-15) (1989)

"Invitation to the Blues"
David Basse
On the album *Strike When Your Iron is Hot* (City Light 2) (2001)

"Invitation to the Blues"
Claudia Bettinaglio
On the album *Saving All My Love* (Taxim HE 024) (2001)

"Invitation to the Blues"
Holly Cole
On the album *Temptation* (Metro Blue CDP 7243 8 31653 2 2) (1995)
Also on the album *Collection* (EMI 97461) (1998)

"Invitation to the Blues"
The Fourth Stream
On the album *The Fourth Stream* (2004)

"Invitation to the Blues"
James Naughton
On the album *It's About Time* (DRG 91473) (2002)

"Invitation to the Blues"
Jan Vayne
On the album *Vanity* (EMI Netherlands) (1994)

"Invitation to the Blues"
Jennifer Warnes
On the album *The Well* (Sindrome 8960) (2001)

"Is There Any Way Out of This Dream?"
Hell Blues Choir
On the album *Greetings from Hell: The Tom Waits Songbook* (Tylden and Co. GTACD 8212) (2003)

"Is There Any Way Out of This Dream?"
Mathilde Santing
On the album *Out of This Dream* (Warner Brothers WEA WX96C) (1987)
Also on the album *So Far, So Good: The Best of Mathilde Santing* (Megadisc) (1992)

"It Rains On Me"
Chuck E. Weiss (co-written by Weiss and Waits; later recorded by Waits)
On the album *Extremely Cool* (Slow River/Rykodisc SRRCD 41) (1999)

"I Want You"
Holly Cole
On the album *Temptation* (Metro Blue CDP 7243 8 31653 2 2) (1995)
Also on the album *Collection* (EMI 97461) (1998)
Also on the album *The Best of Holly Cole* (Blue Note 29064) (2000)

"I Wish I Was in New Orleans"
Brian Rickman
On the album *Ex-Priest* (Aesthetic/EMI) (1996)

"I Wish I Was in New Orleans"
David Roe
On the album *Angel of New Orleans* (Orchard 7667) (2000)

"Jersey Girl"
The Bacon Brothers
On the album *Getting There* (Bluxo 4041-2) (1999)

"Jersey Girl"
Lisa Bade
On the album *Suspicion* (Elektra SP 6-4897) (1982)

"Jersey Girl"
Claudia Bettinaglio
On the album *Sometimes* (Crosscut 12006) (2003)

"Jersey Girl"
Holly Cole
On the album *Temptation* (Metro Blue CDP 7243 8 31653 2 2) (1995)
Also on the album *Collection* (EMI 97461) (1998)
Also on the album *The Best of Holly Cole* (Blue Note 29064) (2000)
Also on the album *Collection: Vol. 1* (Magada 81040) (2004)
Live version on the various artists album *Live from the Mountain Stage* (Blue Plate BPM-312CD) (1998)

"Jersey Girl"
Hell Blues Choir
On the album *Greetings from Hell: The Tom Waits Songbook* (Tylden and Co. GTACD 8212) (2003)

"Jersey Girl"
Jack Mack and the Heart Attack
On the album *Jersey Girl: Original Soundtrack* (Scotti Brothers) (1992)

"Jersey Girl"
Moxy Fruvous
On the various artists album *Live at the World Café: Volume 7* (WXPN WC9807) (1998)

"Jersey Girl"
Pale Saints
On the various artists album *Step Right Up: The Songs of Tom Waits* (Manifesto PT3 41101-2)

"Jersey Girl"
Bruce Springsteen
Live version on the single "Cover Me" (Columbia 04561) (1984)
A different live version on the box set *Live 1975–1985* (Columbia C5X 40558) (1986)

"Jersey Girl"
Dave Van Ronk
On the album *To All My Friends in Far Flung Places* (Gazell 2011) (1994)

"Jesus Gonna Be Here"
The Blind Boys of Alabama
On the album *Spirit of the Century* (Real World 7243 8 50918 2 7) (2001)
Also on the various artists album *Paul Weller: Under the Influence* (DMC UTICD03) (2003)

"Jesus Gonna Be Here"
Ashley Cleveland
On the album *Second Skin* (204 Records 2814) (2002)

"Jesus Gonna Be Here"
Hell Blues Choir
On the album *Greetings from Hell: The Tom Waits Songbook* (Tylden and Co. GTACD 8212) (2003)

"Jesus Gonna Be Here"
Pat the White
On the album *Pat the White* (Bros 14001) (2004)
Also on the various artists album *10 Ans de Blues Au Quebec* (Bros 1402) (2004)

"Jesus Gonna Be Here"
Christopher Williams
On the album *When I Was Everything* (Big Red Van 74) (2005)

"Jockey Full of Bourbon"
Claudia Bettinaglio
On the album *Saving All My Love* (Taxim HE 024) (2001)

"Jockey Full of Bourbon"
The Blue Hawaiians
On the album *Live at the Lava Lounge* (Pascal 88001) (1997)
Also on the album *Savage Night* (Interscope 90305) (1999)

"Jockey Full of Bourbon"
Carlos and the Bandidos
On the album *The Usual Bandidos* (Part 655001) (2003)

"Jockey Full of Bourbon"
Adam Dorfman
On the album *The Difference* (Psycho Poet) (2000)

"Jockey Full of Bourbon"
John Hammond
On the album *Wicked Grin* (Pointblank/Virgin 7243 9 50764 2 8) (2001)

"Jockey Full of Bourbon"
Los Lobos
On the album *Ride This: The Covers* EP (Mammoth/Hollywood 2061-62456)
(2004)

"Jockey Full of Bourbon"
Moxy Fruvous
On the album *Live Noise* (Bottom Line/Velvel 47304) (1998)

"Jockey Full of Bourbon"
Fjorton Sånger (recorded in Swedish)
On the album *Bad Liver and Hans Brustna Hjärtan* (Nonstop Records NSM 33-15) (1989)

"Johnsburg, Illinois" *(retitled "Johnsberg, Illinois)*
Jason Falkner
On the album *Everyone Says It's On* (Air Mail Recordings AIRCD-026/7) (2001)

"Johnsburg, Illinois"
Megan Mullally
On the album *The Sweetheart Break-In* (Supreme Music Program) (2000)

"Johnsburg, Illinois"
Bob Reed
On the 7" single "Johnsburg, Illinois" (Devil in the Woods) (1993)
Also available on RealAudio at http://www.devilinthewoods.com/label/bobreed.htm

"Kentucky Avenue"
Fjorton Sånger (recorded in Swedish)
On the album *Bad Liver and Hans Brustna Hjärtan* (Nonstop Records NSM 33-15) (1989)

"Last Rose of Summer"
Holly Cole Trio
On the album *Treasure* (Alert 81035) (1998)

"Little Boy Blue"
Holly Cole
On the album *Temptation* (Metro Blue CDP 7243 8 31653 2 2) (1995)

"Little Boy Blue"
Hell Blues Choir
On the album *Greetings from Hell: The Tom Waits Songbook* (Tylden and Co. GTACD 8212) (2003)

"Little Boy Blue"
Nastassja Kinski
Performed in the film *One from the Heart* (1981)

"Little Boy Blue"
Astrid Seriese
On the album *Eclipse* (Briga) (1993)

"Little Boy Blue"
Melissa Stylianou
On the album *Bachelorette* (SBM 1001) (2001)

"Little Trip to Heaven"
Holly Robinson
On the album *Beautiful One* (Cameron 291) (1999)

"Little Trip to Heaven"
Astrid Seriese
On the album *Into Temptation* (Briga) (1996)

"The Long Way Home"
Norah Jones
On the album *Feels Like Home* (Blue Note 7243 5 84800 0 9) (2004)
Live version on the video *Norah Jones and the Handsome Band Live in 2004* (Blue Note 7243 5 99793 9 2) (2004)

"(Looking For) The Heart of Saturday Night"
Wolfgang Ambros (recorded in German as "Samstag Nacht")
On the album *Ambros Singt Waits* (BMG Ariola München) (2000)

"(Looking For) The Heart of Saturday Night"
Holly Cole
On the album *Temptation* (Metro Blue CDP 7243 8 31653 2 2) (1995)
Also on the album *Collection* (EMI 97461) (1998)

"(Looking For) The Heart of Saturday Night"
Shawn Colvin
On the album *Cover Girl* (Sony 7464 57875 2) (1994)
Also on the various artists album *Songbird* (Universal International 9818395) (2004)

"(Looking For) The Heart of Saturday Night"
Chris Daniels and the Kings
On the album *Is My Love Enough?* (Flying Fish) (1993)

"(Looking For) The Heart of Saturday Night"
Dion
On the album *Return of the Wanderer* (Lifesong JZ35356) (1978)
Also on the album *Dion and the Belmonts: 24 Original Classics* (Arista AL9-8206) (1984)

"(Looking For) The Heart of Saturday Night"
Hue and Cry
On the EP *Long Term Lovers of Pain* (Circa YRCD 71) (1994)

"(Looking For) The Heart of Saturday Night"
Rickie Lee Jones
Live version never officially released (2004)

"(Looking For) The Heart of Saturday Night"
Mary Elizabeth Mastrantonio
On the album *Limbo: Motion Picture Soundtrack* (Sony 69994) (1999)

"(Looking For) The Heart of Saturday Night"
Marie Mazotti
On the album *This Time From the Heart* (Orchard 5689) (2000)

"(Looking For) The Heart of Saturday Night"
The Picketts
On the album *Paper Doll* (Pop Llama PLCD-0068) (1992)

"(Looking For) The Heart of Saturday Night"
Jonathan Richman
On the album *You Must Ask The Heart* (Rounder 9047) (1995)

"(Looking For) The Heart of Saturday Night"
Fjorton Sånger (recorded in Swedish)
On the album *Bad Liver and Hans Brustna Hjärtan* (Nonstop Records NSM 33-15) (1989)

"(Looking For) The Heart of Saturday Night"
Street Corner Singers
On the album *Reunion* (Collectables) (1994)

"(Looking For) The Heart of Saturday Night"
Jerry Jeff Walker
On the album *It's A Good Night For Singin'* (MCA 2022) (1976)

"Looks Like I'm Up Shit Creek Again"
Nora O'Connor
On the various artists album *Down to the Promised Land: Five Years of Bloodshot Records* (Bloodshot 60) (2000)

"Looks Like I'm Up Shit Creek Again"
Jason Walker (retitled "Up Shit Creek Again")
On the album *Stranger to Someone* (Laughing Outlaw 24) (2002)

"Louise"
Ramblin' Jack Elliot (never recorded by Waits)
On the album *Friends of Mine* (Hightone/Rhino R2 8089) (1998)

"Low Side of the Road"
John Hammmond
On the album *Ready for Love* (Back Porch 80599) (2003)

"Lucky Day"
Mary Coughlan
On the album *Long Honeymoon* (Evangeline 4014) (2001)

"Martha"
Wolfgang Ambros (recorded in German)
On the album *Ambros Singt Waits* (BMG Ariola München) (2000)

"Martha"
John Autin
On the album *Piano Face* (Rabadash 015) (2002)

"Martha"
Tim Buckley
On the album *Sefronia* (Discreet) (1974)
Also on the various artists albums *Step Right Up: The Songs of Tom Waits* (Manifesto PT3 41101-2)

"Martha"
The Carnival Saloon
On the album *The Carnival Saloon Live* (2001)

"Martha"
Andy Cooney
On the album *One For the Ages* (Rego Irish 7025) (2004)

"Martha" *(retitled "Barney")*
Nancy Harrow
On the album *Street of Dreams* (Gazelle 2005) (1995)

"Martha" *(retitled "Those Were the Days of Roses [Martha]")*
Lee Hazlewood
On the album *Poet, Fool or Bum* (Capitol 11171) (1973)

"Martha"
Hell Blues Choir
On the album *Greetings from Hell: The Tom Waits Songbook* (Tylden and Co. GTACD 8212) (2003)

"Martha"
Mitchell Howard
On the album *Everybody Has A Dream* (Cling Peaches 00220) (2000)

"Martha"
Hue and Cry
On the album *Piano and Voice* (Permanent Records CD SPERM 21) (1995)

"Martha"
Meat Loaf
On the album *Welcome to the Neighborhood* (MCA MCAD-11341) (1995)

"Martha"
Bette Midler
Performed on the T.V. series *Saturday Night Live* (1979)

"Martha"
Willis Moore
On the album *So Far* (Orchard 5119) (2000)

"Martha"
Jan Vayne
On the album *Vanity* (EMI Netherlands) (1994)

"Martha"
Freddie White
On the album *Do You Do* (Mulligan) (1981)
Also on the album *Lost and Found* (Little Don) (2002)

"Midnight Lullaby"
Dawn Clement
On the album *Hush* (Conduit 1303) (2003)

"Midnight Lullaby"
Holly Robinson
On the album *Beautiful One* (Cameron 291) (1999)

"Mockin' Bird"
Tindersticks
On the various artists album *Step Right Up: The Songs of Tom Waits* (Manifesto PT3 41101-2) (1995)

"More than Rain"
Elvis Costello and The Brodsky Quartet
On the promo CD *Elvis Costello and The Brodsky Quartet Live at New York Town Hall* (Warner Brothers PRO-CD-6480) (1993)
Also on the promo CD *Plugging the Gaps Vol. 2* (Tone Records 2CD003) (1995)

"Murder in the Red Barn"
John Hammond
On the album *Wicked Grin* (Pointblank/Virgin 7243 9 50764 2 8) (2001)

"Muriel"
Eleni Mandell
On the various artists album *New Coat Of Paint: The Songs of Tom Waits* (Manifesto MFO 42101-2) (2000)

"New Coat of Paint"
The Carnival Saloon
On the album *The Carnival Saloon Live* (2001)

"New Coat of Paint"
Hurricane Sam
On the album *Piano Madness* (Blue Rock-It 109) (1989)

"New Coat of Paint"
Lenny Marcus and Trio
On the album *Jazzaphrenia* (LMT 4) (2000)

"New Coat of Paint"
Lee Rocker
On the various artists album *New Coat Of Paint — The Songs of Tom Waits* (Manifesto MFO 42101-2) (2000)

"New Coat of Paint"
Bob Seger and The Silver Bullet Band
On the album *The Fire Inside* (Capitol CDP 7 91134 2) (1991)
Also on the album *Greatest Hits —Volume 2* (Capitol 52772) (2003)

"New Coat of Paint"
John Slaughter Blues Band
On the album *New Coat of Paint* (Timeless 5326) (1992)

"New Coat of Paint"
Southside Johnny and the Asbury Jukes
On the album *In The Heat* (Atco 90186) (1984)
Also on the album *All I Want Is Everything: The Best of (1979–1991)* (Rhino R2 71426) (1993)

"Nighthawk Postcards (From Easy Street)"
Cheryl Dillis
On the various artists album *Big Change* (self-released by Yahoo Groups Tom Waits List) (2001)

"Nobody"
Jakob Dall
On the various artists album *Big Change* (self-released by Yahoo Groups Tom Waits List) (2001)

"No One Can Forgive Me But My Baby"
John Hammond (never recorded by Waits)
On the album *Got Love If You Want It* (Charisma/Pointblank 92146) (1992)

"Old Boyfriends"
Claire Martin
On the U.K. album *Old Boyfriends* (Linn 028) (1994)

"Old Boyfriends"
Preacher Boy
On the various artists album *New Coat Of Paint: The Songs of Tom Waits* (Manifesto MFO 42101-2) (2000)

"Old Shoes"
David Baerwald and the New Velvet Pillow Orchestra
On the various artists album *Original Soundtrack: Around the Bend* (Rhino 75690)
(2004)

"Old Shoes"
Drugstore
On the various artists album *Step Right Up: The Songs of Tom Waits* (Manifesto
PT3 41101-2) (1995)

"Ol' 55"
Dave Alvin
On the various artists album *Step Right Up: The Songs of Tom Waits* (Manifesto
PT3 41101-2) (1995)

"Ol' 55"
Wolfgang Ambros (recorded in German as "Die Sunn Geht Boid Auf")
On the album *Ambros Singt Waits* (BMG Ariola München) (2000)

"Ol' 55"
Eric Andersen
On the album *Be True To You* (Arista AL 4033) (1975)
Also on the album *Collection* (Archive ACH80017) (1997)

"Ol' 55"
Shawn Colvin
On the promo-only cassette *Someday* (Columbia CAT6452) (1994)

"Ol' 55"
The Eagles
Released on the single "James Dean"/"Ol' 55" (Asylum 45202) (1974)
Also on the album *On the Border* (Asylum 7E-1004) (1974)
Also on the box set *Selected Works: 1972–1999* (Elektra 62575) (2000)
Also on the album *The Very Best of the Eagles* (Warner Strategic Markets/Rhino
R2 73971) (2003)
Also on the box set *Eagles* (Warner Music Group 79681) (2005)

"Ol' 55"
Richie Havens
On the album *Connections* (Elektra 6E-242) (1980)

"Ol' 55"
Jazz Mandolin Project
On the album *The Deep Forbidden Lake* (Doyle Kos DK.E 480806) (2005)

"Ol' 55"
K's Choice
On the album *Extra Cocoon — All Access* (DTM) (1999)

"Ol' 55"
Ian Matthews
On the album *Some Days You Eat the Bear . . . And Some Days the Bear Eats You* (Elektra EKS-75078) (1974)
Also on the album *Discreet Repeat: The Best of Ian Matthews* (Rockburgh 109) (1980)
Also on the album *The Soul of Many Places: The Elektra Years 1972–1974* (Elektra 61457-2) (1993)
Also on the album *Valley Hi and Some Days You Eat the Bear . . . And Some Days the Bear Eats You* (Water 124) (2003)

"Ol' 55"
Sarah McLachlan
On the album *The Liberty Sessions* (Nettwerk W2-6321) (1994)
Also on the original soundtrack album *Boys On The Side* (Arista 07822-18748-2) (1994)
Also on the videotape *Fumbling Towards Ecstasy: Live* (6 West/Nettwerk 07822 15729-3) (1994)

"Ol' 55"
Smashing Pumpkins
From 1999 Bridge School Concert. Never officially released.

"Ol' 55"
Jerry Jeff Walker
On the album *CowJazz* (MCA 5355) (1982)

"On the Nickel"
Carla Bozulich
On the various artists album *New Coat Of Paint: The Songs of Tom Waits* (Manifesto MFO 42101-2) (2000)

"On the Nickel"
Georgette Fry
On the album *Rites of Passage* (Ontario Arts Council SRR002) (1992)

"The Part You Throw Away"
Ute Lemper
On the album *Punishing Kiss* (Decca 289 466 473-2) (2000)

"Pasties and a G-String"
Andre Williams
On the various artists album *New Coat Of Paint: The Songs of Tom Waits* (Manifesto MFO 42101-2) (2000)

"Pasties and a G-String"
Trike
On the album *Charlston Lightshow* (MussMyHair MMHC0011)

"Pasties and a G-String"
Jeffrey Lee Pierce
On the various artists album *Step Right Up: The Songs of Tom Waits* (Manifesto PT3 41101-2) (1995)

"Pasties and a G-String"
Prosegal
On the various artists album *Big Change* (self-released by Yahoo Groups Tom Waits List) (2001)

"The Piano Has Been Drinking (Not Me)"
Dan Hicks and His Hot Licks
On the album *Alive and Kickin'* (Hollywood 167123) (2001)

"Picture in a Frame"
Willie Nelson
On the album *It Will Always Be* (Lost Highway B0002576) (2004)
Also on the various artists album *Lost Highway Sampler* (Lost Highway/UMG 02612) (2004)

"Picture in a Frame"
Kimmy Rhodes and Willie Nelson
On the album *Picture in a Frame* (Sunbird 70007) (2004)

"Please Call Me, Baby"
Morning and Jim Nichols
On the album *My Flame* (Kamei KR-7003CD) (1992)

"Please Call Me, Baby"
Sally Norvell
On the various artists album *New Coat Of Paint: The Songs of Tom Waits* (Manifesto MFO 42101-2) (2000)

"Poncho's Lament"
The Blacks
On the various artists album *New Coat Of Paint: The Songs of Tom Waits* (Manifesto MFO 42101-2) (2000)

"Poncho's Lament"
Rita and Frank Eriksen
On the album *The Water is Wide* (BMG Norway) (1994)

"The Pontiac"
Ron Roberts
On the various artists album *Hey Tom, Look What We Did To Your Songs* (self-released by Yahoo Groups Tom Waits List) (2001)

"Pony"
Ramblin' Jack Elliott
On the album *The Long Ride* (Hightone 8107) (1999)

"Purple Avenue"
Holly Cole
On the album *Blame It on My Youth* (Blue Note/Manhattan CDP 7 97349-2) (1992)

"Purple Avenue"
Ute Lemper
On the album *Punishing Kiss* (Decca 289 466 473-2) (2000)

"Rainbow Sleeves"
Davis Gaines (never recorded by Waits)
On the album *Against the Tide* (Lap 76628-2) (1996)

"Rainbow Sleeves"
Rickie Lee Jones (never recorded by Waits)
On the 10" EP *A Girl at Her Volcano* (Warner Brothers 23805-1) (1983)
Also on the original soundtrack album *The King of Comedy* (Warner Brothers 23765-1) (1983)

"Rainbow Sleeves"
Bette Midler (never recorded by Waits)
Performed in the film *Divine Madness* (1981); removed from video versions because of licensing problems

"Rainbow Sleeves"
Patty Morabito (never recorded by Waits)
On the album *The Delicate Hour* (LML 164) (2003)

"Rainbow Sleeves"
Ian Shaw (never recorded by Waits)
On the album *Soho Stories* (Milestone 9316) (2001)

"Rain Dogs"
The Carnival Saloon
On the album *The Carnival Saloon Live* (2001)

"Rain Dogs"
Fjorton Sånger (recorded in Swedish)
On the album *Bad Liver and Hans Brustna Hjärtan* (Nonstop Records NSM 33-15) (1989)

"Red Shoes by the Drugstore"
The Wedding Present
On the various artists album *Step Right Up: The Songs of Tom Waits* (Manifesto PT3 41101-2) (1995)
Also on the U.K. album *Singles 1995–97* (Cooking Vinyl COOK CD 134) (1999)

"Romeo Is Bleeding"
Wolfgang Ambros (recorded in German as "Romeo Verliert Bluat")
On the album *Ambros Singt Waits* (BMG Ariola München) (2000)

"Romeo Is Bleeding"
Claudia Bettinaglio
On the album *Saving All My Love* (Taxim HE 024) (2001)

"Romeo Is Bleeding"
Dexter Romweber's Infernal Racket
On the various artists album *New Coat Of Paint: The Songs of Tom Waits* (Manifesto MFO 42101-2) (2000)

"Rosie"
The Beat Farmers
On the album *The Pursuit of Happiness* (Curb 1518 77501 2) (1987)

"Rosie"
Gale Force
On the album *Gale Force* (Fantasy 9527) (1978)

"Ruby's Arms"
Wolfgang Ambros (recorded in German as "Es Is Vorbei")
On the album *Ambros Singt Waits* (BMG Ariola München) (2000)

"Ruby's Arms"
Casino Steel
On the album *V.S.O.P.* (Orchard 801097) (2001)

"Ruby's Arms"
Frente!
On the various artists album *Step Right Up: The Songs of Tom Waits* (Manifesto PT3 41101-2) (1995)

"Ruby's Arms"
Megan Mullally
On the album *The Sweetheart Break-In* (Supreme Music Program) (2000)

"Ruby's Arms"
Fjorton Sånger (recorded in Swedish)
On the album *Bad Liver and Hans Brustna Hjärtan* (Nonstop Records NSM 33-15) (1989)

"Ruby's Arms"
Jan Vayne
On the album *Vanity* (EMI Netherlands) (1994)

"San Diego Serenade"
Wolfgang Ambros (recorded in German as "Heimatserenade")
On the album *Ambros Singt Waits* (BMG Ariola München) (2000)

"San Diego Serenade"
Eric Andersen
On the album *Sweet Surprise* (Arista 4075) (1976)

"San Diego Serenade"
Cliff Aungier, Jerry Donohue, and Geoff Bradford
On the various artists album *Blues Brittania* (Blueprint 7) (2000)

"San Diego Serenade"
Barbi Benton
Released as a single "Staying Power"/"San Diego Serenade" (Playboy PB-203 7)
(1976)
Also on the album *Something New* (Playboy PB-411) (1976)

"San Diego Serenade"
Keith Carradine
On the album *Lost and Found* (Asylum 114) (1978)

"San Diego Serenade"
Marcus Dagan
On the album *Old Friends* (MarKas Music 1754) (2000)

"San Diego Serenade"
Baby Jane Dexter
On the album *I Got Thunder* (Elba 5006) (1992)

"San Diego Serenade"
Kate Dimbleby
On the album *Good Vibrations* (Black Box Jazz 1004) (2000)

"San Diego Serenade" *(retitled "Serenade")*
Dion
On the album *Yo Frankie* (Arista ARCD-8549) (1989)

"San Diego Serenade"
David Gogo
On the album *Bare Bones* (Ragged Pup/Cordova Bay 11) (2000)

"San Diego Serenade"
Nanci Griffith
On the album *Late Night Grande Hotel* (MCA D 10306) (1991)
Also on the album *The Complete MCA Recordings* (MCA 00044702) (2003)

"San Diego Serenade"
Freddie Henry
On the album *Get It Out in the Open* (Cloud 8809) (1979)

"San Diego Serenade"
Sarah Leib
On the album *It's Not the Moon* (Panfer Productions) (2003)

"San Diego Serenade"
Ralph McTell
On the album *Right Side Up* (Warner Brothers 56296) (1976)

"San Diego Serenade"
Juice Newton
On the album *Take Heart* (Capitol 12000) (1979)

"San Diego Serenade"
Lynn Rothrock
On the album *This Is Me* (Independent 71410) (2002)

"San Diego Serenade"
Claudia Schmidt
On the album *Out of the Dark* (Flying Fish FF-361) (1985)

"San Diego Serenade"
Spanky and Our Gang
On the album *Change* (Epic 33580) (1975)

"Saving All My Love for You"
Claudia Bettinaglio
On the album *Saving All My Love* (Taxim HE 024) (2001)

"Shiver Me Timbers"
Wolfgang Ambros (recorded in German as "Nach Mir Die Sintflut")
On the album *Ambros Singt Waits* (BMG Ariola München) (2000)

"Shiver Me Timbers"
Laurie Beechman (recorded in a medley with Noel Coward's "Sail Away")
On the album *Listen to My Heart* (Excelsior Ltd. LB CD001) (1990)

"Shiver Me Timbers"
Holly Cole
On the album *Collection: Vol. 1* (Magada 81040) (2004)

"Shiver Me Timbers"
The House Band
On the album *Rockall* (Green Linnet 1174) (1996)

"Shiver Me Timbers"
Bette Midler
On the album *Songs for the New Depression* (Atlantic SD 18155) (1976)
Live version on the album *Live at Last* (Atlantic SD 29000) (1977)
Live version also on the album *Experience the Divine: Greatest Hits* (Atlantic 7 82497-2) (1993)
A different live version is on the album *Divine Madness* (Atlantic SD 16022) (1980)

"Shiver Me Timbers"
Glenn Yarborough
On the album *I Could Have Been a Sailor* (Folk Era 1702) (1995)
Also on the album *Day the Tall Ships Came* (Folk Era 1455) (2000)
Live version on the album *Live at the Troubador* (Folk Era 1704 (1994)

"Shore Leave"
John Hammond
On the album *Wicked Grin* (Pointblank/Virgin 7243 9 50764 2 8) (2001)

"16 Shells From a Thirty-Ought-Six"
John Hammond
On the album *Wicked Grin* (Pointblank/Virgin 7243 9 50764 2 8) (2001)

"16 Shells From a Thirty-Ought-Six"
Bob Seger and The Silver Bullet Band
On the album *It's A Mystery* (Capitol 99774) (1995)

"Soldier's Things"
Holly Cole
On the album *Temptation* (Metro Blue CDP 7243 8 31653 2 2) (1995)

"Soldier's Things"
Hederos and Hellberg
On the album *Ven Stood Still* (Gravitation 010) (2000)

"Soldier's Things"
Eric Leeds
On the album *Things Left Unsaid* (Paisley Park/Warner Brothers 9 45199) (1993)

"Soldier's Things"
Windmill Saxophone Quartet
On the album *This 'N' That* (Global Village 9802) (1998)

"Soldier's Things"
Paul Young
On the album *The Secret of Association* (Columbia CK 39957) (1985)

"Step Right Up"
Violent Femmes
On the various artists album *Step Right Up: The Songs of Tom Waits* (Manifesto PT3 41101-2) (1995)

"Straight to the Top"
Lea Delaria
On the album *Play It Cool* (Warner Brothers 47933) (2001)

"Strange Weather"
Marianne Faithfull
On the album *Strange Weather* (Island 7 90613-1) (1987)
Also on the album *Faithfull: A Collection of Her Best Recordings* (Island 314-524 036-2) (1994)
Also on the album *A Perfect Stranger: The Island Anthology* (Island 314-524 579-2) (1998)
Also on the album *Stranger On Earth: An Introduction to Marianne Faithfull* (Polygram International 585152) (2001)

Also on the album *20th Century Masters — The Millennium Collection: The Best of Marianne Faithfull* (Island 000114602) (2003)
Live version on the album *Blazing Away* (Island 422-842794-2) (1990)

"Strange Weather"
Andi Sexgang
On the album *Faithfull Covers* (Dressed to Kill 375) (2000)
Also on the box set *Complete Sex Gang Children* (Dressed to Kill 428) (2000)

"Swordfishtrombone"
Claudia Bettinaglio
On the album *Saving All My Love* (Taxim HE 024) (2001)

"Swordfishtrombone"
Hell Blues Choir
On the album *Greetings from Hell: The Tom Waits Songbook* (Tylden and Co. GTACD 8212) (2003)

"Swordfishtrombone"
Fjorton Sånger (recorded in Swedish)
On the album *Bad Liver and Hans Brustna Hjärtan* (Nonstop Records NSM 33-15) (1989)

"Take It With Me"
Kitty Margolis
On the album *Left Coast Life* (Mad-Kat 11008) (2001)

"Take It With Me"
Megan Mullally
On the album *Big as a Berry* (Varese 062144) (2002)

"Take It With Me"
Jubilant Sykes
On the album *Wait for Me* (Sony 89107) (2001)

"Take It With Me"
Anne Sofie Von Otter and Elvis Costello
On the album *For the Stars* (Deutsche Grammophon 289 469 530-2) (2001)

"Take Me Home"
Mary Ellen Bernard
On the album *Point of Departure* (Original Cast Records 9351) (1995)

"Take Me Home"
Holly Cole
On the album *Temptation* (Metro Blue CDP 7243 8 31653 2 2) (1995)

"Take Me Home"
Crystal Gayle (different recording than on *One from the Heart* soundtrack)
On the album *Cage the Songbird* (Warner Brothers 23958) (1983)

Also on the album *Best of Crystal Gayle: Talking in Your Sleep* (Castle 122) (2000)
Also on the album *Blue: All Her Greatest Hits* (Hallmark 30864) (2001)

"Take Me Home"
Maria Joao
On the album *Undercovers* (Emarcy 4428) (2002)

"Take Me Home"
Luba Mason
On the album *Collage* (P.S. Classics 423) (2004)

"Take Me Home"
Vonda Shepard
Performed on the T.V. series *Ally McBeal* (1999)

"Tango 'Til They're Sore"
Holly Cole
On the album *Temptation* (Metro Blue CDP 7243 8 31653 2 2) (1995)
Live version on the album *It Happened One Night* (Metro Blue 52699) (1997)

"Tango 'Til They're Sore"
Fjorton Sånger (recorded in Swedish)
On the album *Bad Liver and Hans Brustna Hjärtan* (Nonstop Records NSM 33-15) (1989)

"Tango 'Til They're Sore"
Astrid Seriese
On the album *Into Temptation* (Briga) (1996)

"Telephone Call from Istanbul"
The Carnival Saloon
On the album *The Carnival Saloon Live* (2001)

"Telephone Call from Istanbul"
The Red Elvises
On the album *Your Favorite Band Live* (Shoobah-Doobah 5012) (2000)

"Temptation"
Beekeeper
On the album *Eel Binge* (MussMyHair MMH5550-1) (1995)

"Temptation"
The Bobs
On the album *Sing the Songs Of . . .* (Kaleidoscope K-48) (1991)

"Temptation"
Holly Cole
On the album *Temptation* (Metro Blue CDP 7243 8 31653 2 2) (1995)

"Temptation"
Diana Krall
Released as a CD single "Temptation"/"I'll Never Be the Same" (Verve B0001995-32) (2004)
Also on the album *The Girl in the Other Room* (Verve 000182612) (2004)
Live version on the various artists album *ONXRT: Live from the Archives Volume 7* (SRO Productions 85704) (2004)
Another live version on the video *Live at the Montreal Jazz Festival* (Verve 000378009) (2004)

"Temptation"
Astrid Seriese
On the album *Into Temptation* (Briga) (1996)

"That Feel"
Little Band of Gold
On the album *Little Band of Gold* (Shanachie 6047) (2000)

"This One's from the Heart"
Jazz at the Movies Band
On the album *One from the Heart: Sax at the Movies II* (Discovery 77015) (1995)

"Tijuana"
Meadows (co-written by Jack Tempchin and Waits; never recorded by Waits)
On the various artists album *Hey Tom, Look What We Did To Your Songs* (self-released by Yahoo Groups Tom Waits List) (2001)

"Tijuana"
Jack Tempchin (co-written by Tempchin and Waits; never recorded by Waits)
On the album *Jack Tempchin* (Arista AB4193) (1978)

"'Til the Money Runs Out"
John Hammond
On the album *Wicked Grin* (Pointblank/Virgin 7243 9 50764 2 8) (2001)

"'Til the Money Runs Out"
Bill Perry
On the album *Raw Deal* (Blind Pig 5093) (2004)

"'Til the Money Runs Out"
Fjorton Sånger (recorded in Swedish)
On the album *Bad Liver and Hans Brustna Hjärtan* (Nonstop Records NSM 33-15) (1989)

"Time"
Tori Amos
On the album *Strange Little Girls* (Atlantic 7567-83486-2) (2001)

"Time"
T-Bone Burnett
On the album *T-Bone Burnett* (MCA MCAC-5809) (1986)

"Time"
The Carnival Saloon
On the album *The Carnival Saloon Live* (2001)

"Time"
Sean King and Rob Matthews
On the various artists album *Big Change* (self-released by Yahoo Groups Tom Waits List) (2001)

"Time"
Henk Tack
On the various artists album *Hey Tom, Look What We Did To Your Songs* (self-released by Yahoo Groups Tom Waits List) (2001)

"Tom Traubert's Blues (Waltzing Matilda)"
Wolfgang Ambros (recorded in German)
On the album *Ambros Singt Waits* (BMG Ariola München) (2000)

"Tom Traubert's Blues (Waltzing Matilda)" *(retitled "Waltzing Matilda")*
Bon Jovi
On the CD single "Dry Country" (Polygram International) (1994)

"Tom Traubert's Blues (Waltzing Matilda)"
The Carnival Saloon
On the album *The Carnival Saloon Live* (2001)

"Tom Traubert's Blues (Waltzing Matilda)"
English Country Blues Band
On the album *Home and Deranged* (Rogue FMSL2004) (1983)

"Tom Traubert's Blues (Waltzing Matilda)"
Dave Gannett Jazz Tuba
On the various artists album *Tubas From Hell* (Summit DCD-155) (1995)

"Tom Traubert's Blues (Waltzing Matilda)"
Hell Blues Choir
On the album *Greetings from Hell: The Tom Waits Songbook* (Tylden and Co. GTACD 8212) (2003)

"Tom Traubert's Blues (Waltzing Matilda)"
Jazz Mandolin Project
On the album *The Deep Forbidden Lake* (Doyle Kos DK.E 480806) (2005)

"Tom Traubert's Blues (Waltzing Matilda)"
Royal Rounders
On the album *Playing for Change: Soundtrack from the Documentary Film* (Higher Octave 96369) (2005)

"Tom Traubert's Blues (Waltzing Matilda)"
Rod Stewart
Released as a U.K. single (Warner Brothers International 9362-40718-2) (1992)
Also on the U.K. album *Lead Vocalist* (Warner Brothers International 9362-45258-2) (1992)
Live version on the album *Unplugged . . . and Seated* (Warner Brothers 9 45289-2) (1993)

"Train Song"
Bim Skala Bim
On the album *Eyes and Ears* (BIB Records 2012) (1995)

"Train Song"
Holly Cole
On the album *Temptation* (Metro Blue CDP 7243 8 31653 2 2) (1995)
Also on the album *Collection* (EMI 97461) (1998)
Live version on the album *It Happened One Night* (Metro Blue 52699) (1997)
Live version also on the album *The Best of Holly Cole* (Blue Note 29064) (2000)

"Train Song"
The Carnival Saloon
On the album *The Carnival Saloon Live* (2001)

"Train Song"
The Holmes Brothers
On the album *Promised Land* (Rounder 2142) (1997)
Also on the album *Righteous! The Essential Collection* (Rounder 611588) (2002)

"Train Song"
Jane Siberry
Live version, never officially released.

"Train Song"
Spring String Quartet
On the album *Train Songs* (CC n'C 2022) (2002)

"$29.00"
Claudia Bettinaglio
On the album *Saving All My Love* (Taxim HE 024) (2001)

"2:19"
John Hammond (never recorded by Waits)
On the album *Wicked Grin* (Pointblank/Virgin 7243 9 50764 2 8) (2001)

"Underground"
The Carnival Saloon
On the album *The Carnival Saloon Live* (2001)

"Underground"
Astrid Seriese
On the album *Secret World* (Briga) (1994)

"Union Square"
Eric Ambel
On the album *Knucklehead* (Lakeside Lounge 003) (2004)

"Virginia Avenue"
Knoxville Girls
On the various artists album *New Coat Of Paint: The Songs of Tom Waits* (Manifesto MFO 42101-2) (2000)

"Walking Spanish"
Fjorton Sånger (recorded in Swedish)
On the album *Bad Liver and Hans Brustna Hjärtan* (Nonstop Records NSM 33-15) (1989)

"Way Down in the Hole"
The Blind Boys of Alabama
On the album *Spirit of the Century* (Real World 7243 8 50918 2 7) (2001)

"Way Down in the Hole"
John Campbell
On the album *Howlin' Mercy* (Elektra 7559-61440-2) (1993)

"Way Down in the Hole"
Compulsive Gamblers
On the album *Gambling Days Are Over, Say It With Liquor* (Sympathy for the Record Industry 372) (1995)
Live version on the album *Live and Deadly: Memphis/Chicago* (Sympathy for the Record Industry 698) (2003)

"Way Down in the Hole"
Jon Dee Graham
On the album *Hooray for the Moon* (New West 6036) (2001)

"Way Down in the Hole"
Heavy Metal Horns
On the album *Heavy Metal Horns* (Square Records 4000-2) (1991)

"Way Down in the Hole"
The Neville Brothers
Theme from the T.V. series *The Wire* (2004)

"Way Down in the Hole"
Astrid Seriese
On the album *Into Temptation* (Briga) (1996)

"What's He Building?"
Alicia Fontana
On the various artists album *Big Change* (self-released by Yahoo Groups Tom Waits List) (2001)

"What's He Building?"
Norm Stein
On the various artists album *Hey Tom, Look What We Did To Your Songs* (self-released by Yahoo Groups Tom Waits List) (2001)

"Whistle Down the Wind"
Valerie Carter
On the album *The Way It Is* (ULG 17737) (1996)

"Whistle Down the Wind"
Dave Grismond and Tony Rice
On the album *Tone Poems* (Acoustic Disc 10) (1994)

"Whistling Past the Graveyard"
Screamin' Jay Hawkins
On the album *Somethin' Funny Goin' On* (Demon FIEND CD 750) (1995)
Also on the album *Portrait of a Man: A History of Screamin' Jay Hawkins* (Edsel EDCD414) (1997)
Also on the various artists album *New Coat Of Paint: The Songs of Tom Waits* (Manifesto MFO 42101-2) (2000)

"Who Are You?"
Human Drama
On the album *Solemn Sun Setting* (Triple X 60014) (1999)

"Wrong Side of the Road"
Claudia Bettinaglio
On the album *Saving All My Love* (Taxim HE 024) (2001)

"Wrong Side of the Road"
Nine Pound Hammer
On the album *Smoking Taters* (Crypt 27) (1997)

"Yesterday Is Here"
The Alter Boys
On the album *Exotic Sounds of the Alter Boys* (Fractured Trans 3) (2005)

"Yesterday Is Here"
Cat Power
On the album *Dear Sir* (Runt 006) (1995)

"Yesterday Is Here"
Human Drama
On the album *Pin-Ups* (Triple X CD-51142-2) (1993)

"Yesterday Is Here"
Peter Sanders
On the various artists album *Big Change* (self-released by Yahoo Groups Tom Waits List) (2001)

"Yesterday Is Here"
Astrid Seriese
On the album *Eclipse* (Briga) (1993)

"Yesterday Is Here"
The Walkabouts
On the single *Jack Candy* (Sub Pop SP 81/252) (1993)

"You Can't Unring A Bell"
These Immortal Souls
On the various artists album *Step Right Up: The Songs of Tom Waits* (Manifesto PT3 41101-2) (1995)

NOTES

Personal Interviews

- Aloe, Mary. Telephone interview, 20 Oct. 1999.
- Cohen, Adam. Telephone interview, 17 May 2005.
- Coppola, Francis Ford. Fax to author, 14 Apr. 1999.
- Crivello, Sal. Telephone interview, 20 May 1999.
- Geffen, David. Telephone interview, 10 June 1999.
- Graham, Big Daddy. Telephone interview, 4 June 1999.
- Hennessy, Jill. Telephone interview, 28 Feb. 2004.
- Howe, Bones. Telephone interview, 23 June 1999.
- Howe, Bones. Telephone interview, 14 Apr. 2005.
- Mantegna, Joe. Telephone interview, 12 Feb. 2004.
- McLachlan, Sarah. Personal interview, 22 Mar. 1994.
- Melvoin, Michael. Telephone interview, 25 June 1999.
- Thomas, Rob. Telephone interview, 3 May 2005.
- Yester, Jerry. Telephone interview, 1 June 1999.

Introduction: Little Trip to Heaven

1. Betsy Carter and Peter S. Greenwood, "Sweet & Sour," *Newsweek* 14 June 1976: 84.
2. Mark Rowland, "Tom Waits' Wild Year," *Musician* Jan. 1993: 70–72.
3. Gavin Martin, "Tom Waits," *New Musical Express* 19 Oct. 1985: 30–31.
4. Carter and Greenwood, "Sweet & Sour."

1 Old Shoes and Picture Postcards

1. Tom Waits, concert, Princeton University, Princeton, NJ, 16 Apr. 1976.
2. *Night Flight* [profile of Tom Waits], USA Network 1988.
3. Bill Milkowski, "Tom Waits," *Downbeat* Mar. 1986: 14.
4. Mark Rowland, "Tom Waits Is Flying Upside Down (On Purpose)," *Musician* Oct. 1987: 82–94.
5. Rich Wiseman, "Tom Waits, All-Night Rambler," *Rolling Stone* 30 Jan. 1975: 18.
6. "Tom Foolery: Swapping Stories with the Inimitable Tom Waits," *Buzz* May 1993: 63–64, 109–10.
7. Tom Waits, concert, Apollo Theatre, London, England, 23 Mar. 1981.

8. "Tom Foolery."
9. "Tom Foolery."
10. Tom Waits, concert, Boston Music Hall, Boston, MA, 21 Mar. 1976.
11. Barney Hoskyns, "Tom Waits: The Mojo Interview," *Mojo* Apr. 1999: 72–85.
12. Chris Douridas, *Morning Becomes Eclectic*. KCRW-FM, Los Angeles, CA, 9 Oct. 1992.
13. Gavin Martin, "Tom Waits," *New Musical Express* 19 Oct. 1985: 30–31.
14. Peter O'Brien, "'Watch Out for 16 Year Old Girls Wearing Bell Bottoms Who Are Running away from Home and Have a Lot of Blue Oyster Cult Records under Their Arm,' Says Tom Waits" *Zig Zag* July 1976: 11–13.
15. Tom Waits, concert, Warfield Theater, San Francisco, CA, 31 Dec. 1990.
16. Tom Waits, *VH1 Storytellers*, VH1, 13 June 1999.
17. Hoskyns, "Tom Waits."
18. David McGee, "Smelling like a Brewery, Looking like a Tramp," *Rolling Stone* 27 Jan. 1977: 11–12, 15.
19. Hoskyns, "Tom Waits."
20. "*Swordfishtrombones* Promo Interview," press kit, 1983.
21. David Fricke, "The Resurrection of Tom Waits," *Rolling Stone* 24 June 1999: 37–40.
22. McGee, "Smelling like a Brewery."
23. Wiseman, "Tom Waits."
24. Mick Brown, "Warm Beer, Cold Women," *Sounds* 12 June 1976: 16–17.
25. McGee, "Smelling like a Brewery."
26. Hoskyns, "Tom Waits."
27. "*Bone Machine*: A User's Manual," press kit promo CD, 1992.
28. Hoskyns, "Tom Waits."
29. Rowland, "Tom Waits."
30. Hoskyns, "Tom Waits."
31. Dave Zimmer, "Tom Waits' Hollywood Confidential," *Bam* 26 Feb. 1982: 14–17.
32. "Tom Foolery."
33. Hoskyns, "Tom Waits."
34. McGee, "Smelling like a Brewery."
35. McGee, "Smelling like a Brewery."
36. Rowland, "Tom Waits."
37. Wiseman, "Tom Waits."
38. McGee, "Smelling like a Brewery."

2 Asylum Years

1. Barney Hoskyns, "Tom Waits: The *Mojo* Interview," *Mojo* Apr. 1999: 72–85.
2. Hoskyns, "Tom Waits."
3. Hoskyns, "Tom Waits."
4. Tom Waits, *VH1 Storytellers*, VH1, 13 June 1999.
5. Tom Waits, concert, Boston Music Hall, Boston, MA, 21 Mar. 1976.
6. Tom Waits, interview, WAMU Radio, Washington, DC, 18 Apr. 1975.
7. Waits, interview, WAMU Radio.
8. Tom Waits, interview, KBCO-FM Radio, Denver, CO, 13 Oct. 1999.
9. Dave Zimmer, "Tom Waits' Hollywood Confidential," *Bam* 26 Feb. 1982: 14–17.
10. Rich Wiseman, "Tom Waits, All-Night Rambler," *Rolling Stone* 30 Jan. 1975: 18.
11. Gary Morris, "I'm Not the Statue of Liberty: An Interview with Sylvia Miles," *Bright Lights Film Journal Online* Apr. 1999.

12. Jay S. Jacobs, "Chuck E. Weiss: Chuck E.'s in Love," *Popentertainment.com* Apr. 1999.

13. Stephen Peeples, interview with Tom Waits, *Heartattack and Vine*, press kit, 1980.

14. Waits, *VH1 Storytellers*.

15. Fred Schruers, "Tom Petty: The *Rolling Stone* Interview," *Rolling Stone* 22 July 1999: 88–94.

16. Hoskyns, "Tom Waits."

17. Hoskyns, "Tom Waits."

18. Waits, interview, WAMU Radio.

3 Looking for the Heart of Saturday Night

1. Barney Hoskyns, "Tom Waits: The *Mojo* Interview," *Mojo* Apr. 1999: 72–85.

2. Michael Melvoin, "Michael Melvoin: A Biography," press kit, June 1998.

3. Tom Waits, interview, KPFK-FM, Los Angeles, CA, 10 June 1974.

4. Waits, interview, KPFK-FM.

5. David Fricke, "The Resurrection of Tom Waits," *Rolling Stone* 24 June 1999: 37–40.

6. David McGee, "Smelling like a Brewery, Looking like a Tramp," *Rolling Stone* 27 Jan. 1997: 11–12, 15.

7. Betsy Carter and Peter S. Greenwood, "Sweet & Sour," *Newsweek* 14 June 1976: 84.

8. Fricke, "Resurrection."

9. Fricke, "Resurrection."

10. Barney Hoskyns, "Tom Waits: The *Mojo* Interview," *Mojo* Apr. 1999: 72–85.

11. Don Roy King, email to Blue Valentines (the Italian Tom Waits fan club), 2 July 1999.

12. McGee, "Smelling like a Brewery."

13. "Tom Waits: Twenty Questions," *Playboy* Mar. 1988: 128–31.

14. Stephen Peeples, interview with Tom Waits, *Heartattack and Vine* press kit, 1980.

15. Fricke, "Resurrection."

16. Rich Wiseman, "Tom Waits, All-Night Rambler," *Rolling Stone* 30 Jan. 1975: 18.

4 Warm Beer and Cold Women

1. Tom Waits, interview, KPFK-FM, Los Angeles, CA, 10 June 1974.

2. Tom Waits, concert, Boston Music Hall, Boston, MA, 21 Mar. 1976.

3. Waits, concert, Boston Music Hall.

4. David McGee, "Smelling like a Brewery, Looking like a Tramp," *Rolling Stone* 27 Jan. 1997: 11–12, 15.

5. Peter O'Brien, "'Watch out for 16 Year Old Girls Wearing Bell Bottoms Who Are Running Away from Home and Have a Lot of Blue Oyster Cult Records under Their Arm' Says Tom Waits," *Zig Zag* July 1976: 11–13.

6. Barney Hoskyns, "Tom Waits: The *Mojo* Interview," *Mojo* Apr. 1999: 72–85.

7. McGee, "Smelling like a Brewery."

8. McGee, "Smelling like a Brewery."

9. "Random Notes," *Rolling Stone*, 27 Jan. 1977: 36.

10. Michael Cader, ed., *Saturday Night Live: The First Twenty Years*, New York: Cader/Houghton Mifflin, 1994.

11. *Fernwood Tonight*, syndicated television series, 1 Aug. 1977.

12. Don Roy King, email to Blue Valentines (the Italian Tom Waits fan club), 2 July 1999.

5 Foreign Affairs

1. "Tom Waits: Barroom Balladeer," *Time* 28 Nov. 1977: 77.
2. Delores Ziebarth, "Tom Waits Arrested in L.A.," *Rolling Stone* 14 July 1977: 15.
3. Ziebarth, "Tom Waits Arrested."
4. Jim Jarmusch, "Tom Waits Meets Jim Jarmusch," *Straight No Chaser* Spring 1993: 21–35.
5. Ziebarth, "Tom Waits Arrested."
6. "Random Notes," *Rolling Stone* 11 Aug. 1977: 29–31.
7. Ziebarth, "Tom Waits Arrested."
8. "Random Notes," 11 Aug. 1977.
9. Steve Pond, "Tom Waits on *One from the Heart*," *Rolling Stone* 1 Apr. 1982: 44.
10. Bob Hart, "Flat 'At Tom, the Scrooge of Rock," *Sun* 30 Apr. 1976: 25.
11. "Tom Waits: Barroom Balladeer."
12. Timothy White, *Rock Lives: Profiles and Interviews*, New York: Owl, 1990.
13. White, *Rock Lives*.
14. White, *Rock Lives*.
15. White, *Rock Lives*.
16. White, *Rock Lives*.
17. White, *Rock Lives*.
18. White, *Rock Lives*.
19. Mikal Gilmore, "Tom Waits for His Next Album," *Rolling Stone* 7 Sept. 1978: 17.
20. Gilmore, "Tom Waits."
21. Gilmore, "Tom Waits."
22. George Kanzler, "Side Man," *Newark Star Ledger* 22 May 1999: Spotlight, 1.
23. Kanzler, "Side Man."
24. Gilmore, "Tom Waits."
25. Gianluca Tramontana, "Now for Some Sweetening," *Mojo* Dec. 1999: 139.
26. Tramontana, "Now for Some Sweetening."
27. White, *Rock Lives*.
28. Barney Hoskyns, "The Marlowe of the Ivories," *New Musical Express* 25 May 1985: 28–31.
29. Dave Zimmer, "Tom Waits' Hollywood Confidential," *Bam* 26 Feb. 1982: 14–17.
30. Tom Schnobbel, *Morning Becomes Eclectic*, KCRW-FM, Los Angeles, CA, 3 Oct. 1988.
31. Tom Waits, *VH1 Storytellers*, VH1, 13 June 1999.
32. Zimmer, "Tom Waits."

6 This One's from the Heart

1. Dave Zimmer, "Tom Waits' Hollywood Confidential," *Bam* 26 Feb. 1982: 14–17.
2. Steve Pond, "Tom Waits on *One from the Heart*, *Rolling Stone* 1 Apr. 1982: 44.
3. Barney Hoskyns, "Tom Waits: The *Mojo* Interview," *Mojo* Apr. 1999: 72–85.
4. Elliott Murphy, "Tom Waits: A Drifter Finds a Home," *Rolling Stone* 30 Jan. 1986: 20–21.
5. Zimmer, "Tom Waits' Hollywood Confidential."
6. Stephen Peeples, interview with Tom Waits, *Heartattack and Vine* press kit, 1980.
7. Zimmer, "Tom Waits' Hollywood Confidential."
8. Chris Douridas, *Morning Becomes Eclectic*, KCRW-FM, Los Angeles, CA, 31 Mar. 1998.
9. Peeples, interview.
10. Hoskyns, "Tom Waits."

11. Peeples, interview.
12. Peeples, interview.
13. Peeples, interview.
14. Peeples, interview.
15. Murphy, "Tom Waits."
16. Peeples, interview.
17. Zimmer, "Tom Waits' Hollywood Confidential."
18. Zimmer, "Tom Waits' Hollywood Confidential."
19. Zimmer, "Tom Waits' Hollywood Confidential."
20. Zimmer, "Tom Waits' Hollywood Confidential."
21. Zimmer, "Tom Waits' Hollywood Confidential."
22. Zimmer, "Tom Waits' Hollywood Confidential."
23. Zimmer, "Tom Waits' Hollywood Confidential."
24. Zimmer, "Tom Waits' Hollywood Confidential."
25. Zimmer, "Tom Waits' Hollywood Confidential."
26. Zimmer, "Tom Waits' Hollywood Confidential."
27. Zimmer, "Tom Waits' Hollywood Confidential."
28. Murphy, "Tom Waits."
29. George Kanzler, "Side Man," *Newark Star Ledger* 22 May 1999: Spotlight, 1.
30. Hoskyns, "Tom Waits."

7 Swordfishtrombones

1. Dave Zimmer, "Tom Waits' Hollywood Confidential," *Bam* 26 Feb. 1982: 14–17.
2. Zimmer, "Tom Waits' Hollywood Confidential."
3. Barney Hoskyns, "Tom Waits: The *Mojo* Interview," *Mojo* Apr. 1999: 72–85.
4. John Tabler, ed., *Who's Who in Rock & Roll*, New York: Crescent, 1991.
5. David Fricke, "The Resurrection of Tom Waits," *Rolling Stone* 24 June 1999: 37–40.
6. Tom Schnobbel, *Morning Becomes Eclectic*, KCRW-FM, Los Angeles, CA, 3 Oct. 1988.
7. "Harry Partch," Harmonium Home Page Composers Web site: shift.merriweb.com.au/harmonium/compositions/partch.html
8. "Tom Waits: Twenty Questions," *Playboy* Mar. 1988: 128–31.
9. Fricke, "Resurrection."
10. Chris Douridas, *Morning Becomes Eclectic*, KCRW-FM, Los Angeles, CA, 9 Oct. 1992.
11. Timothy White, *Catch a Fire: The Life of Bob Marley*, New York: Henry Holt, 1983.
12. Qtd. in Mark Rowland, "Tom Waits' Wild Years," *Musician* Jan. 1993: 70–72.
13. Fricke, "Resurrection."
14. *Swordfishtrombones* promo interview, press kit, 1983.
15. *Swordfishtrombones* promo interview, press kit, 1983.
16. Hoskyns, "Tom Waits."
17. Ian Walker, "Waits on His Way," *Observer Magazine* 1984: 30–31.
18. Barney Hoskyns, "The Marlowe of the Ivories," *New Musical Express* 25 May 1985: 28–31.
19. Mick Brown, "Getting High on Low Life," *Time Out* 1984: 52–53.
20. David Sheff, "Tom Waits and His Act," *Rolling Stone* Oct. 1988: 38.
21. Hoskyns, "Marlowe."
22. Elissa Van Poznak, "Lower East Side Story," *Face* Oct. 1985.
23. Elliot Murphy, "Tom Waits: A Drifter Finds a Home," *Rolling Stone* 30 Jan. 1986: 20–21.
24. Hoskyns, "Marlowe."

25. *Late Night with David Letterman*, NBC, 16 Oct. 1987.

26. Van Poznak, "Lower East Side Story."

27. Profile of Jim Jarmusch, *Filmmaker*, Sundance Channel, 1996.

28. Hoskyns, "Tom Waits."

29. Mark Rowland, "Tom Waits Is Flying Upside Down (On Purpose)," *Musician* Oct. 1987: 82–94.

30. Bill Milkowski, *Rockers, Jazzbos and Visionaries*, New York: *Billboard*, 1998.

31. Murphy, "Tom Waits."

32. Hoskyns, "Marlowe."

33. Rowland, "Tom Waits."

34. Hoskyns, "Tom Waits."

35. Rowland, "Tom Waits."

8 Frank's Wild Years

1. Dierdre O'Donohue, *Morning Becomes Eclectic*, KCRW-FM, Los Angeles, CA, Aug. 1987.

2. O'Donohue, *Morning Becomes Eclectic*.

3. Barney Hoskyns, "The Marlowe of the Ivories," *New Musical Express* 25 May 1985: 28–31.

4. Hoskyns, "Marlowe."

5. Hoskyns, "Marlowe."

6. O'Donohue, *Morning Becomes Eclectic*.

7. O'Donohue, *Morning Becomes Eclectic*.

8. Barney Hoskyns, "Tom Waits: The *Mojo* Interview," *Mojo* Apr. 1999: 72–85.

9. Tom Schnobbel, *Morning Becomes Eclectic*, KCRW–FM, Los Angeles, CA, 3 Oct. 1988.

10. Mark Rowland, "Tom Waits Is Flying Upside Down (On Purpose)," *Musician* Oct. 1987: 82–94.

11. O'Donohue, *Morning Becomes Eclectic*.

12. Rowland, "Tom Waits."

13. "Travellin' Man," *Sounds* 17 Oct. 1987: 18–22.

14. Schnobbel, *Morning Becomes Eclectic*.

15. O'Donohue, *Morning Becomes Eclectic*.

16. O'Donohue, *Morning Becomes Eclectic*.

17. *Buried Treasures, Volume 1: The Directors*, Island Visual Arts Video, 1991.

18. O'Donohue, *Morning Becomes Eclectic*.

19. Bill Holdship, "Tom Waits: Town Crier," *Creem* Jan. 1988: 51–53.

20. Rowland, "Tom Waits."

21. Rowland, "Tom Waits."

22. Rowland, "Tom Waits."

23. "Tom Waits: Twenty Questions," *Playboy* Mar. 1988: 128–31.

24. O'Donohue, *Morning Becomes Eclectic*.

25. O'Donohue, *Morning Becomes Eclectic*.

26. Marianne Faithfull with David Dalton, *Faithfull: An Autobiography*, New York: Little Brown, 1994.

27. Faithfull and Dalton.

28. O'Donohue, *Morning Becomes Eclectic*.

29. O'Donohue, *Morning Becomes Eclectic*.

30. *Late Night with David Letterman,* NBC, 16 Oct. 1987.

31. "Tom Waits: Twenty Questions," *Playboy* Mar. 1988: 128–31.

32. Schnobbel, *Morning Becomes Eclectic*.
33. David Sheff, "Tom Waits and His Act," *Rolling Stone* Oct. 1988: 38.
34. Schnobbel, *Morning Becomes Eclectic*.

9 The Large Print Giveth, and the Small Print Taketh Away

1. Mark Rowland, "Tom Waits Is Flying Upside Down (On Purpose)," *Musician* Oct. 1987: 82–94.
2. Rowland, "Tom Waits."
3. Solomon L. Wisenberg, "U.S. 9th Circuit Court of Appeals, Waits v. Frito-Lay, Inc." http://caselaw.findlaw.com/scripts/getcase.pl?navby=search&case=/data2/circs/9th/2/978/1093.html
4. Wisenberg, "Waits v. Frito-Lay."
5. Wisenberg, "Waits v. Frito-Lay."
6. Wisenberg, "Waits v. Frito-Lay."
7. Paul Feldman, "Tom Waits Wins Two and a Half Million in Voice Theft Suit," *Los Angeles Times* 9 May 1990: B1, B8.
8. Wisenberg, "Waits v. Frito-Lay."
9. Feldman, "Tom Waits."
10. Wisenberg, "Waits v. Frito-Lay."
11. Mark Rowland, "Tom Waits' Wild Year," *Musician* Jan. 1993: 70–72.
12. Robert Lloyd, "Gone North," *L.A. Weekly Online* 22 Apr. 1999.
13. Rowland, "Tom Waits' Wild Year."
14. Anthony Bozza, comp., and Shawn Dahl, ed., *Rolling Stone Raves*, New York: Rolling Stone/Quill, 1999.
15. David Sheff, "Tom Waits and His Act," *Rolling Stone* 6 Oct. 1988: 38.
16. Barney Hoskyns, "Tom Waits: The *Mojo* Interview," *Mojo* Apr. 1999: 72–85.
17. Rowland, "Tom Waits' Wild Year."
18. Chris Douridas, *Morning Becomes Eclectic*, KCRW-FM, Los Angeles, CA, 9 Oct. 1992.

10 Who Are You Now?

1. Mark Rowland, "Tom Waits' Wild Year," *Musician* Jan. 1993: 70–72.
2. Rowland, "Tom Waits' Wild Year."
3. Chris Douridas, *Morning Becomes Eclectic*, KCRW-FM, Los Angeles, CA, 9 Oct. 1992.
4. Peter Orr, "Tom Waits at Work in the Fields of Song," *Reflex* 6 Oct. 1992.
5. Douridas, *Morning Becomes Eclectic*.
6. Douridas, *Morning Becomes Eclectic*.
7. Rowland, "Tom Waits' Wild Year."
8. Douridas, *Morning Becomes Eclectic*.
9. "*Bone Machine*: A User's Manual," press kit promo CD, 1992.
10. Rip Rense, "A Few Words about *Bone Machine*," press kit, 1992.
11. Barney Hoskyns, "Tom Waits: The *Mojo* Interview," *Mojo* Apr. 1999: 72–85.
12. Rense, "A Few Words."
13. Douridas, *Morning Becomes Eclectic*.
14. Hoskyns, "Tom Waits."
15. Rowland, "Tom Waits' Wild Year."
16. Douridas, *Morning Becomes Eclectic*.
17. Douridas, *Morning Becomes Eclectic*.
18. Douridas, *Morning Becomes Eclectic*.

19. Hoskyns, "Tom Waits."
20. Douridas, *Morning Becomes Eclectic.*
21. Tom Waits, *The Black Rider* CD liner notes, Island Records, 1993.
22. Hoskyns, "Tom Waits."
23. Hoskyns, "Tom Waits."
24. Dierdre O'Donohue, *Morning Becomes Eclectic,* KCRW-FM, Los Angeles, CA, Aug. 1987.
25. Gavin Bryars, *Jesus' Blood Never Failed Me Yet,* CD liner notes, Point Music, 1993.
26. Bryars, *Jesus' Blood.*
27. Chris Douridas, *Morning Becomes Eclectic,* KCRW-FM, Los Angeles, CA, 31 Mar. 1998.
28. Hoskyns, "Tom Waits."

11 What's He Building In There?

1. "Punk Rocker of the Week," *Entertainment Weekly* 19 June 1998: 75.
2. Bradley Bambarger, "Tom Waits Joins Indie Epitaph for 'Mule' Set," *Billboard* 20 Mar. 1999: 1, 85.
3. David Fricke, "The Resurrection of Tom Waits," *Rolling Stone* 24 June 1999: 37–40.
4. Jay S. Jacobs, "Chuck E. Weiss: Chuck E.'s in Love," *Popentertainment.com* Apr. 1999.
5. Jacobs, "Chuck E. Weiss."
6. Chris Douridas, *Morning Becomes Eclectic,* KCRW-FM, Los Angeles, CA, 31 Mar. 1998.
7. Tom Waits, *VH1 Storytellers,* VH1, 13 June 1999.
8. Douridas, *Morning Becomes Eclectic.*
9. Barney Hoskyns, "Tom Waits: The *Mojo* Interview," *Mojo* Apr. 1999: 72–85.
10. Hoskyns, "Tom Waits."
11. Mark Edwards, "Life in the Old Dog Yet," *Times* (London) 18 Apr. 1999: sec. 11, 10.
12. Rip Rense, "*Mule Variations,*" *Mule Variations* press kit, Apr. 1999.
13. Rense, "*Mule Variations.*"
14. Hoskyns, "Tom Waits."
15. Rense, "*Mule Variations.*"
16. Fricke, "Resurrection."
17. Hoskyns, "Tom Waits."
18. Rense, "*Mule Variations.*"
19. Rense, "*Mule Variations.*"
20. Fricke, "Resurrection."
21. Hoskyns, "Tom Waits."
22. "Waits Lends Voice to Next Sparklehorse LP," *Sonicnet Online* 25 Mar. 1999.
23. Fricke, "Resurrection."
24. Barney Hoskyns, "Tom Waits Talks to Barney Hoskyns," *Mojo* May 1999: 92–94.
25. Hoskyns, "Tom Waits Talks."
26. Hoskyns, "Tom Waits."
27. Fricke, "Resurrection."
28. *Mystery Men: Special Edition,* DVD Universal Video, 1999.

12 The Long Way Home

1. Ross Fortune, "Conformity is a Fool's Paradise," *Time Out* (U.K.) 24 Apr. 2002: 10–12.
2. Edna Gunderson, "Listen to Waits, Hear his Vision of a Unique World," *USA Today* 18 June 2002: D10.
3. Fortune, "Conformity is a Fool's Paradise."
4. "We're All Mad Here," Anti Records electronic press kit 13 June 2002.

5. Gunderson, "Listen to Waits, Hear his Vision of a Unique World."

6. "We're All Mad Here."

7. Jon Pareles, "A Poet of Outcasts Who's Come Inside," *New York Times* 5 May 2002: 43, 51.

8. Gunderson, "Listen to Waits, Hear his Vision of a Unique World."

9. Pareles, "A Poet of Outcasts Who's Come Inside."

10. Pareles, "A Poet of Outcasts Who's Come Inside."

11. *Pollock — Special Edition*, Columbia/TriStar Home Video, 2001.

12. Christina Saraceno, "Waits, Newman Sue MP3.com," *Rolling Stone.com* 9 May 2001.

13. Gunderson, "Listen to Waits, Hear his Vision of a Unique World."

14. "Tori Amos Covers All the Bases," ICE Sept. 2001: 6–7.

15. Gil Kaufman, "Solomon Burke: Return of the King," *VH1.com* 15 Jan. 2003.

16. Ruthe Stein, "Hoffman's Really Big Show," *San Francisco Chronicle* 25 Apr. 2003: D1.

17. "Scoop du Jour," *San Francisco Film Society Website* SFFS.org 25 Apr. 2003.

18. Bruce Bellingham, "Room to Dream," *The San Francisco Examiner*, www.sfexaminer. com, 25 Apr. 2003.

19. "Healing the Divide Benefit Concert," Press release 23 Aug. 2003.

20. Jon Parales, "Star Starts A Show; Tom Waits Ends It," *The New York Times* 23 Sept. 2003: E4.

21. Joel Selvin, "Waits, Raitt, Newstead and Buffalo Jam with S.F. Schoolkids," *San Francisco Chronicle* 23 Oct. 2003: E1.

22. Lyndsey Parker, "Damien Rice Wins Shortlist Music Prize," *Launch.com* 6 Oct. 2003.

23. "Tom Waits Wins Spanish Legal Judgement," *Anti.com* 3 Mar. 2004.

24. Anti Records Newsletter 20 Jan. 2004.

25. "Norah Jones — The Long Way Home," Shore Fire Media Press kit Feb. 2004.

26. Kurt Orzeck, "Los Lobos Goes on *The Ride* of Its Life," ICE Apr. 2004: 6–7.

27. Rip Rense, "A Few Words About *Bone Machine*," *Bone Machine* press kit, 1992.

28. Jonathan Cohen, "Billboard Bits: Waits, Bozulich, Santa Fe Jazz Fest," *Billboard.com* 21 Aug. 2003.

29. Barney Hoskyns, "Long *Gone*," *Rock's Back Pages*, www.rocksbackpages.com, Sept. 2004.

30. Tom Waits, KFOG-FM *Morning Show*, KFOG-FM, San Francisco, CA, 5 Oct. 2004.

31. Tom Waits, *The Dave Fanning Show*, RTE2-FM, Ireland, 8 Oct. 2004.

32. Hoskyns, "Long *Gone*."

33. Vit Wagner, "Songs of Decay from Waits," *Toronto Star* 5 Oct. 2004: C05.

34. Tom Waits, Interview with Mark Coles, BBC Radio 4, U.K., 4 Oct. 2004.

35. Robert Everett-Green, "Old Man Waits Is New Again," *The Globe and Mail* 4 Oct. 2004: R1.

36. George Varga, "This Musical Maverick Waits For No One — Well, Maybe His Wife," *San Diego Union-Tribune* 3 Oct. 2004: F1.

37. Joel Selvin, "Barroom Bard's Next Round," *San Francisco Chronicle* 3 Oct. 2004: 20.

38. Waits, Interview, BBC Radio 4.

39. Waits, Interview, BBC Radio 4.

40. Jonathan Valania, "Magnet Interview with Tom Waits," *Magnet* Oct./Nov. 2004: 72.

41. Tom Waits, "It's Perfect Madness: What the Stars Are Listening To," *The Observer* 20 Mar. 2005: 26.

42. Michael Toland, "Aural Fixations," *HighBias.com* Oct. 2004.

43. Wagner, "Songs of Decay from Waits."

44. Everett-Green, "Old Man Waits Is New Again."

45. *Anti.com* July 2004.

46. Tom Waits, *The Deep End Interview* with Vickie Kerrigan, Radio National Australia, 5 Oct. 2004.

47. Waits, Interview, BBC Radio 4.

48. Sylvie Simmons, "The *Mojo* Interview: Tom Waits Speaks," *Mojo* Oct. 2004: 42–46.

49. Thom Jurek, "*Real Gone,*" *AllMusic.com* Oct. 2004.

50. Rod Smith, "Resident Evil Two," *Seattle Weekly* 13–19 Oct. 2004: 53.

51. Christian Carey, "*Real Gone,*" *Splendid.com* 29 Jan. 2005.

52. Dean Truitt, "Tom Waits: Not Gone Yet," *OneWay.com* Oct. 2004.

53. Steve Hochman, "Waits Tries On Topical For Size," *Los Angeles Times* 27 June 2004: E49.

54. Richard Cromelin, "A Cluttered Harmony," *Los Angeles Times* 26 Sept. 2004: E43.

55. Don Waller, "*Blinking Lights:* Eels Slip Into Guest-Laden Sixth Set," *ICE* Apr. 2005: 5.

56. Adrian Deevoy, "The Son Also Rises: Jakob Dylan — The World's Most Fashionable Wallflower," *GQ Magazine* (U.K.) Oct. 2001.

57. "Guest Edit," *Amazon.com* Oct. 2004.

58. Selvin, "Barroom Bard's Next Round."

59. Mick Brown, "Tom Waits' Theatre of Dreams," *Word* Feb. 2005: 90–101.

60. James Wray, "Tom Waits Returns To the Big Screen In *Domino,*" *MonstersandCritics.com* 17 Dec. 2004.

61. Christopher Morris, "Publisher Sues Warner Music Over Waits Tunes," *ABCNews.com* 2 June 2005.

62. "Billboard" (1982) for Purina Butcher's Blend Dog Food. http://www.clioawards.com/archives

63. Jonathan Valania, "The Man Who Howled Wolf," *Magnet* June/July 1999: 50–59, 93.

64. http://cgi.ebay.com/Master-Recording-of-Tom-Waits-doing-Voice-Over_W0QQitem Z7577508273QQcategoryZ58QQrdZ1QQcmdZViewItem#ebayphotohosting

65. Michael Klein, "Dali-ences," *The Philadelphia Inquirer* 3 Apr. 2005: B2.

66. "Party 2000," *Rolling Stone* 30 Dec. 1999 – 6 Jan. 2000: 47–140.

PHOTOGRAPHS

1. Platt Collection / Archive Photos
2. Simon Fowler / London Features International
3. Phil Ceccola
4. George DuBose / London Features International
5. Corbis
6. Platt Collection / Archive Photos
7. Philip Gould / Corbis
8. Richie Aaron / Redferns
9. Lynn Goldsmith / Corbis
10. Lynn Goldsmith / Corbis
11. Fotos International / Archive Photos
12. Globe Photos
13. Ebet Roberts / Redferns
14. Ebet Roberts / Redferns
15. Ebet Roberts / Redferns
16. Ebet Roberts / Redferns
17. Lynn Goldsmith / Corbis
18. George DuBose / London Features International
19. SAGA / Archive Photos
20. George DuBose / London Features International
21. George DuBose / London Features International
22. George DuBose / London Features International
23. George DuBose / London Features International
24. George DuBose / London Features International
25. Joel Warren / Liaison Agency
26. Tom Sheehan / London Features International
27. Christine Alicino / Corbis
28. Alice Arnold
29. Diana Lyn / Shooting Star

30. Elizabeth Wolynski / Liaison Agency
31. Derek Ridgers / London Features International
32. Henry McGee / Globe Photos
33. Jeffrey Newbury / Outline
34. Alice Arnold
35. Gie Knaeps / London Features International
36. Ebet Roberts / Redferns
37. Greg Gorman / Outline

INDEX